# Shakespeare in the Theatre: Yukio Ninagawa

## SERIES EDITORS

Peter Holland, Farah Karim-Cooper and Stephen Purcell

*Published titles*
*Patrice Chéreau*, Dominique Goy-Blanquet
*The American Shakespeare Center*, Paul Menzer
*Mark Rylance at the Globe*, Stephen Purcell
*The National Theatre, 1963–1975: Olivier and Hall*,
Robert Shaughnessy
*Nicholas Hytner*, Abigail Rokison-Woodall
*Peter Sellars*, Ayanna Thompson
*Trevor Nunn*, Russell Jackson
*Peter Hall*, Stuart Hampton-Reeves

*Forthcoming titles*
*The King's Men*, Lucy Munro

# Shakespeare in the Theatre: Yukio Ninagawa

*Conor Hanratty*

**THE ARDEN SHAKESPEARE**
LONDON · NEW YORK · OXFORD · NEW DELHI · SYDNEY

THE ARDEN SHAKESPEARE
Bloomsbury Publishing Plc
50 Bedford Square, London, WC1B 3DP, UK
1385 Broadway, New York, NY 10018, USA
29 Earlsfort Terrace, Dublin 2, Ireland

BLOOMSBURY, THE ARDEN SHAKESPEARE and the
Arden Shakespeare logo are trademarks of Bloomsbury Publishing Plc

First published in Great Britain 2020
This paperback edition published in 2021

Copyright © Conor Hanratty, 2020

Conor Hanratty has asserted his right under the Copyright,
Designs and Patents Act, 1988, to be identified as author of this work.

For legal purposes the Acknowledgements on pp. x–xi constitute
an extension of this copyright page.

Series design by Dani Leigh
Cover image: *Macbeth* at the Barbican, directed by Yukio Ninagawa
(Photo by Seigo Kiyota, provided by HoriPro Inc.)

All rights reserved. No part of this publication may be reproduced or
transmitted in any form or by any means, electronic or mechanical,
including photocopying, recording, or any information storage or retrieval
system, without prior permission in writing from the publishers.

Bloomsbury Publishing Plc does not have any control over, or
responsibility for, any third-party websites referred to or in this book.
All internet addresses given in this book were correct at the time of
going to press. The author and publisher regret any inconvenience
caused if addresses have changed or sites have ceased to exist,
but can accept no responsibility for any such changes.

A catalogue record for this book is available from the British Library.

Library of Congress Control Number: 2020932968

| ISBN: | HB: | 978-1-3500-8735-4 |
|---|---|---|
| | PB: | 978-1-3502-3946-3 |
| | ePDF: | 978-1-3500-8737-8 |
| | eBook: | 978-1-3500-8736-1 |

Series: Shakespeare in the Theatre

Typeset by Integra Software Services Pvt. Ltd.

To find out more about our authors and books visit www.bloomsbury.com
and sign up for our newsletters.

# CONTENTS

*List of Illustrations* vi
*Series Preface* vii
*Foreword* Thelma Holt, CBE viii
*Acknowledgements* x
*A Note on the Text* xii

1 Introduction 1
2 Foreign Stories, Japanese Images 35
3 Hamlet 85
4 The Sai no Kuni Shakespeare Series 125
5 Conclusion 187

*Appendix* 199
*Notes* 202
*Bibliography* 211
*Index* 222

# ILLUSTRATIONS

1 Ninagawa Yukio in rehearsal for *Hamlet*, Saitama
  Next Theatre, 2012                                                        34

2 *Ninagawa Twelfth Night* (2005): the moon-viewing
  platforms designed by Kanai to replicate the famous
  sand sculpture at Ginkakuji, Kyoto                                        83

3 *Hamlet* (2015): the Players' performance on the *hinadan*
  ends as the entire company (led by Fujiwara Tatsuya)
  moves in slow motion                                                     117

4 *Coriolanus* (2007): the Roman mob atop Nakagoshi's
  impressive set of steps                                                  138

5 *Cymbeline* (2012): the replica of the Kashima single
  pine tree                                                                177

# SERIES PREFACE

Each volume in the *Shakespeare in the Theatre* series focuses on a director or theatre company who has made a significant contribution to Shakespeare production, identifying the artistic and political/social contexts of their work.

The series introduces readers to the work of significant theatre directors and companies whose Shakespeare productions have been transformative in our understanding of his plays in performance. Each volume examines a single figure or company, considering their key productions, rehearsal approaches and their work with other artists (actors, designers, composers). A particular feature of each book is its exploration of the contexts within which these theatre artists have made their Shakespeare productions work. Thus, the series not only considers the ways in which directors and companies produce Shakespeare, but also reflects upon their other theatre activities and the broader artistic, cultural and socio-political milieu within which their Shakespeare performances and productions have been created. The key to the series' originality, then, is its consideration of Shakespeare production in a range of artistic and broader contexts; in this sense, it de-centres Shakespeare from within Shakespeare studies, pointing to the range of people, artistic practices and cultural phenomena that combine to make meaning in the theatre.

*Series editors:*
*Peter Holland,*
*Farah Karim-Cooper and Stephen Purcell*

# FOREWORD

At a certain age, many of us are encouraged to write a memoir of our professional career, not necessarily for publication, but for the pleasure of seeing what we have done with our lives. It is gratifying to know that I will not have to do this, as it has been done for me in this book in relation to the work of my dear friend Yukio Ninagawa.

It is such fun to read; it is also at times heart-breaking. It is not surprising that I could not resist feverishly turning the pages, moving from one production to another, as I worked on so many of them with this inspirational director. What did surprise me was that what I was reading was important both to me personally and to what was happening at the time in classical theatre. On occasion I would go back to something I half-remembered to see if I had in fact invented it. I never had, and all the madness was there.

My first meeting with Ninagawa was at the Edinburgh Festival in 1986, when I was invited by his producer, Tadao Nakane, to see his production of Euripides' *Medea*. The performance was outdoors, and it had poured with rain before the metaphorical curtain went up. I was clutching an inadequate coat round my shoulders, being theoretically dressed for summer, when I saw a slight man running quite quickly to the front of the stalls. He spread out a large piece of plastic sheeting, emblazoned with the word 'Panasonic'. He smiled at me and gestured that I should take my seat in the front row, which I did, picking up the plastic sheeting to protect myself from any further downpour. I knew, without being told, that this modern-day Walter Raleigh had to be Ninagawa. He had the look and behaviour of what I imagined was a sixteenth-century gentleman at his very best.

In this chivalrous performance, he was clearly recalling his brief career as an actor. He was also a painter, and it was not unusual for him to make drawings on a shirt that had been worn. Mrs Ninagawa would often embroider these drawings before the shirt was washed. Eventually, I 'acquired' one of them and I must confess that I do not know if it was a gift or if I knocked it off.

Since I left school I have always kept a copy of the *Complete Works of William Shakespeare* on my bedside table. The only problem this weighty volume has ever had is a certain loneliness. It need not worry now, as it has a companion piece. William Shakespeare can tell Ninagawa where he went wrong, and Ninagawa can explain in very polite Japanese that the Bard has his head up his arse.

Enjoy this homage to a great director, and a dearly missed friend.

*Thelma Holt, CBE*

# ACKNOWLEDGEMENTS

Since my earliest steps towards writing about Ninagawa Yukio, I have met unfailing kindness. Ninagawa was the most generous of all, letting me observe him work for over a year, and he was even indulgent enough to speak with me in my own language at a time when his English was better than my Japanese. Although the focus of his attention could be terrifying, he was very thoughtful and had a wicked sense of humour. It was a privilege to spend time with him and watch him at work.

In the middle of August 2005, thanks to a series of judicious emails, I managed to arrange a meeting with the producer Thelma Holt in the bar of a Tokyo hotel. Thelma, who was responsible for bringing Ninagawa's work to the UK, was due to have lunch with Ninagawa the following day and agreed to make a case for me if I could have a letter – in Japanese – written to Ninagawa by the time she was due to leave the hotel the following morning. I got the letter written, and delivered, and thanks to an introduction from this extraordinary and generous lady I was invited to attend rehearsals very soon afterwards. I first attended a rehearsal midway through the creation of the *Tenpo Juninen no Shakespeare* in August 2005. I stayed for over a year and had the privilege of observing *The Comedy of Errors*, *Titus Andronicus*, *Byakuya*, *Tis Pity She's A Whore*, *Orestes* and *Tango at the End of Winter* before my time in Tokyo ended in late 2006. Hers has been an extraordinary contribution to world theatre, and without her intercession this book would never have happened. I am reasonably sure that everyone working with Ninagawa was so hospitable to me because I was introduced by Seruma-san. To her, and to all of the artists and staff of Ninagawa's various companies, I owe a debt of enormous gratitude.

# ACKNOWLEDGEMENTS

The list of those who have helped me along the way – sharing their time, their thoughts, their research, their company or their homes – is a testament to the goodwill I have encountered. This small listing is poor recompense, but I am very grateful to them all. Thank you to Brian Singleton, Steve Wilmer, Dennis Kennedy, Marianne McDonald, Amanda Wrigley, Oliver Taplin, David Wiles, Platon Mavromoustakos, Fiona Macintosh, Edith Hall, the staff of what was the Theatre Museum in Covent Garden, the National Theatre archive, the Archive of Performances of Greek and Roman Drama, the Shakespeare Birthplace Trust, Cian O'Brien, Avery Willis Hoffman, Lynda Radley, Maria Sehopoulou, Yu Moriyama, Andrew Meehan, Rachel Walzer, Nicky Faint, Angela Peachey, Jo Thurley, Shane Killoran, Jonah Salz, Erika Fischer-Lichte, Carol Sorgenfrei, Stanca Scholz-Cionca, Marilena Zarouila, Melinda Powers, Tomatsuri Akiko, Maria Iosifidou, Mary Hart, Eike Grossmann, Yamagata Harue, Sakaguchi Midori, Brian August, Naomi Daly, Gordon Bell, Sian Thomas, Jenny O'Connor at the Japanese Embassy in Dublin, Loughlin Deegan, Lynne Parker and my fellow Rough Magic SEEDS, Okamuro Minako and Mikami Hiroko and their students at Waseda University, Yamaguchi Hiroko, the staff of the Japan Foundation in London, Kimata Fuyu, Matsuoka Kazuko, Kasamatsu Yasuhiro, Nomura Mansai, Kanamori Miyako at HoriPro and Ninagawa's assistants Okouchi Naoko and Inoue Shonsho, who were especially kind and patient with me. Stephen Purcell, Lara Bateman and Mark Dudgeon at The Arden Shakespeare, and Farah Karim-Cooper who said yes in the first place, have been of tremendous help.

This journey began with a chance encounter, when my mother recorded an early 1990s Open University documentary featuring footage of Ninagawa's *Medea* and insisted that I watch it. She and my father were the kind of enthusiastic, supportive parents that took great interest in the random fascinations of their children, curious to see where they might lead. Twenty-five years later, it is bittersweet that this book must be dedicated to her memory. I hope she would have loved it.

# A NOTE ON THE TEXT

All quotations from Shakespeare's plays are taken from *The Arden Shakespeare: Shakespeare Complete Works,* revised edition, ed. Ann Thompson, David Scott Kastan and Richard Proudfoot (London: Arden Shakespeare, 2011).

Japanese names are rendered in natural Japanese order, with the surname first, except when a name includes a non-Japanese element (e.g. Lily Komine). Since Japanese does not use capital letters, I have limited their use to proper nouns. For the ease of non-Japanese speaking readers, I have omitted macrons. The romanization of Japanese words and names is sometimes inconsistent, but I have endeavoured to use actors' preferred versions of their names (hence Otake Shinobu but Ohtori Ran). Technical terms and words in Japanese (and other languages) are italicized throughout.

# 1

# Introduction

The first part of this introduction examines the productions that Ninagawa Yukio directed between October 2004 and November 2006, when I lived in Tokyo. Ninagawa turned seventy in 2005, and the year was focused on celebrating this milestone, at the Bunkamura Theatre Cocoon and the Saitama Arts Theatre in his hometown. Ninagawa was the artistic director of both venues,[1] and he created distinctly different programmes for each. Bunkamura presented a series responding to Ninagawa's career to date, while in Saitama Ninagawa began a new phase of the Sai no Kuni Shakespeare series, his ambitious attempt to stage all Shakespeare's plays. The eighteen shows Ninagawa directed between 2004 and 2006 reflect specific aspects of his career. Some projects were nostalgic, but many were innovative and forward-looking; several major initiatives and collaborations in the final decade of Ninagawa's life trace their origins to this period. This book focuses specifically on Ninagawa's Shakespeare productions, but these were by no means created in a vacuum. Besides almost fifty separate productions, of nearly all Shakespeare's plays, Ninagawa directed over a hundred plays by other writers. The decade after my time in Tokyo showed no relaxation of pace: between 2007 and his death on 12 May 2016, Ninagawa directed over seventy-five more plays. For ease of reference, given this extraordinary output, I use the list of shows created during my time in Japan as a lens through which to examine certain interests and approaches that appear throughout Ninagawa's career.

# Biography

Ninagawa Yukio was born in October 1935 in Honmachi, part of Kawaguchi City in Saitama Prefecture, north of Tokyo. Of its busy foundries, Ninagawa remembered how 'the labourers came from all over Japan; Kawaguchi itself gave the impression of a human slag heap. Scenes of masses of people were burned into my memory from childhood' (Miyashita, 1987: 402). His mother took him to *kabuki* performances from a very early age, and these frequent visits had a strong impact on Ninagawa's sense of the theatrical. He applied, unsuccessfully, to study painting at Tokyo University of the Arts, and instead became an actor. In 1955 he joined Gekidan Seihai (Young People's Theatre Group) and began studying with its director Kurahashi Ken, a professor at Waseda University. Ninagawa was eventually made a full member of the group and stayed with Seihai for the best part of a decade. He acted in a variety of projects, including a performance as the queen in Jarry's *Ubu Roi*. He also appeared in several films and television shows, among them Matsumoto Toshiro's *Funeral Parade of Roses*, set in the underworld of 1960s Tokyo. His most memorable screen performance was as a theatre director in the award-winning 1984 film *W's Tragedy*.

Gekidan Seihai was founded in the early 1950s by former members of the Bungakuza, Japan's foremost *shingeki* company. Translated literally as 'new drama', *shingeki* developed during the early twentieth century as a modern theatre style, eschewing the traditional performing arts and emulating the realism of modern European and American drama. Working with Seihai, Ninagawa was drilled in the Stanislavski-inspired, text-based approach integral to many *shingeki* companies. Script analysis was a central tenet of their approach to any play, and while Ninagawa would eventually rebel against much of what he learned with the company, this textual analysis remained central to his working method throughout his life. When Kurahashi left the company, Ninagawa soon followed, and, now in his early thirties, turned his attention to directing.

# July–December 2004

My first experience of Ninagawa's work was in the mid-1990s, when I saw excerpts from his *Medea* in a BBC documentary. I was fascinated by its beauty and its dramatic power. It inspired me to study Greek at school and then drama at university, before combining these with an MA in Greek Theatre Performance at Royal Holloway in London. My thesis analysed Ninagawa's 2002 *Oedipus Rex*. Happily I saw the show in Athens as part of the Cultural Olympiad in 2004, weeks before I finished the dissertation. While I completed it, Ninagawa was back in Japan, directing an all-male *As You Like It* for the Sai no Kuni series. The experiment marked a turning point in his interpretation of Shakespeare and led to a series of several all-male productions in Saitama, discussed in Chapter Four.

After my MA I was awarded a Japanese Government Monbukagakusho Scholarship, and I moved to Tokyo in October 2004. Before I left, I saw Ninagawa's English-language *Hamlet* at the Theatre Royal in Plymouth. This was his second English-language Shakespeare production, after a *King Lear* with the Royal Shakespeare Company (RSC) at the turn of the millennium that was savaged in the press. A similar fate had befallen Ninagawa's 1992 *Peer Gynt*, presented as part of the cultural programme of the Lillehammer Winter Olympics and performed in London and Oslo. English critics consistently praised Ninagawa's vision and ability when he presented works in Japanese, but his English-language productions were never as well received.

In late 2004 Ninagawa remounted two plays that had been instrumental to his early success. In December a new production of *Romeo and Juliet* opened at the Nissay Theatre in Tokyo, marking thirty years since Ninagawa's first production of the play. The 1974 version was a major success, launching his commercial career. The majority of the plays Ninagawa directed during the 1970s reappeared throughout his career; among these were *King Lear*, *The Water Magician*, Mishima Yukio's *Modern Noh Plays*, *Oedipus Rex*, *Medea* and *Hamlet*.

The theatrical approaches Ninagawa devised for each of these plays evolved over the years, but a seam of interpretative continuity in each can be traced back to this highly creative experimental period. The 2004 *Romeo and Juliet* toured Japan and proved that even thirty years later Ninagawa still had new things to say with the play. Casting Fujiwara Tatsuya as Romeo ensured its commercial success, and the young film star developed into a fine actor under Ninagawa's tutelage. He had played Hamlet in Ninagawa's most recent Japanese-language production. It was a *Hamlet* very much for young people, starring popular young actors in a new translation of the play. *Romeo and Juliet* continued in this vein.

Late 2004 marked three decades since Ninagawa's first Shakespeare and a quarter of a century since the debut of his career's most successful production, Akimoto Matsuyo's *Suicide for Love*. The play is an ingenious interweaving of stories and characters from three plays by 'Japan's Shakespeare' Chikamatsu Monzaemon. Chikamatsu was the poet par excellence of Japan's puppet theatre, *bunraku*. He wrote over three hundred plays, several of which deal with love suicides. Stories of such pacts between doomed lovers were so popular in Chikamatsu's time that they led to alarming numbers of real-life copycat deaths.[2] Although the source material was written for *bunraku*, Akimoto's play and Ninagawa's production successfully translated the stories into performances by live actors. The production was an early example of Ninagawa's supreme gift for spectacle. The design featured astonishing evocations of eighteenth-century Osaka, vibrant crowd scenes and an extended snowstorm during the climactic double suicide of Chubei and Umegawa. Theatre critic Senda Akihiko has written that Ninagawa was the first director to match the scale and ambition of Akimoto's theatrical ideas in performance (Senda, 1997: 104).

*Suicide for Love* was enormously successful and was performed over a thousand times between 1979 and 2005, substantially more than any other Ninagawa production. He directed several other plays by Akimoto over the subsequent decades, including *Namboku Love Story*, *Kaison: The Priest of Hitachi* and *Genroku Harbour Song*, his last ever show at the Theatre Cocoon in early 2016. *Suicide for Love* was the most enduring of their collaborations, and its final performances at the Hakata-za in Fukuoka were a fitting start to Ninagawa's celebratory year of 2005.

## *Ninagawa x Cocoon*

As *Suicide for Love* opened, Ninagawa began rehearsals in early January for the first of four productions in a programme celebrating his seventieth birthday at the Bunkamura Theatre Cocoon. Ninagawa's first production at Bunkamura had been in 1996, and he became the theatre's artistic director in 1999. Each of the four plays in the *Ninagawa x Cocoon* programme responded to a particular element of Ninagawa's work. The series featured a play by Shimizu Kunio, an 'angry young man' play from the 1960s, a Greek tragedy and a play about Japan's relationship with Shakespeare. Each was a response to (or a celebration of) a significant aspect of Ninagawa's career.

Opened in 1989, Bunkamura (which translates as 'cultural village') is an entertainment complex owned by the Tokyu Group in Shibuya, Tokyo. It houses a concert hall, cinema and museum, as well as the 747-seat Theatre Cocoon, the site of over fifty Ninagawa productions between 1996 and 2016. These included works by Shakespeare and Sophocles alongside important Japanese playwrights such as Mishima, Noda and Shimizu. For *Ninagawa x Cocoon* it might have been feasible to remount, say, *Hearty But Flippant*, *Medea*, *Suicide for Love* and *NINAGAWA Macbeth* – his first ever play, the first ever to tour internationally, the most successful and the most critically acclaimed of his Shakespeare productions. Four such revivals might have been a mouthwatering prospect for anyone who had not seen these landmark productions but would have been utter anathema to Ninagawa. Despite the consistent attention to the passage of time, and repeat engagements with particular plays, his focus was always on forward motion and improvement, on addressing problems that he had not quite solved. An obvious indication of this drive is his eight separate productions of *Hamlet*, discussed in Chapter Three.

*Ninagawa x Cocoon* relied on groundwork laid by earlier productions. In his first decade there Ninagawa had already presented an eclectic mix of plays, including Greek tragedy, Shakespeare, the *kabuki*-derived ghost story *Yotsuya Kaidan*, Chekhov, Brecht, Tennessee Williams and a new production of the aforementioned *Hearty But Flippant*. The 2005 programme bridged the gap between nostalgia and forward motion, acknowledging earlier successes but also presenting works that were new to Ninagawa. The first production of the series was by one of Ninagawa's earliest collaborators, Shimizu Kunio. Ninagawa directed more plays by Shimizu than by any other writer apart from Shakespeare, and their collaboration was a critical part of Ninagawa's career.

Ninagawa met Shimizu during the 1960s when they were introduced by Kurahashi Ken at Gekidan Seihai. When Seihai declined to produce one of Shimizu's early plays – despite Ninagawa's support – they both felt their days with the company were numbered, leaving soon afterwards to found Gendaijin Gekijo (the Contemporary People's Theatre). Theirs was one of a great number of companies within Tokyo's Little Theatre Movement, often known as *angura*, from the Japanese transliteration of 'underground' (*andaguraraundo*). Gendaijin Gekijo's first production was Shimizu's 1969 play *Hearty But Flippant*, performed at the Art Theatre Shinjuku Bunka, a cinema that permitted live performances after its final screening every evening. This was a play about waiting in line, an all too common feature of contemporary Japanese life. Tokyo had seen countless riots and demonstrations through the tumultuous 1960s, between the resistance to Japan's renewal of the controversial ANPO Security Treaty in 1960 and the violent student protests in 1968. Tokyo citizens had accordingly become used to the sight of the *kido-tai*, the riot police. Shimizu's play ends with an execution, but Ninagawa's final *coup-de-théâtre* was to surround the applauding audience with actors costumed as the aforementioned riot police, barring the exits. The stunt had an enormous impact, launching Ninagawa as a director to watch. Ninagawa soon directed Shimizu's *Let's Lay Flowers There Tomorrow* – the play that Seihai had earlier rejected. Shimizu and Ninagawa remained collaborators after Gendaijin Gekijo disbanded in 1971, and launched another company, the Sakura-sha, or Cherry Blossom Company. Ninagawa directed five further plays by Shimizu, all presented at the Art Theatre Shinjuku Bunka.

In 1974 Nakane Tadao, a young producer from the entertainment conglomerate Toho, invited Ninagawa to direct a commercial Shakespeare production for the Nissay Theatre. Ninagawa accepted, but members of the Sakura-sha felt that his taking the job was a betrayal. The company was in something of a creative rut, but there were still numerous plans afoot for further productions. All of these would have to be abandoned if the director absconded to direct for a huge commercial venue. Ninagawa took the job, and the Sakura-sha ceased operations soon afterwards. The resulting feeling of ostracization haunted Ninagawa for much of his career. One project in development at the time of this crisis was a proposed version, by Shimizu, of the story of *Masakado*. Taira no Masakado, famous from *The Tale of the Heike*, led a massive rebellion against the government in Kyoto. The Sakura-sha were trying to find a way to frame the ancient story in a way that reflected contemporary politics.

> I was thinking about doing [...] a play on Masakado, who rebelled against the establishment of the time somewhat like Macbeth. It would be about a lost war leader's revival – the story of a leader who died in Kyoto and whose head suddenly appeared in Otemachi in Tokyo. I wanted the story of a leader's revival to connect with our theatre company's revival. What I was asking Shimizu to write was quite different from what we had been doing before. (Ninagawa, 1995: 209–10)

Ninagawa was hoping, too, for a different style of writing, a different way of communicating even, and Shimizu endeavoured to factor all of this into the play he eventually wrote and completed in 1975. The play tells the story of Masakado from the perspectives of several of the people in his life as he himself goes through a fever dream of madness. The historical character was eventually decapitated, and the play's full title has an inference similar to the English phrase 'lost his head'. By the time Shimizu finished it, the Sakura-sha had been disbanded and Ninagawa had taken the leap into the commercial unknown, directing the aforementioned *Romeo and Juliet*.

Ninagawa and Shimizu reunited in 1982 for Shimizu's *In that Rainy Summer, Thirty Juliets Came Back*. This beautiful play features a homage to Takarazuka, Japan's distinct genre of all-female musical theatre. The story is built around a company's efforts to stage a production of *Romeo and Juliet*. It is surely no coincidence that *this* was the play-within-the-play in the project that reunited Shimizu and Ninagawa, since the same play had precipitated the dissolution of their company. Ninagawa directed several more plays by Shimizu in the 1980s and 1990s, including *Tango at the End of Winter*, performed in Edinburgh and the West End in 1991. The play tells the story of an actor who has travelled back to his hometown, where his family runs a cinema. Having abandoned the stage, he is haunted by memories of past performances, and as his mind collapses the people in his life try to help him. Ninagawa directed the premiere in Japanese starring Hira Mikijiro, and then in English it starred Alan Rickman. Of the four productions that Ninagawa directed in English in the course of his career, *Tango* was perhaps the best received. Revisiting what might have happened if he had not directed that first *Romeo and Juliet*, Ninagawa finally brought his spectacular interpretation of *Masakado* to the Cocoon stage in 2005, three decades after Shimizu finished it.

After *Masakado* came Wesker's *The Kitchen*, written in 1959. It was translated into Japanese by Odashima Yushi, known primarily for his translations of Shakespeare. Odashima's translations were the basis for many of Ninagawa's most famous productions, and he also translated a wide variety of English-language playwrights, including Tennessee Williams, Lillian Hellman and Harold Pinter. Ninagawa also staged Odashima's versions of Chekhov's *The Cherry Orchard*, *The Seagull* and *Three Sisters*, all at the Theatre Cocoon.

*The Kitchen* has been performed in over sixty cities worldwide, and it was an early success for Ariane Mnouchkine's Théâtre du Soleil. Ninagawa had always been eager to tackle it, not least since its young protagonist was exactly the same age as Ninagawa when the play was first produced. The play's major set piece – the recreation of a London kitchen during a busy lunch service – was performed entirely in mime during the production. Ninagawa staged the play in traverse, arranging the space as in his extraordinary production of *The Greeks*. Rehearsals included instruction from professional chefs, and everything was precisely choreographed, despite the fact that no food was actually cooked.

One might wonder how well Wesker's socialist critique was communicated, presented as it was within the entertainment complex of a large department store. During the interval, members of the Theatre Cocoon's predominantly female audience were invited to buy items featured on the lunch menu prepared within the play, rather undermining Wesker's focus on the plight of the individual within the machine of capitalism. Much of the play's investigation of race and class in 1950s' London was eradicated by the necessity of hiring a homogeneous Japanese company of actors. Instead it became the story of yet another angry young man, not markedly different from, say, *Hamlet*, or even *Caligula*, which Ninagawa directed at Bunkamura in 2007. While Ninagawa may have hoped to encourage his audiences out of their comfortable seats and back into the kind of spirited revolution he witnessed in the 1960s, most likely his 2005 audience saw *The Kitchen* as a period piece, akin to Ninagawa's Shakespeares or Greek tragedies.

*The Kitchen* was not particularly revolutionary, despite the director's best efforts, but its successor in the series, *Medea*, was a concerted attempt to reimagine a 'classic'. Within this festival celebrating Ninagawa's work, it was to be expected that the programme would celebrate the director's successes with Shakespeare and Greek tragedy. A radical response to Ninagawa's Japanese Shakespeare would round out the series, but first came a new version of Euripides. Ninagawa's original production of *Medea* premiered in 1978 and is arguably the most famous Japanese production of a Greek tragedy ever. It was presented all over the world for over twenty years before its final performance in Nagano in October 1999.[3]

Just as *Masakado* was not the first Shimizu play Ninagawa directed at the Theatre Cocoon, so *Medea* was not the first Greek tragedy. He directed *Oedipus Rex* in 2002 and *Electra* in 2003, both in new translations by Yamagata Harue. She was also responsible for the 2005 *Medea* and would translate *Orestes* in 2006. The new *Medea* starred Otake Shinobu, a popular actress and regular fixture at Bunkamura, where her roles with Ninagawa had already included Electra, Blanche DuBois and Lady Macbeth. Decades before, Ninagawa had commented rather controversially that he did not feel that a woman could play the role as he perceived it – primarily because his production was so reliant on his adaptation of several aspects of *kabuki*. The most obvious of these was the tradition of *onnagata*, male actors who play female characters. Ninagawa's original *Medea* was designed to subvert and manipulate this *kabuki* tradition, and in order for its subversive presentation to work it was imperative that a woman not play the part. In 2005, armed with a new translation (by a female translator), he revisited the play with an all-female chorus and no trace of *kabuki*.

Outside Japan, Ninagawa's original *Medea* is considered a landmark of intercultural theatre. It was remarkable primarily for its beauty and impressive staging, but it was a structurally traditional production of the Euripides text. To Japanese audiences, it was much more experimental and transgressive (as discussed in Chapter Two) and the 2005 production aimed for similar impact. This time, however, he wanted to concentrate on the acting, particularly that of Otake.

> If you get too carried away with the lighting and electronic development, you forget about the actors. At the moment I feel that theatre should be given back to the actors, so my sets are getting simpler and I am putting more demands on the actors. They are happening right there in front of you. That is what theatre is about. (Irvin, 2003: 97)

This focus was immediately obvious in the minimalist designs for his Bunkamura productions of *Oedipus Rex* and *Hamlet*, but less so in *Medea*, wherein he covered the whole stage of the Theatre Cocoon with water. The heart of this production was not a typical Ninagawa 'concept' or a new recontextualization of the play, but Otake's spirited performance as the heroine. Its ending was particularly interesting. Having transported the audience to this strange, waterlogged nether-world, which featured a hyper-realistic performance from its heroine, Ninagawa's final *coup-de-théâtre* could simply have been his filling the entire theatre with light when Medea appeared aloft in her dragon-borne chariot. Even as the obviously artificial chariot was slowly withdrawn, Ninagawa had another trick up his sleeve: the back doors of the stage opened, revealing the Bunkamura car park. This final move undercut any and all artifice, allowing the mundane reality of the outside world to seep onto the stage.

Ninagawa had opened the theatre doors on various other occasions. The mechanicals of his *Midsummer Night's Dream* wandered in from the street via an open door, and his 2001 version of *Hearty But Flippant* ended with a similar stunt. It was an attempt to show the audience that what was happening on stage was immediately relevant to what was happening on the street outside the theatre, now visible through these opened doors. *Hearty But Flippant* is a play about trying to stand up to authority. Central to it is a quest for an active sense of 'self' – always a preoccupation of Ninagawa's theatre. In *Medea*, the incursion of the outside world had a different message. The doors opened after the most acrimonious interactions between Medea and Jason; the children had been slaughtered, and Medea was ready to leave Corinth for a new life. Opening the rear doors to reveal a car park at such a climactic point in the play was a deliberately bathetic move. Ninagawa was provocatively questioning the seriousness of such an argument. As the doors closed and the lights faded, the audience heard an increasing number of crying children. Ninagawa appeared to be saying that, no matter how spectacular the divorce, the children are the ones who suffer in the end.

# Reinventing Japanese theatre

After *Medea*, Ninagawa decamped to Saitama to revive his production of Mishima's *Modern Noh Plays*. This double bill of *Sotoba Komachi* and *Yoroboshi* was another of the successful 1970s productions, and a revival had toured to the Barbican in London in 2001. The new dates in Saitama were programmed in advance of another tour, this time to Lincoln Center's White Lights Festival in July. Mishima had always wanted his *Modern Noh Plays* to be performed on Broadway, and he and his translator Donald Keene had worked hard to create a viable English-language version. Thirty-five years after Mishima's death (and almost thirty years after Ninagawa's first production) this Japanese-language production finally brought the plays to an American audience.

*Sotoba Komachi* reimagines the story of the Heian poetess Komachi, turning her into an elderly beggar reminiscing about happier days. A young poet, entranced by her story, dies of love for her at the end. *Yoroboshi* was Mishima's particularly bleak interpretation of the story of a blind boy whose parents fight for custody with the couple who adopted him after a wartime air raid. The original *noh* play is about a reunion between a father and son, but Mishima's version is significantly darker. As his case worker describes the blazing sunset bursting into the court room, Toshinori agrees that he can see it, but in fact all he sees is the inferno that cost him his sight. Ninagawa's production ended with a spectacular surprise, as the entire set collapsed and Mishima's final speech before his suicide played in the background. Just as the play's anger and passion started to subside, Ninagawa interrupted the theatrical artifice with a chilling reminder of the reality of the world beyond the theatre. The production's approach had not changed much since 1976. Once again *Sotoba Komachi* was performed by an all-male cast, and red camellia blossoms cascaded onto the stage throughout. This revival featured Jo Haruhiko and Takahashi Yo as the two central characters, while Fujiwara Tatsuya reprised his performance as Toshinori in *Yoroboshi*. The production was an appropriate choice for export in this celebratory year. It showcased Ninagawa – known in New York primarily for his Shakespeare – as a director capable of staging innovative readings of Japanese plays *as well as* his more feted versions of European classics.

In the first half of 2005 Ninagawa revisited most of his signature theatrical genres, including Greek tragedy, polemical dramas from the 1960s and 1970s and works by major Japanese playwrights of the twentieth century. Thereafter Ninagawa turned to Shakespeare, the playwright with whom he is most associated. Immediately after Mishima's modern interpretation of *noh*, Ninagawa scored the huge coup of being invited to direct a *kabuki* production.

Non-Japanese critics have used the words *noh* and particularly *kabuki* to describe any and all Japanese elements in Ninagawa's work since it was first seen abroad in the early 1980s. Thanks to the successes of *Medea* and *NINAGAWA Macbeth*, which both manipulated elements of *kabuki*, he was for decades considered a director of '*kabuki* Shakespeare'.[4] This assumption overlooks the fact that *kabuki* invariably does not even have a director. A supervisory role is often taken by the leader of the troupe performing a given month's programme, but the concept of a director, responsible for a production's overall interpretative strategy, is alien to the form. Ninagawa had cast *kabuki* actors in several productions, but their presence no more made a show a *kabuki* production than his casting a Takarazuka star such as Rei Asami in *Oedipus Rex* could turn Sophoclean tragedy into a glitzy musical. The most recent such project had been *The Greeks*, featuring the young *kabuki* star Onoe Kikunosuke V as Orestes. Following this collaboration Kikunosuke commissioned a new *kabuki* translation of *Twelfth Night* and asked Ninagawa to direct it. It was entirely in keeping with the mood of this celebratory year that the one Shakespeare play Ninagawa directed in 2005 would be such a major event: Ninagawa would, at last, create an actual *kabuki* Shakespeare.[5]

## *Tenpo Juninen no Shakespeare*

Ninagawa *Twelfth Night* (discussed in Chapter Two) was perhaps the production that audiences always expected he would create; a legitimate fusion of Ninagawa's Shakespearean expertise and Japan's most popular traditional theatre. By contrast, his choice for the fourth and final production of the *Ninagawa x Cocoon* season was one that turned Shakespeare completely inside out. Ninagawa liked to be a maverick, and to do the unexpected. It was unsurprising that, in a festival celebrating his work, this famed interpreter of Shakespeare chose not to direct a Shakespeare play at all. Instead, he chose a play that draws on elements from *all* of Shakespeare's works, woven together in a sprawling new Japanese story: Inoue Hisashi's *Tenpo Juninen no Shakespeare* (Shakespeare in the Twelfth Year of the Tenpo Era). Inoue (1934–2010) was one of Japan's foremost playwrights, and an almost exact contemporary of Ninagawa. They had never worked together before this production in 2005, but their collaboration was a very happy one. Ninagawa directed seven more Inoue plays in the final years of his life, including *Musashi*, written especially for him.

*Tenpo* was written in 1974 – not coincidentally the year Ninagawa first began working on Shakespeare. Japan was enjoying a boom of Shakespearean production at the time, which is why a young producer like Nakane had the means to recruit an up-and-coming director such as Ninagawa. Inoue's play is a response to this popularity. As he explained at the time, 'Essentially, Shakespeare should be splendid, varied and amazingly amusing. So, we will present our Japanese Shakespeare including all these essences' (Tanaka, 2002a).

Given *Tenpo*'s four-hour running time and its enormous cast (Ninagawa's production featured forty-three actors), it is seldom performed; there had been only two significant previous attempts to stage it.[6] Ninagawa's version was a huge success. Even allowing for Ninagawa's penchant for celebrity casting, the *Tenpo* company was astonishing; job offers must have felt like invitations to his birthday party. He cast a galaxy of stars from Japanese film, television and theatre, including favourites such as Fujiwara Tatsuya, Shiraishi Kayoko, Kiba Katsumi, Natsuki Mari, Jo Haruhiko, Karasawa Toshiaki, Shinohara Ryoko and Yoshida Kohtaloh. The performance sold out within hours of going on sale, months before it opened.

During rehearsals, Ninagawa often joked that whatever reputation he had earned over the years would be destroyed by this production, designed to be irreverent, bawdy and disrespectful. He often referred to the text that had inspired him since his first Shakespeare production, Mikhail Bakhtin's *Rabelais and His World*. The book completely changed Ninagawa's impression of Renaissance Europe, and deeply influenced his interpretation of Shakespeare. While *shingeki* may have been more interested in the nobility and aristocracy of Shakespeare's worlds, Rabelais led Ninagawa to explore the bottom of the slag heap, reminiscent of his early memories of Kawaguchi. Reading Bakhtin encouraged him to celebrate the chaos, the outsiders and the danger inherent in Shakespeare's plays. *Tenpo* was the perfect play to celebrate Ninagawa's 'Bakhtinian' relationship with Shakespeare. The play's pageantry and carnival, its inversions and interpolations, its choruses of builders, thieves and prostitutes, match wonderfully with Ninagawa's own ideas about Shakespeare.

In the following quotation, Bakhtin is discussing carnival, but could easily be reviewing Ninagawa's *Tenpo*:

> all the symbols of the carnival idiom are filled with this pathos of change and renewal, with the sense of the gay relativity of prevailing truths and authorities. We find here a characteristic logic, the peculiar logic of the 'inside out', of the 'turnabout', of a continual shifting from top to bottom, from front to rear, of numerous parodies and travesties, humiliations, profanations, comic crownings and uncrownings. A second life, a second world of folk culture is thus constructed; [...] a parody of the extracarnival life, a 'world inside out'. [...] Folk humour denies, but it revives at the same time. (Bakhtin, 1984: 11)

The world of *Tenpo* was certainly a world 'inside out'. As the audience took their seats, they saw a reconstruction of the interior of Shakespeare's Globe Theatre in London. Actors paced the set in period costumes worthy of the most obsequious *shingeki* production. At show time, a gong sounded and Uzaki Ryudo's raucous music completely changed the mood, as a motley crew of dirty builders marched through the audience. Some of them carried night-soil buckets, and others raced onto the stage to pull apart the Globe set while they sang. The world of Shakespeare's theatre was torn down and replaced with Japanese scenery, and the story began in earnest.

The show's opening number asks 'what if Shakespeare had never existed?' The answer is that English literature students would not receive their PhDs, publishers who print Shakespeare in translation would go broke and the world of *shingeki* would be entirely at a loss. Inoue was responding to the Shakespeare boom in the 1970s, but in 2005 he could have been writing for Ninagawa. The director spent most of his career resisting academic criticism (of his own work) and rejecting *shingeki* tradition, and this play was the ideal conclusion to his Theatre Cocoon celebration. Shakespeare, the song concludes, is a 'rice chest' – and as long as he exists, Japanese theatre-makers (Ninagawa foremost among them) would never go hungry.

Never one to miss a trick, Ninagawa inserted nods to other Shakespeare directors throughout. A wry example was the moment after the play's King Lear character was expelled by his daughters. The actor, Yoshida Kohtaloh, walked painfully slowly around the stage in a physical manner obviously reminiscent of the work of Suzuki Tadashi. There was a healthy rivalry between Ninagawa and Suzuki; while both were leading figures in the experimental underground theatre scene of 1960s Tokyo, Suzuki received consistent critical acclaim while Ninagawa achieved enormous popular success. Neither was above making an occasional dismissive comment about the other's work, but they were united by *King Lear*. Both had presented significant productions of *King Lear* in England, and both were roundly criticized in the press. Whether it was a nod of solidarity or just a little playful mockery, the small reference to Suzuki was very funny. Ninagawa made comparably knowing reference to another Japanese Shakespeare at the end of the play.

Ninagawa was not the first interpreter to create a successful, internationally acclaimed, Japanese version of *Macbeth*; that honour went to Kurosawa Akira and his magnificent 1957 film *Kumonosujo* (*Throne of Blood*). Many compared the two directors, since they both loved Shakespeare, drew on traditional Japanese arts and imagery for their versions of the story and enjoyed substantial acclaim for the results. At the end of *Tenpo*, its villain is killed after scheming his way to power throughout the play. Ninagawa staged the execution in a manner deliberately reminiscent of Mifune Toshiro's death in *Kumonosujo*. If *Twelfth Night* was Ninagawa's exuberant answer to a career's worth of comparisons with *kabuki*, then this little homage was a nod to Kurosawa, acknowledging a lifetime of comparisons with another great Japanese Shakespearean.

At the end of *Tenpo*, all the actors/characters reappeared, climbing out of their 'graves' as ghosts, singing a reprise of the opening song. This time, however, as 'what if Shakespeare had never existed' rang through the auditorium, the Globe Theatre set was reassembled and 'order' was restored after Ninagawa's epic, freewheeling carnival. Ninagawa's notes from some of his earliest work included a short essay entitled 'the laughter of ghosts' (Ninagawa, 2002b: 44). At the end of *Tenpo*, as their laughter filled the theatre, this 'folk humour' restored Shakespeare's status, but only after having denied it throughout a terrifically entertaining, thoroughly Japanese evening.

# Spring 2006

Ninagawa's seventieth birthday fell one week before the end of *Tenpo*, and after its tour to Osaka he took a short break. Rehearsals began in December for his first production of 2006, *The Comedy of Errors*, his second Saitama Shakespeare with an all-male cast. There had been no Sai no Kuni productions in 2005, since the year's two major Shakespearean projects were elsewhere. Once rehearsals started the company would be busy for almost six months. As *The Comedy of Errors* opened, rehearsals began for a revival of *Titus Andronicus*, preparing for its tour to Stratford-upon-Avon for the RSC *Complete Works* season.

Discussed in detail in Chapter Four, *The Comedy of Errors* was a very welcome romp before the company tackled the grim horrors of *Titus Andronicus*. The latter was first staged in 2004, but this revised version had a number of new cast members, among them Oguri Shun as Aaron. In Shakespeare's play Aaron is a Moor, but in a homogeneous country such as Japan it is extremely difficult to find an ethnically appropriate actor who could speak Japanese well enough to play the part. Side-stepping race (by necessity rather than any disrespect),

Ninagawa had Oguri play the part as a sexually aggressive punk, with a look reminiscent of the worst kinds of Tokyo hoodlum. Oguri's youth made for a significant age gap between his Aaron and Rei Asami's Tamora, heightening the transgressive, sexually inappropriate reading of the character. The production presented a compelling version of Shakespeare's grisliest play without spilling a drop of blood.

Ninagawa began *Titus Andronicus* with a kind of pre-show, with actors on the stage warming up, lights being focused and a general feeling of theatrical activity being prepared. At showtime, Ninagawa told the actors to begin, and those playing Bassianus and Saturninus whipped around and began their opening speeches. The device of having the company on stage before showtime stemmed from Ninagawa's lifelong distaste for *shingeki* and its lip service to foreign acting styles. Ninagawa preferred to acknowledge and dispel any sheepishness about his company's Japanese identity, and to make an audience complicit in the imaginative creation of a show. He introduced the acting company (and occasionally the crew) in numerous productions, showing them as actors before they began the play. The story began once this agreement had been made – the audience and the performers on stage were all well aware that this was a Japanese production, and nobody was going to pretend otherwise. Variations on this kind of pre-show dated back at least as far as *The Tempest* in 1987 and continued to appear throughout the decade after *Titus* rehearsed in Saitama in early 2006. This kind of pre-show induction was one of Ninagawa's signature techniques, discussed throughout the book.

Before *Titus* departed for England, Ninagawa directed a new production of Noda Hideki's 1985 play *Byakuya no Valkyrie* (Valkyrie of the Midnight Sun), the first of his trilogy loosely based on Wagner's *Ring* cycle. Noda's company, The Dream Wanderers, presented all three plays in a huge event at Yoyogi Stadium in 1986, attended by over 26,000 people. Ninagawa had long considered Noda the most talented playwright in contemporary Japan. Early in his time at Bunkamura, he had directed Noda's play *Pandora's Bell* starring Otake Shinobu. *Byakuya* was staged to mark the play's twentieth anniversary and Ninagawa's ten years at Bunkamura. His four Cocoon productions in 2006 continued the inventive strand of programming devised for the previous celebratory year, this time with a focus on new versions of older works.

The two summer productions were Ford's *Tis Pity She's a Whore* and Euripides' *Orestes*. Neither was well known in Japan, and neither had ever been staged with the scale or resources available to a Ninagawa production. Although Ninagawa's focus had always been on Shakespeare, Odashima Yushi had translated Marlowe, Johnson, Middleton and Ford in the mid-1990s. Odashima's version of *Tis Pity She's a Whore* was Ninagawa's first production of a Jacobean play not by Shakespeare – perfect for the programming focus at Bunkamura. The design for the show was particularly impressive, featuring a split-level set evocative of the Romanesque architecture of Renaissance Italy. Streams of red ribbon – a marker of the transgressive or the disturbing from as far back as *Medea* – filled the entire space. This was a clear sign of the transgressive, incestuous passions that drive Ford's play. The play's shocking depiction of Catholic Italy was made manifest in a sharp, unsettling production, a fascinating testament to how provocative Jacobean tragedy can be.

## *Orestes*

Euripides' *Orestes* is a difficult play, relying heavily on an audience's awareness of its story. It was written as a parody of Aeschylus' *Oresteia*, and Euripides often mocks the structure of his predecessor's tetralogy. It is a minor miracle that both plays have survived the lottery of time, since without the surviving Aeschylus plays for comparison, *Orestes* would be very confusing indeed. At several points Euripides does the unthinkable and makes actual jokes – best among them the hapless, noisy attempts of the chorus to discuss the sleeping protagonist without waking him. Ninagawa was only able to stage this play because he had already directed *The Greeks* in 2000 and *Electra* in 2002. Had his audiences not already encountered these stories, the play would have been fiendishly difficult to communicate.

In Ninagawa, Euripides' cockeyed potboiler may just have found its ideal interpreter. Ninagawa was a sly, irreverent director who despite his age was determined constantly to challenge and to reinvent. *Orestes* came about because Fujiwara Tatsuya was eager to perform in a Greek tragedy for Ninagawa, after the wide variety of their recent collaborations, invariably featuring troubled, fractured young men. Ninagawa challenged the young actor to read the works of the Polish director Jerzy Grotowski. The production, and particularly Fujiwara's approach to the lead role, were heavily inspired by Ryszard Cieslak's performance in Grotowski's production of *The Constant Prince*.

If, as is believed, three actors performed all of a Greek play's speaking roles, Euripides really tested the versatility of his actors in *Orestes*. In an almost belligerent challenge to the convention, *Orestes* includes a very wide range of speaking roles, which would have forced a fascinating array of doublings. For Ninagawa, however, it was an opportunity to employ a large number of his favourite actors in a single production. Electra, Helen, Hermione, Pylades, Tyndareus, Menelaus, an Old Mycenaean and a Trojan Slave (one of the strangest roles Euripides ever created) all have speaking parts, making it one of the most populous surviving plays. While Fujiwara was doubtless the star, he was surrounded by a particularly seasoned and talented cast, including Yoshida Kohtaloh as a brilliant, petulant Menelaus. As he had since *The Greeks*, Ninagawa also employed a very strong group of actresses as the chorus.

*Orestes* was the last Greek play Ninagawa directed at Bunkamura, and he directed very few further tragedies.[7] In his final decade, the focus of Ninagawa's programme at the Theatre Cocoon remained inventive and wide ranging. He staged an increasing number of Japanese plays, by Inoue, Mishima, Kara Juro and Terayama Shuji, and by several younger playwrights. There were occasional Shakespeare revivals, juxtaposed with plays such as Christopher Hampton's *Total Eclipse*, Tom Stoppard's nine-hour epic *The Coast of Utopia*, an in-the-round version of *Twelve Angry Men* and even a Japanese adaptation of *Farewell My Concubine*.[8]

## Tango at the End of Winter

*Masakado* forged a new rapprochement between Ninagawa and Shimizu Kunio and led to several new productions in the following years. Among these were a version of the 1980 play *My Soul is Shining Water*, starring the unlikely combination of a *kyogen* star, Nomura Mansai, and a *kabuki* star, Onoe Kikunosuke. The play is an allegory drawn from Japanese history, using the past to comment on the present in the kind of theatrical dialogue at which Shimizu is such a master. For his final mainstage show in 2006 (and the last of my time in Japan), Ninagawa directed a new production of *Tango at the End of Winter*.[9] Shimizu's plays are notably filled with references to Shakespeare. *Gakuya* features actresses reminiscing about performances of *Macbeth*, *Romeo and Juliet* haunts *In that Rainy Summer* and *Tango* has echoes and quotations from *Othello* and many other plays. Erudition and nostalgia are woven through his works, and they are a beautiful complement to Ninagawa's own eclecticism.

Ninagawa began *Tango* with an evocation of the story's cinema in its heyday, filling it with nearly a hundred young people. The production featured Ninagawa's largest cast in many years. Rehearsals for this opening sequence were quite literally a masterclass, as Ninagawa lectured and directed the young actors. It was an impassioned recreation of the excited, engaged cinema audiences of the 1960s – in the kind of small cinema where Ninagawa and Shimizu first started working together. These were the young people who fought and protested, resisting the government and showing up to the cinema bandaged and wounded. The shock of this introduction was that, as the action in the film these young people were watching turned violent, the line between film and reality was blurred. The young people's movement turned to slow motion, as the performers attempted to escape from attack. Without specifying the nature of the onslaught, Ninagawa created a horrifying, moving sense of the tumultuous experience of being young in late 1960s Tokyo, when something as simple as going to the cinema could end in police brutality.

This opening sequence was one of the noisiest and most aggressive inductions Ninagawa ever staged and is a clear example of how he liked to start a production. Framing devices, acknowledgements of theatrical artifice or arresting inductions all served to explain the rules of a given production. Here, the introduction served as a clear indication of the parallels between the director and the play's protagonist. *Tango* is the story of a man of the theatre, reminiscing about the passionate youth he left behind when he became a professional. The sense of nostalgia, of longing for a more engaged, violent and exuberant life, haunted Ninagawa almost as much as it haunted Kiyomura. Unlike Shimizu's protagonist, of course, Ninagawa was in control of his memories, and he ended his production by having the crowd of young people return to the cinema, as exuberant and excited as they had been at the beginning. Here again was the passionate audience of politically engaged, rebellious young people that Ninagawa left behind at the beginning of the 1970s. They had always been in the background, glimmering in the shadows.

# Critical approaches

Discussing Native American dance, Roland Barthes once asked 'can we Westerners really consume a fragment of civilization totally isolated from its context?' (Barthes, 1985: 121). The question of context – and of how cultural difference can influence the reception of an artist's work – is central to this book's analysis of Ninagawa's work. I must obviously acknowledge my own non-Japanese status, mitigated by extensive research and time spent in Ninagawa's rehearsal rooms in Tokyo. This book examines how Ninagawa interpreted Shakespeare primarily for his Japanese audiences. It has at its core two related ideas. The first is Barthes' question about whether a fragment of a civilization (or a work of art, or indeed any 'text') can ever be consumed outside its cultural context. For Ninagawa's theatre, cultural context is vitally important, and feeds directly into the book's second key idea, the centrality of the spectator as ultimate creator of meaning in the theatre. The spectator is 'the object of the verbal and scenic discourse, the receiver in the process of communication, the king of the feast' (Ubersfeld, 1982: 303). The viewer is central to the production of theatrical meaning, and the pleasures this entails:

> There is the pleasure of discovery, of analysing the signs of performance, of invention (when the spectator finds her own meanings for the theatrical signs), of identification, of experiencing temporarily the impossible or the forbidden, and finally there is the total pleasure suggested by the Indian *rasa*, 'the union of all effective elements, plus the distancing that gives peace.' (Carlson, 1993: 510)

> Theatrical pleasure, properly speaking, is the pleasure of the sign; it is the most semiotic of all pleasures ... It would not be going too far to say that the act of filling the gap is the very source of theatrical pleasure. (Ubersfeld, 1982: 129)

In Ninagawa's theatre, the audience was presented with multiple layers of meaning, and invited to enjoy the 'pleasure' of creating their own meaning from his varying systems of signification. Ninagawa's references only combined in the imagination of the spectator. This, however, could only fully happen within Ninagawa's intended Japanese context, since context so deeply influences interpretation.

# Interculturalism

Japan has, for over a millennium, been subject to external cultural forces. China was a dominant influence for many centuries, and European culture was becoming fashionable before the Tokugawa Shogunate banned all outside influence between 1603 and 1868. Despite this prolonged isolation, the Japanese language is a constant site of 'intercultural' activity. The written language's *kanji* are quite literally Chinese characters, and while some of these ideograms can mean the same thing in both languages, they represent very different sounds in each. Japanese has two further syllabaries, each representing every spoken syllable in the language. One set is used for Japanese words and the other exclusively for words of any foreign origin. The two syllabaries also identify the various readings of a particular *kanji*, since almost every ideogram will have both a Chinese and a Japanese reading. European influence is also evident in certain everyday words, such as *pan* (bread), or *arubaito* (job, from the German *Arbeit*). Contemporary Japanese is suffused with loan words, often modified to an almost unrecognizable extent. *Angura* is a good example, as is *pokémon*, which comes from the contraction of '*pocke*t *mon*ster'. There are intercultural negotiations at every turn of phrase.

Lacanian theory suggests that one's character is intricately connected to language. 'Before language assigns us an "I," we possess no sense of self' (Rivkin and Ryan, 1998: 123).

So, one's identity and one's way of looking at the world are determined by one's language. Given that Japanese language is a site of such intercultural readings and adaptations, it can be argued that the Japanese identity is likewise predisposed to the absorption and incorporation of 'foreign' material. Finding a *Japanese* 'sense of self' was a major preoccupation throughout Ninagawa's career: 'I'm still struggling with this disadvantage in our culture – we don't have a definite "self," "self" as an agent, an assertive, aggressive self. The core of my artistic struggle is actually to discover such a self' (Ninagawa, 1995: 211).

In this context, Ninagawa's long-standing fascination with key texts of Western drama dealing with personal agency is understandable. Transposing *Hamlet* (or *As You Like It*, or *Coriolanus*) to a Japanese context helped him to investigate and present Japanese equivalents to the active, 'European' self in these plays. Ninagawa presented a twin-layered staging of the Japanese self – primarily in the protagonists of the plays themselves, and secondly in the 'intercultural' tendency of the Japanese character as evidenced in its language.[10]

As was gently parodied in the film *Lost in Translation*, Japanese appropriation and assimilation of Western culture is extremely widespread but often happens on strictly Japanese terms. Given the 'repackaging' that can take place (as exemplified by the linguistic cases above, and the often wholly unconscious assimilation of foreign music[11]), 'Western' cultural artefacts can become so much a part of Japanese culture that they can no longer be considered 'foreign'.

Ninagawa's work first began to appear as an example of intercultural theatre in the 1980s. In *The Dramatic Touch of Difference* (Fischer-Lichte et al., 1990) he received minimal attention compared to Suzuki Tadashi, but the small reference was quite influential. James Brandon wrote 'The director, Ninagawa Yukio, produced a *Macbeth* specifically for production in London while using a wholly Japanese cast' (Brandon, 1990: 91). NINAGAWA *Macbeth* was actually produced in Tokyo in 1980, and it was half a decade before it toured outside Japan. It was first presented in Edinburgh, and then came to the National Theatre in London in a double bill with *Medea*, thanks to the determination of Thelma Holt. Ninagawa asserted throughout his career that his primary concern was for his Japanese audience, and that when he did travel abroad it was at the behest of others. Almost all of his productions began in Tokyo, and they toured with hardly any modification. Productions created in English were either given a Japanese production first (*Peer Gynt*, 1990, *Tango at the End of Winter*, 1991) or developed and first performed in Japan (*King Lear*, 1999). Stating that productions were specifically created for overseas performance is problematic, as this overlooks Ninagawa's stated philosophy and approach. Commentators have remained committed to the importance of his outward-leaning interest, insisting on Ninagawa's status as a global 'purveyor' of Shakespeare.[12] There is obviously some truth to this – after all, Ninagawa's work toured annually for thirty-five years – but his primary artistic focus was on telling stories to his own people. The idea that Ninagawa's work was conceived *specifically* (or worse, exclusively) for foreign consumption overlooks and undermines a lifetime commitment to his Japanese audience.

Said's *Orientalism* (1978, published the same year as Ninagawa's first *Hamlet*) was the first study to analyse the traffic of artistic ideas between 'East' and 'West', while landmark 'intercultural' productions by Peter Brook and Ariane Mnouchkine generated heated discourse in the 1980s and 1990s for their manipulation of Asian iconographies. Ninagawa's work was comparably foreign and exotic, but the images he interpolated were from his *own* culture, and the subtleties of their employment were often lost on non-Japanese audiences. Ninagawa's work – a different kind of intercultural project by virtue of its position outside the 'Western' world of Europe and America – engendered less heated debate, since the cultural traditions he used were generally his own. As 'global Shakespeare' has become an increasingly vital academic discourse, Ninagawa's work has often featured as an example of an international product designed for multiple markets – as his consistent touring schedule would attest. Some critics repeatedly contended that there was a deliberate *japonisme* operating in Ninagawa's productions, designed to fascinate foreign audiences with seductive glimmers of Japan. Ninagawa resented this, insisting that his Japanese references were designed to communicate to a *Japanese* audience.[13]

Regardless, Ninagawa is mentioned in Brian Singleton's survey of interculturalism:

> directors such as Japan's Ninagawa Yukio [...] have sought not to reinvigorate their own national theatre practices but to reject authenticity and embrace hybrid multiple realities. Thus one of the reasons why First World interculturalism has become a global phenomenon is that it purloins the surfaces of other cultures in order to attain the greatest market share, by reaching out for the largest common denominator of mythologized cultural icons. Ninagawa [is] very much part of the transnational circus of the supra-cultural festival circuit (joining Western directors such as Brook, Robert Lepage, and Robert Wilson), whose constituency has no real national or social hinterland other than the globalized community of high-art consumers, many of whom experience theatre as cultural tourists. (Singleton, 2003: 629)

Certainly Ninagawa's productions were seen abroad (i.e. outside Japan) at various international festivals, but these productions constituted only a fraction of his overall output. Singleton's description of a globalized 'supra-cultural festival circus' without a 'national or social hinterland' ignores the vast majority of Ninagawa's productions, which were only performed in Japan. With remarkably few exceptions, Ninagawa's international productions premiered in Tokyo before touring abroad, and often toured extensively within Japan. Singleton's listing of Ninagawa alongside Brook, Lepage and Wilson is problematic, since the 'mythologized icons' that he 'purloined' belonged to *his own* culture. Commentators may criticize his use (or abuse) of these cultural signifiers, but his frame of reference is not 'other'. Shakespeare had been part of the Japanese imaginative landscape for a century by the time of Ninagawa's first encounter. Writing about both Ninagawa and Suzuki Tadashi, Brokering argued that they

> can be labelled neither Orientalists, Occidentalists, post-colonialists, nor multi-culturalists. [...] they resist classification – perhaps a testament to the success with which they have syncretised Japanese and Western theatre traditions. ... Their approaches and methods have restored to Japanese theatre the music, dance, theatricality, and physicalized acting that were characteristic of all other Japanese performing arts. (Brokering, 2002: 87–9)

Since the vast majority of Ninagawa's work was created for a Japanese audience by a Japanese director whose main visual, musical and theatrical references are all Japanese, calling Ninagawa's work 'intercultural' is inadequate. Only a third of Ninagawa's Shakespeare productions were seen outside Japan, and indeed the total number of touring productions constitutes only about a tenth of his overall output. While his work may appear intercultural to a non-Japanese spectator, the designation recalls Daryl Chin's criticism of Barthes' *The Empire of Signs*, which

> discusses Japanese culture in terms of its sheer 'otherness,' thereby rendering the working of a complex social structure as quaint, in the manner that Edward Said has described as 'Orientalism.' At no point [...] is there any cognisance of the fact that, for a Japanese person living in Japan, the culture is not 'Other.' The culture is, in fact, the dominant culture, and the inscrutability, the impassivity, and the unfathomability of the culture are not constructs designed to tease the Western imagination. For a Japanese person, they are not inscrutable, impassive or unfathomable at all. (Chin, 1991: 85–6)

The process of intercultural traffic in contemporary Japanese theatre is very different from its equivalent in the Western world: 'one could argue that interculturalism was born out of a certain ennui, a reaction to aridity and the subsequent search for new sources of energy, vitality and sensuality through the importation of "rejuvenating raw materials"' (Bharucha, 1996: 207).

In Japan, 'intercultural' directors such as Ninagawa and Suzuki emerged at a time when theatre practitioners were dissatisfied with *shingeki*, but they sought 'rejuvenating raw materials' from *inside* Japan. Ninagawa's directing career began in a curious milieu between traditional performing arts such as *kabuki*, to which he would have had no access because he was not born into it, and the kinds of *shingeki* Shakespeare interpretation that he spent his career trying to supplant. As his work evolved he found his own distinct space between these two Japanese performance cultures. His 'rejuvenating raw materials', Japanese cultural signifiers transported from the performing arts, from religious rituals and from contemporary life, are certainly not 'foreign', and their employment is not so much 'intercultural' as '*intra*-cultural', which 'refers to the search for national traditions, often forgotten, corrupted or repressed, in order to reassess the sources of a style of performance, to situate it better in relation to external influences and to understand more deeply the origins and the transformation of its own culture' (Pavis, 1996: 5).

Although reinterpretation and modification are characteristic of Japanese culture in general and Ninagawa's theatre in particular, Japanese society is so 'transculturated' (Taylor, 1991) that 'intercultural' lacks the nuance to explain Ninagawa's complicated semiotics. Thanks to the work of such projects as the Interweaving Performance Cultures initiative at the Freie Universität Berlin, the reductive dichotomies inherent in early discussions of 'intercultural' performance have long been supplanted by more sophisticated modes of approach.

In their introduction to *Shakespeare in Asia* (2010: 1–20) Dennis Kennedy and Yong Li Lan analyse Ninagawa's use of flowers (among them cherry blossoms, irises and lotus leaves) from a sophisticated variety of perspectives. They acknowledge that context is essential, and that 'all these ways of "seeing" Ninagawa's use of flowering plants were available at the same time in one production, if not all to the same spectator' (2010: 20). While Ninagawa's work absolutely deserves attention as an example of the interweaving of different cultures (Japanese and foreign), its sophisticated, deliberate manipulation of Japanese images for *Japanese* viewers suggests an alternative, intertextual approach.

# Intertextuality

Although the term 'intertextuality' was only formulated and theorized in the 1960s, the process of intertextual reading is much older, particularly in the theatre. Intertextuality insists that no 'text' exists within a closed system, but that 'the work of art is inevitably shot through with references, quotations and influences of every kind [...]; what is produced at the moment of reading is due to the cross-fertilization of the packaged textual material ... by all the texts which the *reader* brings to it' (Worton and Still, 1990: 1).

Ninagawa's theatre is a deliberately rich kind of intertextual performance. The majority of its references, although recognizable to a Japanese spectator, communicated little to a non-Japanese viewer without extensive programme notes. A foreign audience would not have the same frame of reference as a Japanese one and was not equipped with the 'texts' required for the cross-referencing that Ninagawa's theatre was designed to encourage. Barthes' dilemma about digesting materials outside their cultural context is particularly relevant here, since it was only within a production's Japanese context that Ninagawa's intertextual references could make complete sense.

The most immediate site of intertextual meaning in Ninagawa's theatre was his casting of recognizable stars.

> The very concept of a film *star* is an intertextual one, relying as it does on correspondences of similarity and difference from one film to the next, and sometimes too on supposed resemblances between on- and off-screen personae. (Reader, 1990: 176)

> the star is a 'structured polysemy,' or a bearer of many different intertextual meanings, that makes him or her able to signify many things to many audience members. (Pearson and Simpson, 2001: 423)

Ninagawa himself acknowledged that his employment of stars – from traditional theatre, film or even pop music – had a clear purpose: 'casting stars in a play's leading roles helps to structure and prepare the people's desires and feelings even before the curtain goes up. There is no more favourable condition for entering into theatrical time than this' (Ninagawa, 1993: 110, my translation).

The presence of stars in Ninagawa's productions operated like a cinematic synecdoche:

> All forms of intertextuality rely on the capacity of the spectator to recognise the references and make the connections. This does not mean that if the reading competence is absent then the *meaning* ... is lost or misread, but rather that different meanings are produced depending on the sense of the intertextual reference. ... In the operation of synecdoche, the intertextual is formed through the part of one film relating to a much larger order, including another film entirely, or a filmic form ... the synecdoche tends to operate at a level less invested in the strictly textual and more in the associative. (Fuery, 2000: 52)

'Associative' references – to the lives and careers of his actors, and sometimes even to their previous Ninagawa performances – were undetectable to most foreign spectators, but in context they were immediately apparent. Ninagawa's intertextual allusions to Japanese traditional performance were also reliant on an audience's familiarity with the original forms (although it could not be guaranteed that all Japanese audience members could or would understand all Ninagawa's references). As Kishi Tetsuo (1998) insists, Western spectators were seldom equipped to spot them. Without these 'associative' references, his productions were considerably less moving or interesting. While a Ninagawa Shakespeare production would always present a clear account of a given play, the production's power came in large measure from the intertextual meaning invited in the mind of the spectator. References to popular culture, to Japanese myth and national identity, or even helpful nods to comparable stories or historical events, all enriched and elaborated the narratives for his local audiences. These were virtually invisible, however, to the uninformed spectator.

To the foreign spectator of Ninagawa's productions, familiar with the original narratives and cultural contexts of Shakespearean drama, a Brechtian kind of alienation was produced by his 'Japanification' of these plays. The reverse happened for his intended Japanese audiences; in translating them to Japanese settings, Ninagawa *familiarized* these foreign plays, in a process that relied on their ability to identify his intertextual references.

Focused on these two central points, context and audience, this book analyses Ninagawa's work in three distinct chapters. Chapter Two investigates the expressly Japanese-inflected productions that made Ninagawa famous abroad, charting the different ways he approached foreign texts over several decades. Chapter Three discusses his eight productions of *Hamlet*. Chapter Four analyses his productions for the Sai no Kuni Shakespeare Series, investigating particular programming strands such as the all-male Shakespeare series and a variety of experimental productions. The series initiated a fecund new phase of Shakespeare production in Ninagawa's career, and by the time he died there were only five plays left that he had not directed.[14]

There are references throughout to Bakhtin's seminal *Rabelais and His World*. Bakhtin discusses carnival, the popular and the grotesque, which combine, like Ninagawa's astonishing variety of allusions, in 'the true feast of time, the feast of becoming, change and renewal ... hostile to all that [is] immortalised and completed' (Bakhtin, 1984: 45). The book concludes with a discussion of some paradoxes and apparent inconsistencies in the study of Ninagawa's theatre and presents some alternative approaches to his work. However difficult his work may be to classify, Ninagawa was for over forty years the most popular and commercially successful theatre director in Japan. Like Rabelais,

> [his] enigma can be solved only by means of a deep study of [his] popular sources ... His images are completely at home within the thousand-year-old development of popular culture. ... To be understood he requires an essential reconstruction of our entire artistic and ideological perception, the renunciation of many deeply rooted demands of literary taste, and the revision of many concepts. (Bakhtin, 1984: 3)

FIGURE 1 *Ninagawa Yukio in rehearsal for* Hamlet, *Saitama Next Theatre, 2012. Photo by The Asahi Shimbun via Getty Images.*

# 2

# Foreign Stories, Japanese Images

Ninagawa's was a career of immense productivity and versatility. He was one of very few Japanese directors whose name alone could sell out a production of even the most obscure Greek tragedy or Shakespeare play. This chapter charts the various ways in which he recontextualized the narratives of the foreign plays he directed, and how he interpreted Shakespeare with Japanese imagery.[1] Most of the productions discussed are Shakespeare plays, but the chapter begins with a discussion of how some key productions – among them Greek tragedies and Japanese plays – were integral to Ninagawa's developing approach. Throughout his career Ninagawa employed a wide variety of techniques to help Japanese audiences access or understand the stories he was telling. These evolved over the years, but at the heart of his works was a dedication to beauty and theatricality as he understood them.

> When I turned thirty and chose to become a theatre director, I decided to incorporate into my work the traditional performing arts that *shingeki* had discarded as old and worthless. During my time in the *shingeki* world [as an actor] I had learned much from European theatre, which was one school to me, *kabuki* and *bunraku* were my other school. From this school I learned many things, and its

influence should be quite evident throughout the plays that I have directed. (Ninagawa, 1993: 250, my translation)

This chapter discusses Ninagawa's most recognizably 'Japanese' productions, both of Shakespeare and of plays that directly informed his directorial approach.

Japan's theatre culture is extraordinarily diverse. The traditional performing arts, among them *noh*, *kabuki* and *bunraku*, date back several hundred years and coexist with several significant forms of dance theatre, ranging from the traditional to the aggressively contemporary. In 1868 Japan's borders reopened after a long period of isolation, and a flood of new ideas became available. Theatre transitioned into modernity with *shinpa* (the 'new school', as opposed to the 'old school' – *kyuha* – of *kabuki*) before it was supplanted by *shingeki*, 'new theatre'. *Shingeki* became the dominant theatrical style for most of the twentieth century. In the 1960s an astonishing variety of experimental and avant-garde practices burst out of the *angura* movement, many of them actively seeking to supplant *shingeki* in favour of more contemporary Japanese modes of expression. There is also a long history of musical theatre in Japan, a field currently dominated by the all-female Takarazuka company and the theatre conglomerate Shiki, which stages Japanese translations of Broadway musicals. Commercial theatre also has its place, with high-profile productions by Japanese and foreign companies drawing consistent audiences. There are various National Theatres – Tokyo has one building dedicated to the traditional performing arts and another that houses more contemporary work and a substantial programme of opera and ballet.[2] All of these different genres and houses happily coexist within the Tokyo theatre scene, but other than the occasional movement of actors from one style to another, there is little crossover between them. This is not to suggest any express hostility or disinterest between these various forms of Japanese theatre, so much as a consistent focus on delivering a particular product. A theatregoer would not buy a ticket from Shiki in the hope of seeing *noh*, nor would one go to the Kabuki-za to see a play by Chekhov.

## Kabuki

Ninagawa's own theatrical taste grew from his early exposure to *kabuki* in the company of his mother. In the 1930s *kabuki* was a vibrant, politically engaged art form at the heart of the Japanese imperial project. Since the restoration of the Meiji emperor in the 1860s, Japan had quickly risen to the status of a superpower, having waged successful wars against China and Russia. When Ninagawa was born, Japan controlled Korea, Manchuria and Taiwan. As explained in James Brandon's excellent *Kabuki's Forgotten War*, *kabuki* was until 1945 a thriving art form, where new plays were consistently written to reflect (and support) the war effort. American censorship of *kabuki* in the aftermath of Japan's defeat and surrender in 1945 effectively ended its status as a living art. Only a small number of plays were permitted to be performed. No new plays were written any more, and *kabuki* turned itself into a more reverential, classical art form. Ninagawa experienced several manifestations of *kabuki* in his own lifetime: the new plays written to support the war, the extreme censorship in its aftermath, its reconfiguration and rebranding as Japan's 'classical' theatre, and eventually its attempts to innovate and attract new audiences.

*Kabuki* began as a transgressive, female-dominated art form. Markedly different from *noh*, it began with the popular and provocative performances by a woman called Izumo no Okuni (ca. 1572–ca. 1613). At exactly the same time as Shakespeare was writing in London, Okuni titillated Kyoto with her all-female dance troupe, performing in the dry riverbed of the Kamo River. She often hired prostitutes and trained them in singing and dancing for her dances and skits, wherein women played male roles and men often played women. Okuni was notorious for her suggestive performances and her androgynous clothing, sometimes even bedecked with rosary beads appropriated from Portuguese interlopers – a kind of seventeenth-century version of what brought Madonna to fame in the early 1980s.

Okuni's performances quickly gained popularity and she became known throughout Japan. Popularity led to emulation, and brothels began to present similar performances by their own all-female troupes. These entertainments grew so popular, and led to so much intermingling of the classes, that in the early 1640s the shogun had to intervene. Performances by women were outlawed, since their charms were too often for sale after performances and posed too much of a threat to public morals. As a result, female roles were then given to very young men, long cited as a comparison to the boy players of Shakespeare's theatre. The Japanese boy players were also available for private hire, and a further ban soon followed. Thanks to this steady traffic between the futon and the footlights (as deftly described by Senelick, 2000: 76), it was eventually decreed that only adult males should perform, and *kabuki*'s all-male codification of performance began to develop. What began as a female-led, transgressive genre evolved into an intractably all-male performing art form.[3]

*Kabuki*'s popularity grew from its seductive appeal. The original female performers, and later the young men who replaced them, were selling an eroticized art. Once adult male performers assumed the roles of women and could no longer rely on the same kind of innate physical beauty as a selling point, the erotic charms that had made *kabuki* so popular had to be performed rather than merely presented. The concept of *iroke* (something between charm and sex appeal) became integral to how men played women on stage. The art of the *onnagata* – an actor who plays female roles – was born. At its heart was (and is) the cultivation of this *iroke*. As *kabuki* evolved, no longer merely an advertisement for more private engagements, it began to rely on acting and narrative more than dance alone. The actors concentrated on their craft, and the form attracted better and better writers. Different kinds of acting also developed for male characters, in parallel with the codification of *onnagata* female roles. The two most significant styles to develop were *aragoto* ('rough') and *wagoto* ('young male') *kabuki* – plays focused on stories about two different kinds of male characters. *Aragoto* performances use exaggerated, masculine speech and feature the heavily exaggerated *kumadori* make-up for which *kabuki* is famous. *Wagoto kabuki* focuses on more realistic characters and does not use this heavily lined make-up. A simplified delineation would be that *aragoto* plays are about fighters and *wagoto* plays are about lovers. As these styles became popular, playwrights began to experiment with their forms. Some developed scenarios in which female characters might perform typically male activities, or complicated things further by having a male character dress as a woman, only to reveal his true masculine identity at a key moment. Such experiments have an equivalent in Shakespeare's comedies, which also make inventive use of the restrictions of their form by having boys who play girls who play boys, and so on. Gender is highly codified in *kabuki*. An entire semiotic language (combining costume, gesture, physicality, voice, language, make-up and more) is used to construct every character, whether male or female. At least part of the viewing pleasure is still derived from watching the actors' immense skill in creating their characters.

With the rise of *aragoto kabuki*, scenes of battles and sword fights became increasingly necessary, and highly choreographed scenes called *tachimawari* became enduringly popular. In these battles, a lead character can take on a whole crowd of enemies and summarily despatch them with his sword. Significantly, these fights are not performed in real time, and the slower motion enables the hero's aggressors to do backflips and various other acrobatic tricks when they fall victim to his attacks.

Comparable innovations happened with costume, where special techniques developed that even allow performers to change their appearance on stage. As well as the aforementioned stories of disguise, some plays have characters that transform into animals; famous examples include foxes, lions and butterflies, and even snakes and demons. Disappearances, stage trickery and even flying became very popular. These effects, known as *keren*, would be impossible without the participation of *kabuki*'s stagehands, or *kuroko* ('the children in black'). They are so called because they are dressed entirely in black and have their faces covered with black gauze. *Kabuki* convention is such that someone dressed in black is considered invisible.

As the quality of acting and writing for *kabuki* became more sophisticated, so did its stage technology. Revolving stages, trap doors and dramatic changes of scenery became and remain very popular aspects of a *kabuki* performance. Particularly influential was the development of the *naminuno*, or wave-cloth, used in *kabuki* to depict the sea. Painted with wave designs evocative of ink-paintings, it was adapted and expanded from *bunraku*, but in *kabuki* they can expand to sizes large enough to cover the entire stage. Sometimes they are flat, but in dramatic storm scenes they can be manipulated by stagehands and made to billow and surge, in a technique that has inspired theatre-makers all over the world. The predominant architectural feature of a *kabuki* stage is a walkway that leads from the audience to the stage, entitled a *hanamichi* (flower path). Used for dramatic exits and entrances, it brings actors into thrilling proximity of the audience.

One of *kabuki*'s most dynamic and prevalent features is its music, often played by on-stage musicians. Flutes, *shamisen* and drums dominate, accompanied by the *tsuke*, a kind of large wooden clapper beaten on the floor to accompany moments of particular intensity. In addition to the *tsuke*, a wide variety of sound effects underscores every performance. Evocative but not naturalistic, these sounds can, among other things, develop tension, indicate the weather or emphasize dramatic moments in the action. The most identifiable sound in *kabuki* is that of the *hyoshigi*, wooden clappers that produce the *ki* sound indicating the start of a performance. They are also struck at particularly dramatic moments, often accompanying an actor in a *mie*, the iconic pose struck by *aragoto* characters.

Spectacle, music, play with gender, fight scenes, sound effects, costume and eroticism all combine in *kabuki*, and its influence on Ninagawa was indelible. *Kabuki*'s distinctive brand of pageantry appealed to the visual artist in Ninagawa. Its distinctive richness informed his sense of the 'theatrical' from a very early age. 'If I were pressed to say how much theatrical methodology I have acquired from *kabuki*, *noh* or popular theatre, it is in fact quite limited. [...] As for practical stage technique, however, I have undoubtedly been influenced' (Ninagawa, 1998a).

From his very earliest productions at the Art Theatre Shinjuku Bunka, Ninagawa showed a distinct gift for arranging bodies in space. The Art Theatre was primarily a cinema, so the available acting space was very shallow, and any set pieces that his Gendaijin Gekijo used had to be easily removed after each performance. Ninagawa staged his first play *Hearty But Flippant* on several sets of risers. The theatre's restrictions inspired him to play with height and this arrangement of bodies in space, in modes not dissimilar to the pageantry of *kabuki*, but with an inventiveness and a visual imagination that was utterly contemporary. Photographs in his collected *Notes* (2002) show the rudimentary nature of this first performance, but as Ninagawa's work gained popularity his designs became more impressive. His 1970 production of Shimizu's *Ten Thousand Years of Memories of Japan* took place on an enormous mound of *sotoba*, the wooden placards inscribed with the names of the dead that are a recognizable sight in Japanese graveyards. Ninagawa gave theatrical form to the tensions between old (and dead) Japan and life in contemporary Tokyo. The names of Shimizu's plays provocatively distanced themselves from old-fashioned *kabuki* titles.[4] Non-Japanese commentators have made light of these early productions, assuming that their titles bespoke a shallowness of content and missing the irony Shimizu wove into them.[5] Ninagawa, a trained *shingeki* actor who had grown up watching *kabuki*, was their perfect interpreter. He was not trying to create a 'new' *kabuki*, but rather developing a theatrical aesthetic that rejected *shingeki* and celebrated the dramatic possibilities *kabuki* had inspired.

The beginning of the 1970s was a difficult time to be an artist in Japan. Mishima Yukio killed himself in revolt against

Japan's spiritual decline in November 1970. The turn of the decade saw many of the passionate theatre groups of the previous decade either disband or fall apart. Many artists despaired watching the passionate energy of the 1960s end in failure. The Security Treaty was renewed for another decade in 1970, the student revolts were well and truly suppressed and a pall of gloom fell over the very idea of revolution. Gendaijin Gekijo also disbanded, but one of their final productions is significant for having been Ninagawa's first production of a play not written by Shimizu. This was *Tokaido Yotsuya Kaidan*, Ninagawa's contemporary version of the 1825 *kabuki* play by Tsuruya Nanboku IV. Performed (appropriately) at a public hall in Yotsuya, Ninagawa filled the play with rock music and directed the story as a metaphor for young people. *Yotsuya Kaidan* (Ghost Stories from Yotsuya) is a perennially popular play, both in *kabuki* and other formats. Ninagawa staged two further productions of the play, and its story formed the basis of two of the four films he directed.[6] Significantly, this production pre-dated any encounter with Shakespeare, but demonstrated a comparable desire to drag classical *Japanese* theatre into an engaging, accessible new context for contemporary audiences.

## *Romeo and Juliet*

Ninagawa's second company, the Sakura-sha, disbanded after Nakane invited Ninagawa to direct *Romeo and Juliet* for Toho in 1974. Understandably for the company responsible for the Godzilla franchise, the budget was enormous. There was even enough money to send Ninagawa to Italy on a research trip. He visited Rome and various other cities, and the primary impression that he took away from the trip was the sensation of young people running in public – still a comparatively rare sight in Japan. This would become a major element of all his interpretations of the play. Having seen Peter Brook's *A Midsummer Night's Dream* when it toured to the Nissay Theatre the previous year, Ninagawa was inspired to think that Shakespeare could be more interesting than *shingeki*'s recreations of European performances by Japanese actors.

Ninagawa and Nakane cast the *kabuki* actor Matsumoto Koshiro IX as Romeo. His was in no way a *kabuki* performance, but rather a performance by a *kabuki* actor in a contemporary Shakespeare production. (A comparable equivalent might be if an opera singer took a non-singing role in a play.) Ninagawa's desire was to fill the theatre with the youthful energy of a 'whirlwind' world in which two teenagers meet, fall in love and die passionately within the space of a few days (Miyashita, 1987: 404). Ninagawa's approach was a synthesis of various inspirations. Jan Kott's *Shakespeare Our Contemporary* (1964), Brook's *The Empty Space* (1968) and Bakhtin's *Rabelais and His World* (1965) had all been recently translated into Japanese. He encouraged his actors to watch Fellini rather than Shakespeare, eagerly hoping to bring a sense of the vibrant physicality of Fellini's cinema to this Verona. It was barely a quarter of a century since Japan's nobility had been abolished, and Ninagawa was interested in a version of the Renaissance that had more to do with Breughel and Bakhtin than stately copies of foreign productions.[7] There was a distinct tension between Ninagawa's desire to develop a fresher way of communicating and the staid modes of delivery that the commercial actors employed. He worried that every sentence they spoke sounded as if it was coming from a samurai warrior in a television period drama. Deeply unsatisfied with this, Ninagawa drowned out the opening minutes of the play with music by Elton John, hoping to mask any lack of clarity in the text. Tales of Ninagawa's reputation as a martinet and the stories of his throwing ashtrays at actors first emerged during this intense period, as he tried to find a new means of creating an accessible, popular Shakespeare.[8]

Thirty years later, Ninagawa directed another production of *Romeo and Juliet*, again at the Nissay Theatre, with a set design that replicated the spatial arrangement of the original. Both took place on a large curved set arranged over three levels, with doors and connecting stairs on each. The 2004 version was updated and decorated with a huge variety of photographs of people of all ethnicities. These were taken from a high school yearbook but could equally have been so many funeral photographs or the kinds of footage presented in the aftermath of a high-school shooting. Ninagawa heightened this impression by starting the play with a funeral procession, which was then derailed by the young men's brawl. The overall feeling of both productions was of energetic, passionate young people, running and filling every inch of the performance space.[9]

Although the expansive set for each production allowed for a dizzyingly energetic interpretation, there was very little Japanese influence on the design of either show. In 1974 the costumes were not unlike those of Zeffirelli's 1968 film, which had inspired Nakane to produce the play in the first place.[10] In 2004, they were more contemporary and fashionable, without looking expressly Japanese. In both instances, a recent hit film version of *Romeo and Juliet* (by Zeffirelli and Luhrmann, respectively) guaranteed a certain level of familiarity with the play's story, and so Ninagawa did not use a framing device to bring the play closer to a Japanese audience.

After *Romeo and Juliet*, Kara Juro invited Ninagawa to direct his version of *The Water Magician*, based on a novel by Izumi Kyoka. The book had already been filmed by Mizoguchi Kenji and was one of the best-loved films of the silent era. Ninagawa's production was staged at Daiei's Tokyo studios, the only available space large enough to house the spectacular water effects central to Kara's play. This production was especially meaningful because Kara's offer came soon after the Sakura-sha disbanded, leaving Ninagawa with a sense of ostracization that haunted him for decades. *The Water Magician* would remain one of Ninagawa's favourite stories, to which he returned several times throughout his career.

# 1970s productions

Ninagawa's experiments with European classics continued with his first productions of *King Lear* and Sophocles' *Oedipus Rex*. Both starred Matsumoto, then known as Ichikawa Somegoro VI. Successful *kabuki* actors often perform under several names during their careers, usually taking a new name when a predecessor dies or retires. Having spent his early career as Ichikawa Somegoro VI, he became Matsumoto Koshiro IX (that is, the ninth actor to perform under that name) in 1981. In 2018 he took the name Matsumoto Hakuo II, his son graduated from Ichikawa Somegoro VII to Matsumoto Koshiro X and his grandson became Ichikawa Somegoro VIII. Actors' names are important in the preservation and acknowledgement of *kabuki*'s long legacy, and Matsumoto's family remains one of the foremost in that world. Matsumoto is a graduate of Waseda University and starred in a great variety of non-*kabuki* productions, including several musicals. He was thirty-four when he played *King Lear* in Ninagawa's next Shakespeare production, which opened in 1976.

A central element of Ninagawa's productions of *King Lear* and *Oedipus Rex* was the size of their respective casts. He actually provided his Lear with an impressive retinue of unruly knights, who made total sense of his daughters' concerns about having to accommodate them. Not since Max Reinhardt can there have been an *Oedipus Rex* with a chorus as big as Ninagawa's 1976 production, which presented a Thebes populated with over 160 actors. The effect was startling and gave a real sense of the community over which Oedipus and Jocasta presided, and how they suffered as a result of the plague. The success of these monumental productions confirmed Ninagawa's taste for putting large crowds of people on stage. Much later in his life he explained that 'as I see it, one of the traits of Asianness is multitude, which is why I like to use more than fifty actors on stage. I now want to show the power of life, of multitude, rooted in Asian theatre, in contrast to European theatre and its obsession with psychological realism' (Salz, 2016: 535).

The desire to move away from psychological realism sprang from Ninagawa's dissatisfaction with *shingeki* and his eagerness to create a more Japanese kind of contemporary theatre. He acknowledged a debt to Kara Juro and Hijikata Tatsumi, a leading figure of *butoh*, whose disruptive and experimental work in the 1960s felt far more relevant and Japanese than *shingeki* attempts to present beautiful and dignified recreations of European plays. After his own *angura* work with Gendaijin Gekijo and then the Sakura-sha, Ninagawa sought to bring a similar spirit to his productions of foreign plays. Instead of a literary, *shingeki* approach, he was aiming to build a dynamic, Japanese world in which the plays made visceral sense to a contemporary audience.

Another important production happened in 1976, when Ninagawa was invited to direct a double bill of Mishima Yukio's *Modern Noh Plays*. These were performed at the National Theatre, as part of a Mishima retrospective. The *Modern Noh Plays* were a project that occupied Mishima over a period of several years. He wrote at least eight interpretations of classical *noh* plays, reimagining them as contemporary dramas. Ninagawa directed *Sotoba Komachi* and *Yoroboshi*, and the production was his first collaboration with the actor Hira Mikijiro. Hira played the Heian poetess in *Sotoba Komachi*, here transformed into an ancient, homeless beggar who rhapsodizes over her former beauty. Even though Mishima wrote Komachi with a female performer in mind, Ninagawa cast his production with an all-male company, as a nod to the all-male performance practices of classical *noh* and, perhaps, to some of the more controversial aspects of Mishima's personal life. Although primarily known as a novelist, Mishima was one of the finest Japanese playwrights of the twentieth century. The *Modern Noh Plays* were a literary equivalent to what Ninagawa wished to do with both foreign and Japanese classics – reimagining them for his Japanese audience in inventive, beautiful and contemporary ways.

## *Medea*

Ninagawa's next major production was Euripides' *Medea*, his most transgressive, avant-garde production to date. It would be the first of Ninagawa's productions to be seen abroad, and to non-Japanese audiences it was enormously impressive. It was exotic, it was spectacular and it was brilliantly performed, but it was technically a faithful production of the Euripides text. It is a mark of Ninagawa's particular ability as a director that within the traditional framework of this foreign play he also created a remarkably subversive, postmodern piece of Japanese theatre.

Like *Sotoba Komachi*, *Medea* was performed by an all-male company, primarily because that is how plays were performed in ancient Greece. Such a move would not have been especially surprising to the original audience at the Nissay Theatre, since so many of the traditional theatres of Japan remain the exclusive preserve of male performers. Ninagawa exploited the potential of having a male actor playing Medea throughout, making use of the varying levels of politeness and humility that are central to the Japanese language. Medea was not played as a *kabuki onnagata*, but the production manipulated *kabuki*'s coded representations of gender and the opportunities created by having a man play the role. As frequently happens in *kabuki* plays, the lead character began the performance in one costume and gradually revealed a contrasting inner nature by the removal of several outer layers. By the time she exited to murder her children, Medea had removed her enormous headdress (which visually echoed the golden fleece), her artificial breasts (suggesting an exaggerated, performed femininity) and her huge cloak, constructed from countless *obi* sashes that were cut up for the costume. Having stripped off and renounced all the trappings of her history, along with her position as a woman and a wife, she was reduced to an essential self, sheathed in a red smock and ready to exact her revenge.

Mae Smethurst (2002) describes *Medea* in great detail in an article that parses the Japanese iconography it manipulated.

Ninagawa and the show's art director Tsujimura Jusaburo subverted an array of *kabuki* images throughout. Most memorable was the staging of the first choral ode, which begins 'Holy rivers flow back to their sources – reversed is the order of all things'. The chorus comments on how everything is inverted for Medea; her husband has left her, she is a foreigner and oaths to the gods appear meaningless. To highlight this upset, Ninagawa had Medea and the chorus invert a specific *kabuki* convention, a dance wherein a young woman coyly puts a red ribbon in her mouth to display her love. Instead Medea and all sixteen chorus members drew red ribbons *out* of their mouths, in an extraordinary and now iconic inversion of the *kabuki* image.[11]

The music of the production was as eclectic as Ninagawa's audiences had come to expect. The chorus all held a *shamisen*, the three-stringed instrument that is deeply associated with *kabuki*. *Medea* featured the *tsugaru shamisen*, a rougher, rustic version of the instrument that was enjoying a revival in Japan's folk music scene at the time. Juxtaposed with this particularly evocative and Japanese sound were various pieces of Western classical music that Ninagawa used to underscore Medea's emotional state. Among these were a Handel sarabande and Barber's *Adagio*.[12] Ninagawa also used the sound of the *ki* clappers to punctuate Medea's thoughts. The contrast between Western classics and traditional Japanese music insisted that although this was a foreign story it could absolutely resonate with a Japanese audience.

Ninagawa's *Medea* was his first show to feature a prolonged and direct manipulation of elements of *kabuki*. It must be stressed that this was *not* a *kabuki* performance, but audiences familiar with its tropes could easily appreciate what Ninagawa was trying to communicate. Unlike *Romeo and Juliet*, *Oedipus* and *King Lear*, *Medea* did not feature a *kabuki* actor as its protagonist. In the lead role, Hira Mikijiro incorporated several elements of *kabuki*, most astonishing being his subversion of the tradition of *mie* poses, ordinarily reserved for *aragoto* male characters. Striking such poses at the height of Medea's emotional distress was a key example of the theatrical excitement of this production. Allowing this most transgressive of female characters to subvert the masculine codes of traditional theatre made for an electrifying effect. In some subsequent revivals the role of Medea was played by an actual *onnagata*, Arashi Tokusaburo, who further exploited the possibilities for such subversion.

The opening minutes of *Medea* were filled with neither *shamisen* nor western music, but with a contemporary pop song by Mikami Hiroshi. The song was called *Daikanjou* (Deep Feeling) and its lyrics encourage the listener to travel back in time, thousands of miles, thousands of years, to various ancient locations in Japan, inviting a connection between the ancient Greek story of the play and the mythological origins of the country. Japan traces its origins to the goddess of the sun, Amaterasu, while in Greek mythology the sun is also Medea's grandfather. The lyrics of *Daikanjou*, although mysterious and unspecific, invite the listener to visit ancient lands populated with such children (or grandchildren) of the sun – whether Greek or Japanese. This overture to *Medea* was Ninagawa's way of arresting the audience's attention in the first three minutes of the play, introducing them to the world he was presenting. These initial three minutes eventually became essential to how Ninagawa presented any play, as he insisted that it was during this time that he had to jolt an audience away from their own lives and into the shared experience of watching a play.

> He wanted his audience [for *Medea*] to be engrossed in the performance within the first three minutes and to feel for at least three minutes after the end of the play two things: first, as a group, a sense of anarchy (his word) and, as individuals, a resolute sense of self, as was not the social norm for women in Japan. (Smethurst, 2002: 32)

That final feeling of anarchy, and particularly the search for 'a resolute sense of self', were central to his next production in 1978, his first staging of *Hamlet*. Ninagawa's life long fascination with the play – and his eight separate productions of it – are the focus of Chapter Three.

## *Suicide for Love*

From his earliest productions of foreign plays, Ninagawa was in a kind of conversation with traditional performing arts. Whether this was in the casting of an actor such as Matsumoto or in the multilayered deconstruction of its codes in *Medea*, *kabuki*'s powerful influence on his sense of the 'theatrical' was always palpable. *Medea* and *Hamlet* manipulated and reconfigured Japanese images to dramatic effect, but while they used Japanese images in their attempt to make these foreign stories more accessible, the productions were not ostensibly set in Japan. In 1979, Ninagawa scored an immense success with *Suicide for Love*, probably the most Japanese (and certainly the most popular) show he ever directed. It might seem strange to highlight his shift from European plays with avant-garde costumes to Chikamatsu and kimono, but this production marked a major turning point for Ninagawa. Until now, his focus had been on contemporary plays and non-Japanese texts. Since his move to commercial theatre in 1974, the only Japanese texts he had directed were *The Water Magician* and the *Modern Noh Plays*; all of his other productions had been of foreign material, which he picked precisely because he felt commercial theatres would never present them otherwise (Irvin, 2003: 94). The very Japanese-ness of *Suicide for Love*, a sumptuous, life-size evocation of eighteenth-century Osaka, was a novelty. A full decade after Ninagawa's riotous debut, it was just as important to his development as *Medea* or *Hamlet*.

The original production of *Suicide for Love* had a cast of over 100, and its first three minutes were particularly impressive. In the darkness, a spotlight picked out the tiny figure of a *bunraku* puppet. This was at once a deferential nod to the story's origin and an indication of the lighting and technical capacities available to this production precisely because it was *not* a traditional performance. Moments later a massive street scene shimmered into view. This evocation of eighteenth-century Osaka was teeming with life, and was the first of many remarkable images in Asakura Setsu's design. A courtesan in scarlet, shielded by a servant holding an enormous parasol, made her stately way through the audience to the stage, copying the entrances of *kabuki* actors along the *hanamichi*. Over the course of the production Ninagawa used spectacular lighting to evoke everyday life in Genroku-era Japan. The most impressive staging happened at the end of the show, when one couple attempted suicide in an actual river flowing across the stage, while a second ended their lives in the snowstorm that became one of Ninagawa's signature moments. The late 1970s and early 1980s were a period of enormous economic growth in Japan, but the rising tide of wealth did not float all boats. Many people found themselves in severe financial difficulty, to the extent that there was a marked rise in the number of people taking their lives to escape significant debt. Spotting the correlation between this worrying trend and the period when Chikamatsu's plays reflected comparably high numbers of desperate suicides, Ninagawa created the production in the hope of examining the sad phenomenon (Billington, 1989).

*Suicide for Love* was another example of Ninagawa's inventive and wilfully anachronistic use of music. Using traditional music for this play, set in Genroku-period Osaka, would have made it sound very much like a *bunraku* production. Instead, Ninagawa punctuated the story with a soundtrack of *enka* – Japan's distinctly twentieth-century brand of sentimental music. The music was so integral that some subsequent productions incorporated its theme song into the show's title. In Japanese the play is called *Chikamatsu's Stories of Love Suicide*. Later revivals also incorporated the show's theme song 'That's Love' by Mori Shinichi, with lyrics contributed by Akimoto. The English title *Suicide for Love* was coined for its tour to Europe in 1989.

## *NINAGAWA Macbeth*

After the big budget productions of the 1970s, Ninagawa began the 1980s with a production of *Macbeth*. His producer Nakane Tadao had originally suggested setting the production in Azuchi Castle, the residence of Oda Nobunaga, a warlord from Japan's Sengoku (Warring States) period. Nakane's suggestion was that the reference to Oda would make Macbeth's 'vaulting ambition' relatable to a Japanese audience otherwise unfamiliar with the play. Ninagawa chose to place the action in the Azuchi-Momoyama period – the final phase of the Sengoku Era – before comparative order was restored to Japan with the rise of the Tokugawa Shogunate. The Azuchi-Momoyama period was characterized by intense infighting and extreme political instability, which made for an effective equivalent to the bloody chaos of Duncan's Scotland. Ninagawa's production was never 'just' going to be a period drama wherein he relocated a version of Scottish history to a particular moment in Japan's past. This had already been done in Kurosawa's *Throne of Blood* – already over twenty years old by the time that Ninagawa approached the play. Instead, he turned it into a dialogue with the dead, inspired by a chance moment when he was paying his respects to the deceased members of his own family.

> when I ... opened up our family butsudan (Buddhist home altar) to light a candle and pray for my father, at that moment, I thought 'this is the right image'. I had two overlapping complex ideas: ordinary people watching *Macbeth*, and a Japanese audience looking at the stage and seeing through it to our ancestors. When I was in front of the butsudan, my thoughts were racing. It was like I was having a conversation with my ancestors. When I thought of *Macbeth* in this way, I thought of him appearing in the butsudan where we consecrate dead ancestors. (Ninagawa, 1995: 217–18)

Ninagawa often acknowledged that such inspirations came to him by surprise. He maintained that the idea of having camellia blossoms fall to the stage throughout *Sotoba Komachi* came to him while he was walking through a cemetery. The thud of a falling blossom startled him, and he replicated it in the Mishima piece to heighten the constant interplay between beauty and death (Ninagawa, 1998a: 87–8). Ninagawa's acknowledgement that his inspirations came during such ordinary activities as remembering his father or going for a walk also emphasize his commitment to finding expressly relatable imagery. His aim was always to enhance his interpretations of foreign or obscure material with imagery drawn from ordinary Japanese lived experience.

Ninagawa had been experimenting with scale and the interpretation of text with varying degrees of success. *Macbeth* was the first foreign play that he framed in a specifically Japanese setting, and the idea was a risk. Comparisons with Kurosawa were inevitable, and he certainly did not want to replicate the dull *shingeki* Shakespeares that had prompted his own retirement from stage acting. Ninagawa's primary concern was to avoid the feeling of awkwardness and embarrassment he so often felt when he saw Japanese actors trying to play Caucasians.

> One further reason that I transfer foreign plays to Japanese settings is the clear artificiality of our attempts to mimic the outward form of foreigners. By this I mean visible aspects such as gesture and make-up. The very sight of people wearing tights and blond wigs on stage fills me with a feeling of embarrassment, enough to alienate me from the theatre altogether. In order to avoid this kind of theatre, I must come up with directing solutions that resolve these various problems. For example, this is why I set *Macbeth* within a Buddhist altar. (Ninagawa, 1993: 106, my translation)

An unfortunate characteristic of *shingeki* was its almost slavish emulation of European performers – including earnest attempts to look like white Europeans. Like many of his fellow *angura* practitioners, Ninagawa's career took off precisely because of his determination to avoid this kind of work. His focus was on left-wing politics, the plight of the individual in Japanese society and the quest for a Japanese sense of self. None of these would be served by the literary, hierarchical and Western-looking productions by the likes of the Bungakuza. The ten years between *Hearty But Flippant* and *Suicide for Love* saw Ninagawa's work evolve and expand in scale and ambition, although his commitment to exciting and even unsettling his audiences did not diminish. *Hamlet* and the two iterations of *Romeo and Juliet* grew out of an aim to shake the dust off the text-focused and boring imitations of Shakespeare that *shingeki* had encouraged. His *Macbeth* grew organically from the trifecta of previous productions: it combined the framing of the play with an introduction from *Medea*, the manipulation of a familiar household image from *Hamlet* and an exuberantly Japanese theatricality from *Suicide for Love*. While the title *NINAGAWA Macbeth* rather immodestly announces just whose interpretation it is, it should be noted that in Japanese, as a kind of acknowledgement of the two-way traffic of interpretation, Ninagawa's name was written in Roman characters and 'Macbeth' was written in Japanese.

The *butsudan* idea was a stroke of genius – a very clear lens through which Ninagawa could examine and refract Shakespeare's play. As an example of its lasting effect, I must tell a story against myself. I spoke at an event in late 2017 at King's College London with the writer Yamaguchi Hiroko, co-author with Ninagawa of an excellent book about his directing career (Ninagawa and Yamaguchi, 2015). I made a passing reference to the production's reputation as a 'samurai' or 'cherry-blossom' production, and Yamaguchi insisted that Japanese people would really only refer to the show as Ninagawa's *butsudan Macbeth*. All of the show's other features – the samurai setting, the cherry blossoms and the various *kabuki*-derived elements – were secondary to the monumental metaphor of the family altar, which gave the entire production its distinctly elegiac feeling. The primacy of this image and its resonance are central to understanding *NINAGAWA Macbeth*.

The key thread running through Ninagawa's approach to foreign material was his desire to bridge the gap between their European (or occasionally American) sources and his Japanese audience. In several interviews over the years, he described the aforementioned discomfort of watching actors pretend not to be Japanese, and in later life articulated an even more revealing long-held insecurity. This was a concern as to whether the work he was making would be in any way meaningful, or have any genuine substance, when viewed by a Japanese audience in light of their personal experience.[13] These two thoughts operated like a kind of artistic conscience for him throughout his career, and on close inspection their influence is evident in nearly all of his productions, particularly those of foreign material.

The opening sequence of *NINAGAWA Macbeth* was a perfect example of how Ninagawa wrestled with this concern. Two stooped and elderly women came onto the stage, opened the doors of the greatly oversized *butsudan* and then took their seats on either side of the stage. They observed the action, ate, drank tea, wept and eventually closed the doors again at the end of the performance. They remained visible throughout the performance, active witnesses to the story of the play. They wore modern dress – reviewers consistently mentioned that one of them had a thermos flask – and acted as a link between the costume drama inside the *butsudan* and the audience's contemporary reality. By including these women as witnesses, Ninagawa mitigated his own concerns about what ordinary Japanese people might think of his work and turned *Macbeth* into a play-within-a-play. The women remained on stage throughout almost as a reminder that this was a performance, and that the action being represented on stage was already long over. Their stooped bodies and the physical exertion of opening the doors evoked the more basic realities of life in Japan – and the sense that while communion with the dead could be a daily ritual, ordinary life must continue. The presence of such 'real' Japanese bodies also allowed for the imaginative leap of seeing Japanese actors – albeit this time in Japanese costume – enacting Shakespeare's play.

Several distinct sign-systems combined to foreground Ninagawa's concept of the production as a dialogue with the dead. The *Sanctus* from Fauré's Requiem underscored the old women as they opened the doors and allowed the story to begin.[14] This was juxtaposed with gongs and Buddhist chanting, which itself faintly echoed the Barber *Adagio*. These pieces appeared at specific moments throughout the show, as did a passionate string sextet by Brahms that operated as a leitmotif for the Macbeths' relationship.

Much has been written of the significance of the cherry blossoms in *NINAGAWA Macbeth*. To outside audiences, they were a beautiful evocation of Japanese culture, of which the falling petals are a recognizable icon. (A programme note for some productions explained the wide range of references it evoked.) In Japanese culture, cherry blossoms are a symbol of transience, the epitome of the concept of *mono no aware*, an awareness and appreciation for the beauty of things that do not last. Blossom viewing parties are a cherished fixture in the spring calendar, and familiar stories and turns of phrase to do with *sakura* are very common. Beneath the transient beauty of the petals lies a more sinister set of images. The short story *Under the Cherry Trees* by Kajii Motojiro features a consistent refrain that 'there are corpses buried under the cherry trees!' Cherry blossoms have long been associated with death and dying young, and by extension those whose lives ended in ritual suicide – whether by *seppuku* or, later, *kamikaze* pilots. The cherry blossoms fell only at very specific moments in *NINAGAWA Macbeth*: during Macbeth's scenes with the witches and the murder of Banquo. The falling petals in these specific scenes, all expressly focused on Macbeth's realization of his ambitions, foreshadowed the impermanence of his success. They also adorned Lady Macbeth's kimono, which

Macbeth wrapped around himself when he learned of her death. Ninagawa saved the most impressive use of the cherry blossoms for the final scenes of the play. Spectacularly, when Birnham Wood came indeed to Dunsinane, the soldiers carried branches of flowering cherry trees, allowing for the entire stage to present a forest of moving blossoms. The impermanence of the cherry blossom was a perfect metaphor for Macbeth's rise to power; the falling petals insisted subtly but unmistakably that his reign could not last.

The cherry blossoms also evoke a short poem by the warrior monk Saigyo, which says 'I hope I can die under the spring blossoms, in the light of a full moon in the second month.'[15] Ninagawa staged the final duel between Macbeth and Macduff in front of a huge red full moon, and when Macduff struck the crucial blow all music stopped and the moon snapped from red to blue. Macbeth was granted the heroic death that Saigyo had wished for, and in several Japanese performances his death was given a round of applause.

In his published directing notes, Ninagawa makes frequent reference to the Japanese Red Army in connection to *NINAGAWA Macbeth*. He had been sympathetic to the politics of Japan's New Left during the 1960s but disassociated himself from the overtly political as demonstrations became increasingly violent towards the end of the decade. Early in the 1970s, the country was horrified to hear about the actions of the United Red Army, a terrorist faction formed by communists and those violently opposed to Japan's Security Treaty. They spent the winter of 1971–2 hiding in the mountains, but it was eventually discovered that as many as fourteen members of the group had been brutally executed for lack of commitment. Eventually the surviving members were arrested after a nine-day police siege. Ninagawa was horrified by the cruelty of these summary executions. The idealism and spirited protest of the 1960s – such a formative period for experimental theatre in Tokyo – had been in steady decline since the 1970s began, and the United Red Army incident was a final nail in its coffin. As well as the dialogue with his own ancestors, Ninagawa felt that the dead commemorated within the *butsudan* were echoes of the revolutionaries murdered by their own colleagues in the United Red Army.

Elsewhere in his sketches and discussions of the play, there is an intriguing, half-finished sentence suggesting that an unspecified scene is dedicated to the Red Army. The militants were certainly on his mind as he developed the production, more for their having fallen in their prime, like cherry blossoms, than for any particular devotion to their cause. The notes also mention anachronistic sound effects – of riot police and tear gas canisters, for example – which were sparingly used, but like the presence of the old women as observers, they constituted another aspect of Ninagawa's very personal response to the play: 'Ninagawa's own opposition to the repressive politics of those years, his dreams of resistance, lying somewhere at the bottom of his heart, seemed somehow still apparent, however dimly we might now perceive them' (Senda, 1997: 128).

Ninagawa's production transferred the play from a Christian to a very obviously Buddhist setting. Besides the *butsudan*, which literally framed the entire play, there were other nods to Buddhism, most notably in the England scene, wherein Malcolm warily tests Macduff before revealing his true feelings. For this scene Ninagawa filled the stage with several enormous statues, reminiscent of the kind that usually guard the entrances to Buddhist temples. These statues, called *nio* or *kongorikishi*, are the wrathful guardians of the Buddha, or manifestations of the *bodhisattva* of power. A particular branch of Buddhism known as *nio-zen* had a brief flourishing during the Azuchi-Momoyama period in which Ninagawa set the production. *Nio-zen* advocates meditated on these statues in order to cultivate their power. Setting this scene in a space filled with so many *nio* was a very meaningful choice. The powerful statues posed a sharp contrast to Macduff's response to the news that Macbeth had murdered his family. In a space dedicated to aggressive, martial virtues, his outburst of grief was as inappropriate as it was moving. Dwarfed by these hyper-masculine statues, Malcolm enjoins Macduff to dispute it 'like a man', and Macduff insists that he 'must also feel it as a man'. The scene's setting made sense of Macduff's outburst, and the juxtaposition between supernatural masculinity and Macduff's all-too-human grief was particularly harrowing. When the ambitious Malcolm then advised him to 'let grief convert to anger' and the men resolved to take revenge, under the watchful glare of the *nio*, Ninagawa's reading of the scene came full circle.

Ninagawa wrote in his notes that his entire concept and approach for this *Macbeth* were designed for the reality of Macbeth's late soliloquy in Act 5, Scene 5. He is alone, surrounded by flickering candles 'just like the candles at Nenbutsu Temple'. Nenbutsu is a Buddhist temple in Kyoto, famous for its enormous number of statues. They are all dedicated to those who died without family, and during O-Bon, the Festival of the Dead, the entire precinct is filled with candles. While its specific inspiration may not have reached audiences, the image was a beautiful one. Setting the play within the *butsudan* suffused with cherry blossoms and costuming it to evoke a remote historical period all but insist on the understanding that everyone in the play is already dead. This scene emphasizes that Macbeth will die alone. He learns that his wife has died, and as Macduff proclaimed earlier in the play 'he has no children!'. This setting made the 'tomorrow and tomorrow and tomorrow' speech exceptionally powerful. The notes suggest that Macbeth 'can light the candles as if trying to use the activity to conquer his fears, and then lie down among them. The dead!' Macbeth's realization of his own mortality, that 'all our yesterdays have lighted fools/the way to dusty death' was brilliantly conveyed.

A fascination with the intercultural politics of Ninagawa's work has busied critics for most of the three decades since it was first seen outside Japan. If an audience member does not speak Japanese or cannot digest the specifically Japanese cultural references manipulated in a given production's *mise-en-scène*, are they merely participating in an orientalist transaction? Is Ninagawa's repurposing of specific Western cultural artefacts (the plays of Shakespeare or Euripides or Ibsen) in fact a kind of *occidentalist* activity, with the same political complications as Western, orientalist consumption of material from the East?[16] Ninagawa's work – particularly *NINAGAWA Macbeth* – appears frequently as an example in critical discussion of the possibilities and failures of intercultural theatre.[17] The waters are often muddied by a kind of inequality of authenticity: is Ninagawa's position as a director who does not speak English automatically disadvantageous?

By contrast, some English-language criticism of Ninagawa's work questions not being able to speak Japanese.[18] But even as critics acknowledge that any nuance or poetry from the text is unavailable to them, some feel entitled to insist that because audiences outside Japan do not understand the spoken language of a play, Ninagawa's work relies on a kind of *japonisme*, a calculated manipulation of Japanese aesthetics designed to impress and intrigue foreigners.[19] There is no question that a certain level of planning went into the overseas presentation of so many elaborate productions, nor can it be ignored that Ninagawa worked for over forty years as a commercial theatre director – with considerable economic as well as artistic success. The suggestion that Ninagawa was exclusively interested in marketing a kind of globalized Shakespeare product, capitalizing on pseudo-Japanese iconographies that were bastardized for ease of foreign consumption, wilfully overlooks his career-long focus on his Japanese audiences.[20] Ninagawa himself adamantly refuted charges of *japonaiserie* or *japonisme*, insisting that this was a misreading of his work (Ninagawa, 1995: 211). If some audiences responded to the surface visuals of his productions rather than the nuanced meanings they were designed to infer, Ninagawa was happy for them to appreciate even that much.

Ninagawa found a formidable opponent in the scholar Kishi Tetsuo, who was a major dissenting voice against Ninagawa's Japanese framings of Shakespeare.[21] Kishi also had strong words for the manner in which English reviewers attempted to discuss it. Ironically his indictment of such critics made Ninagawa's work (deservedly) seem far more nuanced and sophisticated than foreigners' attempts to describe it. While Kishi rightly questions an English reviewer's description of *NINAGAWA Macbeth* as a '*kabuki* ritual', he also makes the rather reductive suggestion that the sliding screens inside the *butsudan* are a literal depiction of the 'fourth wall' of European realist theatre. Ninagawa was thereby attempting to turn Shakespeare into psychological realism – and failing in the attempt by having actors enter from the back of the auditorium. Shakespeare, Kishi also insists, wrote for a bare stage, and therefore Ninagawa's visual interpretations of the plays are fundamentally at odds with how the plays are written (Kishi, 1998: 115–16).

## *The Tempest*

The early 1980s saw several new collaborations with the playwrights who had been instrumental to Ninagawa's early career, including Kara (*Shitaya Mannencho Monogatari*, *Black Tulip*), Shimizu (*In That Rainy Summer Thirty Juliets Came Back*, *Tango at the End of Winter*, *Between 95kg and 97kg*, *Blood Wedding*) and Akimoto (*Genroku Harbour Song*, *Namboku Love Story*). It was not until 1987 that Ninagawa returned to Shakespeare, for a production of *The Tempest*, again at the Nissay Theatre. The production came at a time of crisis, during which Ninagawa was considering giving up directing. It was, he explained,

> [a] midlife crisis. That's the way I was: not seeing anyone and thinking about retirement. My own situation at that time seemed to relate to Prospero's thoughts in the play when he says, 'Our revels now are ended.' I was convinced that I had lost my talent for directing and that this would be my last chance to make a successful production. If it failed I would retire. (Ninagawa, 1995: 213–14)

Ninagawa went on holiday to Bermuda to find inspiration for Shakespeare's island play. The experience was rather miserable for a man who had quipped previously that he would rather read about the Mediterranean than swim in it. Of all things, the holiday made him focus in particular on the idea of exile, which led to the idea of setting *The Tempest* on Sado Island, to the north-west of Japan's main island. Zeami, perhaps the greatest figure in the history of *noh* theatre, was exiled to Sado when he fell foul of the shogunate. Ninagawa was intrigued by its preponderance of open-air *noh* stages. It became increasingly obvious that Ninagawa's *Tempest* would feature elements inspired by Japan's oldest continuously observed performing art form.

*Noh* theatre derives its name from the word for 'talent' or 'skill' and is the most respected form of traditional performance in Japan. Highly codified, it is a refined and minimalist art form, and its aesthetics are particularly austere. All plays take place on the same bare stage, with no design other than a painted pine tree at the back of the stage, symbolizing an ancient and holy tree in the former capital city of Nara. Actors enter and exit the stage via a long walkway called the *hashigakari*, along which three further pine trees are painted. Performers and musicians are all male, and an air of refined elegance and simplicity permeates. *Noh* developed from various forms of dance drama and festival performances at temples. In the fourteenth century it began to take shape in its own distinctive form, codified by its greatest proponent Zeami Motokiyo. Patronized by samurai, it became increasingly associated with the social elite, an association that still persists. Different categories of plays feature gods, warriors, ordinary people, demons and madwomen. A typical *noh* programme will include plays from different categories, with *kyogen* – comic interludes – interspersed between them. *Kyogen* is a form as old as *noh*, and like *noh* has its own schools, traditions and repertoire.

Ninagawa, now in his early fifties, was still reacting to that 'clear artificiality' of *shingeki* performance. Twenty years of directing had not lessened his distaste for Japanese actors trying to hide their innate Japanese-ness, and the majority of plays he directed between *NINAGAWA Macbeth* and *The Tempest* were Japanese. As he had for *Romeo and Juliet*, *Hamlet* and *Macbeth*, Ninagawa was eager to find a means of acknowledging the distance between his company's Japanese identity and the foreignness of Shakespeare's play. The solution was fascinating.

Just as his production of *Macbeth* included his own name, Ninagawa's version of *The Tempest* came with a subtitle. It has been frequently mistranslated, but the Japanese reads 'A Rehearsal on a Noh stage on Sado Island'. Translations rendering it as 'a rehearsal of a noh play' are incorrect, suggesting an attempt to turn *The Tempest* into a *noh* play. This was resolutely not the case.[22] Ninagawa staged the play as a rehearsal *on* Sado Island, already so richly associated with theatre and exile. His way into the play was to have the entire company on stage for thirty minutes before curtain. The audience entered and saw actors warming up, technicians and stage management making final preparations, and even Ninagawa himself giving notes. As showtime approached, the actor playing Prospero (Hira Mikijiro) took control, so that by the time the play began the audience was completely invested in the dynamics of the company. Actors stayed on stage throughout the performance, and even visibly contributed to the sound effects.

This meta-theatrical framing of the play – a Japanese company on a Japanese island covered with traditional Japanese theatre stages, rehearsing a Shakespearean play that contains within it several kinds of performance – allowed for a multiplicity of meanings. 'A single mirror will no longer suffice to reflect our complex world. My production of *The Tempest* ... can be likened to the intermingling reflections of a shattered mirror' (Miyashita, 1987: 404). Prospero became the leader of the company, running the rehearsal on the stage. When he spoke of 'drowning his book', it was the working script for the play that he threw away. The resonances between Zeami and Prospero were clear in 'the imaginative parallel between the isolated playwright-sage Prospero and the two great playwrights of East and West, at the moment when all three relinquish their magic' (Mulryne, 2006: 6). The production did not rely on any particular biographical details of Zeami's life – it was enough for the audience to remember that Sado was his place of exile. Any audience members who also knew that Zeami was allowed to return to the mainland and there lived out the rest of his life in peace might have assumed a similar fate for Prospero at the end of the play. A key to the show's artistic success was that Ninagawa made Prospero a version of himself. Ninagawa had been on the brink of abjuring *his* rough magic; he was also a theatrical magician with not one but two daughters, suffering from a midlife crisis. Hira did not make his performance an imitation of Ninagawa, although he did clap his hands to start or interrupt scenes, imitating a habit very familiar to anyone who ever spent time in Ninagawa's rehearsal room.

The only actual evocation of *noh* during *The Tempest* happened during the masque in Act 4, Scene 1, conjured up by Prospero to display the 'vanity' of his art. The parade of Iris, Ceres and Juno was originally Shakespeare's imitation of a Jacobean court masque. Here it became Ninagawa/Prospero's interpretation of Japan's equivalent court performance, a *noh* play. The three goddesses were not performed by actual *noh* actors, and as Kishi hotly insisted, the performers of this masque came down off the *noh* stage during their performance, which would never happen in a real *noh* play.

Interviewed in 1995, Nakane Tadao explained the kind of synthesis that he and Ninagawa were hoping for in the theatre they tried to create.

> For example, while *kabuki* was appreciated in style, and modern plays (*shingeki*) for their words, there were also underground theatre groups focusing on using the body for expressive rather than narrative purposes, and commercial plays which relied on the actors' presentation of personality

in a character role. All of these approaches existed, but almost without connection to each other. So I wondered if I could mix them together in the same production. However, there wasn't a single playwright available who could write for such a new genre. (Ninagawa, 1995: 210)

*The Tempest* was the first production that really brought these approaches together. The spectacular storm sequence owed a debt to *kabuki*'s *naminuno* fabrics for its billowing waves, but Ninagawa insisted that his 'waves' be made of quilted rather than painted fabric, and that the sound effects not attempt to replicate *kabuki* for fear of any misapprehension. The translation was by Odashima Yushi, still the presiding Shakespeare translator of choice. *The Tempest* certainly relied on the presence of commercially viable actors in key roles. Hira Mikijiro was by now one of Japan's foremost Shakespearean actors, and his previous collaborations with Ninagawa were on their way to becoming the stuff of legend.[23] Ninagawa cast pop idol Hatakeyama Hisashi and the very popular television actress Tanaka Yuko as Ferdinand and Miranda, happily capitalizing on their fame to imbue the characters with an aura of romance and glamour frequently missing from the two young lovers. Ninagawa was never afraid of this kind of strategic casting. Matsumoto was emerging as a big star (in *kabuki* and in foreign musicals) when he cast him as Romeo, and throughout his career Ninagawa cast pop idols and film or television stars in his productions: 'A star represents the greatest common measure of the people's desire. As such, casting stars in a play's leading roles helps to structure and prepare the people's desires and feelings even before the curtain goes up. There is no more favourable condition for entering into theatrical time than this' (Ninagawa, 1993: 110, my translation).

Casting recognizable – and bankable – stars helped to ensure the commercial viability of Ninagawa's expansive, often crowded productions. In a country where government subsidy for theatre is as visible 'as a teardrop in the eye of a sparrow', as one producer very poetically lamented, celebrity casting was also an economic strategy. It was also a part of Ninagawa's recontextualization of a play, since the associations surrounding a given performer could be used to manage the audience's narrative expectations. Ninagawa had a casting pool of several regular actors who appeared for him in supporting roles – in some instances for decades. To be a reliable actor in Ninagawa's company could mean a lifetime of employment. His supporting players were in many ways the backbone of his work, since his approach so relied on the number of actors on stage: as Shakespeare's Benedick might say of a Ninagawa production, 'the world must be peopled!'.

Ninagawa also cast his productions with notable performers from Japan's various different theatrical genres, developing significant collaborations with luminaries from various disciplines. He worked frequently with *kyogen* star Nomura Mansai and younger *kabuki* personalities such as Onoe Kikunosuke V and Ichikawa Kamejiro. A number of Ninagawa's leading ladies were retired stars from Takarazuka. The all-female revue was founded in Takarazuka, a small town close to Osaka, in the early twentieth century. It has become one of Japan's most lucrative performance traditions, militantly organized and managed. The unmarried women who perform within Takarazuka do so only until they turn thirty, at which time they 'graduate'. There have been a wide variety of recent performances employing Takarazuka stars; for example, a recent all-female production of the Broadway musical *Chicago* was an enormous success and was brought to the Lincoln Center Festival in New York in the summer of 2016. Takarazuka audiences are almost entirely female, and its stars enjoy massive adulation from a particularly devoted fan base.

In his superlative recent *History of Japanese Theatre*, Jonah Salz uses the very elegant phrase 'calculated intimacies' to describe layers of meaning that can develop over time between performers in traditional theatre and their audiences (Salz, 2016: 383). Salz is referring specifically to meta-patterns and codes within traditional theatre performance, but the idea also illuminates Ninagawa's repeated choice of certain actors, and his manipulation of their personae to help 'prepare the people's desires and feelings' (as in the 1993 quotation above) for a given performance. A clear example is the long-standing collaboration between Ninagawa and Shiraishi Kayoko, one of the great champions of interdisciplinary performance in post-*shingeki* Japanese theatre. Her casting brought the wealth of her experience and an aura of gravitas, earned throughout a formidable career as one of late twentieth-century Japan's most versatile actresses.

Shiraishi came to prominence as one of Suzuki Tadashi's early collaborators, starring in his version of *The Trojan Women* and many other productions. Famed for the range of colours she can achieve with her extraordinary voice, she had worked with an impressive range of directors before her first collaboration with Ninagawa – the list includes Miyamoto Amon (*Mary Stuart*), Noda Hideki (*The Tiger*), Kokami Shoji (*Waiting for Godot*),[24] and Julie Taymor (Stravinsky's *Oedipus Rex*). Shiraishi's first production with Ninagawa was in 1994, when she played Titania/Hippolyta in his production of *A Midsummer Night's Dream*. She performed in many subsequent productions, including *Coriolanus*, *Tenpo Juninen no Shakespeare* and *The Trojan Women*.

## *A Midsummer Night's Dream* (1994)

In 1984 Ninagawa founded a new company, the Ninagawa Company,[25] to provide young actors with a place to train. Their first production was *Three Sisters, Staged as a Rehearsal*, and thereafter Ninagawa created several studio productions with the company, often of plays written by Shimizu Kunio. The first was *Blood Wedding*, which was also given the surtitle 'Performed by the Young Men and Women of the Ninagawa Company'. Shimizu's work had been integral to Ninagawa's own development, so he was eager to share it with his younger colleagues. The Ninagawa Company's work revolved around scenes and atelier presentations, which eventually Ninagawa would shape into an evening's worth of material for public presentation. Under the title *Waiting*, the company presented several such performances throughout the 1990s and into the new millennium.[26] Ideas developed by the Ninagawa Company were often formative, leading to large-scale productions elsewhere. The idea of presenting *Three Sisters* as a rehearsal was the first in a clear progression that led to the concept behind *The Tempest*.

For several years the Ninagawa Company operated at a studio space called the Benisan Pit, in Morishita, Tokyo, significantly smaller than the commercial theatres in which Ninagawa often worked. The work there was more immediate and intimate, created free from the pressure of commercial investment. In 1996 Ninagawa dismayed Nakane by proposing to direct a full-scale production of *A Midsummer Night's Dream* there. The company had been making more and more ambitious work in recent years, including impressive productions such as *Gipisu* and *Bacteria of the Rainbow* – both designed by Nakagoshi Tsukasa, emerging as Ninagawa's preferred set designer. The profit margins were impossible, and a variety of compromises were necessary to facilitate the demands of *Midsummer*. (Stories abound of Nakane personally providing lunch to the company.)

The visit of Peter Brook's *A Midsummer Night's Dream* to Tokyo in the early 1970s was very significant. Ninagawa had found it a liberating experience, since it departed so radically from all that had preceded it. For his own production of the play, Ninagawa wanted to out-Brook Brook, and certain interpretative similarities appeared.

> In 1970, Peter Brook staged his 'Dream' at the Nissay Theatre in Tokyo. At the time, it shocked us young generation of thesps and opened our eyes to the possibility of staging Shakespeare as modern theater. It was a revolutionarily

shocking production to us young Asian actors at the time – it was Shakespeare as we had never seen it before. So when I was looking around for a [Shakespeare] comedy to direct, 'Dream' seemed the natural choice. It occurred to me that it would be the perfect opportunity to fashion my own response to Brook – and to come up with a response as a Japanese dramatic artist. (Ninagawa, 2002a)

Both productions featured sumptuous costumes (by now a Ninagawa hallmark), athletic, circus-derived performances and a bright white setting. Brook's box set was a literal manifestation of his 'empty space'. Ninagawa translated this into a distinctly Japanese setting, staging the play in a Japanese rock garden, evoking the famous dry landscapes of Ryoan-ji in Kyoto.

Ninagawa's notes are filled with references to art history, to a variety of styles and movements within European painting from mannerism to the invention of perspective. Considering perspective to be a significant philosophical difference between European and Japanese art, he was drawn to the artistry of Ryoan-ji's dry-stone garden precisely because it is an example of a *Japanese* use of forced perspective. He had for a long time wanted to direct a production set in a Japanese garden, since it could be an entirely enclosed universe in which anything could happen. Columns of sand trickled down in vertical shafts of light throughout the play, suggesting the passage of time and an invitation to sleep. An enormous quantity of rose petals also fell throughout, echoing the camellias in *Sotoba Komachi* and the cherry blossoms in *NINAGAWA Macbeth*. Ninagawa undercut all this visual beauty by insisting that characters wore wigs made out of black refuse bags. His assistant Okouchi Naoko told me hilarious stories of the stress involved in getting these and other elements of the production ready for the company's eventual performances of the play in London. Ninagawa opened the doors of the performance space for the arrival of the mechanicals, allowing them to bring the 'reality' of the streets outside directly into the world of the play.

Bottom cooked noodles on the stage, filling the space with the smell of his dinner, and Snug arrived on a tiny bicycle. Shiraishi was a very powerful, regal Titania, which made her falling for Daimon Goro's Bottom all the more humorous. Daimon was a stalwart member of the companies of *NINAGAWA Macbeth* and *Medea* and appeared regularly in productions of *Suicide for Love* from 1979 until 2005. He played a great variety of Shakespearean comic characters, most notably Bottom, the Porter and Trinculo, as well as brilliant interpretations of the First Player and the Gravedigger in several versions of *Hamlet*.

As in *The Tempest*, Ninagawa combined a variety of acting styles within *A Midsummer Night's Dream*. He cast a Chinese opera acrobat, Yung-Biau Lin, as Puck and had a Japanese actor speak the role from beside the stage. The speaking actor was obscured with a black mask, in a nod to the *kuroko* of *kabuki*. At key moments, an increasing number of identically costumed doubles appeared, making Puck appear to have remarkable magical abilities. Splitting the role between performers was at once an avant-garde theatrical device, but a Japanese audience familiar with *kabuki* performances would not have been perturbed by such a division. For certain dance pieces it is entirely customary for a narrator and accompanist to speak from the side of the stage while an actor presents the character physically – and non-verbally.

To date, Ninagawa's approach to Shakespeare's plays had shown a consistent interest in their inherent performativity. *The Tempest* and *Hamlet* were both dominated by Ninagawa's interpretations of the plays within these plays, and even *NINAGAWA Macbeth* was 'performed' in front of witnesses. *A Midsummer Night's Dream* has one of Shakespeare's most famous internal performances, and, unlike *The Murder of Gonzago* or Prospero's masque, it is an opportunity for genuine humour. The mechanicals in Ninagawa's *Dream* were presented as earthily and realistically as possible, not only to force the contrast between Bottom and Shiraishi's stately Titania, but particularly for the comic potential of *Pyramus and Thisbe*. As he did for nearly all presentations of *Hamlet*'s mousetrap, Ninagawa announced the play's theatricality with an arrangement of candles. The mechanicals actively burlesqued the performance traditions of *kabuki*, exaggerating their amateur performance at the wedding feast with gusto. Daimon's Bottom and Fukazawa Atsushi's Flute also brought sincere charm to the performance, despite its ridiculousness, and Ofuji (a beloved Ninagawa regular and former sumo wrestler) stole the show as the Lion. Like *The Tempest*, Ninagawa's *Dream* ended with a single character on stage for the epilogue. This time it was Puck, and while the off-stage speaker ended Shakespeare's text, the physical performer treated the audience to a few final acrobatic tricks before extinguishing the *kabuki*-inspired candles. Ninagawa saw the division between physical and verbal performance as a generalized difference between European and Asian forms of theatre:

> [I was] thinking about the characteristics of Asian theater that set it apart from its European counterparts. It struck me that it was the importance of physical as well as verbal expression in the Asian dramatic vocabulary that makes it so special. Traditional forms of Asian theater, such as Chinese opera, are extremely physically demanding, whereas European theater is less so, and the focus is on verbal expression ... (Ninagawa, 2002a)

This experiment of sharing the physical and vocal parts of a Shakespearean character was never repeated. During the late 1990s, Ninagawa began to refer to himself as an Asian director, and placed more emphasis on this aspect of his identity. The differences between European and Asian performance were thrown into very sharp relief in *King Lear*, his next Shakespeare production to travel abroad.

*King Lear* was the fourth in the Sai no Kuni series, and it was a significant landmark in Ninagawa's career – his first time directing Shakespeare in English. Ninagawa's first English-language production was a translation of Shimizu Kunio's *Tango at the End of Winter*, which was performed in Edinburgh and London and starred Alan Rickman. A few years after *Tango* he had earned the worst reviews of his international career to date with a production of Ibsen's *Peer Gynt*. His concept, an attempt to rationalize the fantastical layers of Ibsen's play by likening them to the levels of a video game, was panned by critics in Norway and England alike. By contrast, all of Ninagawa's touring versions of Shakespeare – *Macbeth*, *The Tempest*, *A Midsummer Night's Dream* and the 1998 tour of *Hamlet* – were praised as revelatory interpretations of the plays. The logical next step, therefore, was for Ninagawa to direct a production in English. He was the first non-English-speaking artist ever invited to direct a new production for the RSC. The co-production brought together a company of (mostly) English actors and a design team and crew of Ninagawa's Japanese regulars. They rehearsed and performed in Saitama before transferring to Stratford-upon-Avon and then the Barbican in London. With designer Horio Yukio, Ninagawa conceived a performance space inspired by the aesthetics of *noh*.

> The format of the *noh* stage was perfected as an 'empty space' in the 15th century – long before Peter Brook – and it continues to be a fundamental and defining influence on contemporary Japanese theatre. However, Ninagawa's setting of *King Lear* is not a real *noh* stage in the traditional sense. It is his version of the 'empty space', the basic structure of which is inspired by the *noh* stage. (Nakane, 1999)

> Horio's set is dominated by a huge black wooden walkway sloping gently towards you and widening into an immense platform. At the back the walkway seems to disappear into black darkness, whence the actors emerge like mythological figures, both real and remote. All this suggests the structure of the classical *noh* stage, where the curtained entrance also leads somewhere indeterminate: a primeval darkness that holds no moral secrets ... this reinforces the uncomfortable Shakespearean vision of a world where you are left without the consolation or guidance of a moral order. (Peter, 1999)

These *noh* aesthetics extended to the design for the shelter taken during the storm and the tent in which Lear sleeps towards the end of the play. They were designed to look like *noh*'s rudimentary stage properties known as *tsukurimono* ('disposable items'), which are evocative rather than realistic. Variations of a simple frame can be used to suggest a palace, a boat, a carriage or even a spider web, and here Ninagawa capitalized on this representational economy. There was a feeling that everything was moving towards increased simplicity – if not outright nihilism. This is the driving narrative force of the play, which begins with 'nothing' and reaches its nadir in Shakespeare's most extraordinarily bleak line in Act 5, Scene 3: 'Never, never, never, never, never!' For Ninagawa it was a new aesthetic turning point. While *King Lear* delivered all the customary spectacle of his earlier productions, it also physically staged Ninagawa's shifting interpretative focus. Lear began the show bedecked in voluminous furs and an impressive crown, but the journey of the play stripped all of this away, rather as *Medea* had, two decades earlier. The Japanese elements of *King Lear* were themselves simpler and less spectacular than previous productions – an impressive but minimalist set design, costumes that echoed but were not actually kimono and no dramatic make-up. The percussive and indicative sound effects from *kabuki* were still in use, but even Uzaki Ryudo's impressive music fell towards silence as the production reached its inexorably bleak conclusion. As the twentieth century ended, Ninagawa was moving away from the extravagant framing devices of his earlier Shakespeare productions. The move towards a new kind of production began in the aftermath of his first *Othello* in 1994. This reunited Ninagawa with Matsumoto Koshiro IX, who played Othello, with Kiba Katsumi as Iago. Ninagawa later acknowledged that too much emphasis had gone into its scenic elements, and that the production simply 'didn't work' (Ninagawa, 1995: 217).

*King Lear*'s intermingling of sources (from Brook, *noh* and elsewhere) epitomized Ninagawa's personal feelings about

Shakespeare. Brook's influence on Shakespearean performance is inescapable, and Ninagawa found it both an inspiration and a challenge. His productions sought the same achievement and 'freedom' that Brook had accomplished in a Japanese context that a local audience could digest.

*King Lear* was announced as Sir Nigel Hawthorne's farewell to the stage, at least partially inspired by his Oscar-nominated performance in Nicholas Hytner's *The Madness of King George*. Beloved of British audiences for his award-winning run as Sir Humphrey Appleby on *Yes Minister*, Hawthorne was also a much-lauded stage actor. A meticulous thinker, he devoted careful attention to his portrayal of Lear, particularly from the perspective of contemporary scientific investigations of Alzheimer's and dementia. His Lear was a powerful, competent man who was starting to lose his mind. The character's rage, madness and volatility were all charted with this in mind, and for many audience members it was a remarkably moving interpretation. Unfortunately, his choices were found to be at odds with Ninagawa's production, with which English critics had a field day, and no turn was left unstoned. The consensus of the London press was that the production was ridiculous, the performances unsatisfactory and, cruelly, that Hawthorne was incapable of playing the part.

Ninagawa became the victim of the kind of Bakhtinian, carnivalesque inversion of authority that his productions sought to invite. He was toppled from his pedestal as a Shakespeare director of acclaim, and successive reviews seemed to compete to find new expressions of contempt. These ranged from 'bumbling' (Nightingale, 1999) and 'a waste' (Spencer, 1999) to 'woeful' (Coveney, 1999) and 'pathetic' (Parry, 1999).[27] Most critics mentioned that the production's set, lighting and costumes were beautiful, but they seem to have expected such delights in a Ninagawa production, and now almost resented being given more of the same.

While Horio's set was praised for its elegance, the critics were universally vituperative when it came to Ninagawa's concept for the play's central storm scene. As an indication of the scene's earth-shattering chaos, the trickling sand and falling petals of previous productions were replaced with falling rocks. These were carefully constructed and rehearsed, timed and cued by stage management between the actors' lines. Critics uniformly loathed this, determinedly seeing panic on the actors' faces and lamenting the distraction caused by the rocks and pebbles falling and rolling on the stage. Michael Coveney, an erstwhile champion of Ninagawa's work,[28] witheringly suggested that the effect would better suit Falstaff in *The Merry Wives of Windsor*, when he cries 'let the sky rain potatoes!'. Dennis Kennedy went so far as to suggest that 'the device seemed to underline the cultural indeterminacy of the production, and of Ninagawa's approach to Shakespeare' (Kennedy, 2001: 324). Ninagawa had been dropping flowers, water and sand for decades, all as a means of activating the visual space of his stages and insisting on the immediacy of the theatrical experience. The *Richard III* that immediately preceded *King Lear* in Saitama had opened with a dead horse being dropped from the flies – *Lear's* rocks were dramatic, but hardly surprising to an audience in any way familiar with his work.

The critical ferocity was a terrible blow to Ninagawa, and to Hawthorne, who died of pancreatic cancer soon afterwards. Only Sheridan Morley seemed willing to take the production on its own terms, and in his positive response he seemed as isolated as Lear himself.

> As the production was rehearsed in Tokyo, opened in Tokyo, has a Japanese director, designer and Fool, not to mention a largely Japanese backstage staff, the objection [that the production's priorities 'appear to be somewhat Japanese'] is much akin to the complaint that Kurosawa's *Throne of Blood* is doubtless a wonderful movie but somehow not quite *Macbeth* as we used to know and love it at the Old Vic. (Morley, 1999: 66)

Morley had particular praise for Hawthorne's reading of the part:

given the Japanese reverence for old age, and his own talent for portraying a mind diseased, it was also surely a safe bet that [Hawthorne] would deliver in Act V a touching and heart-rending old man and this he unquestionably does. Indeed, I have never seen a Lear which ends better: instead of the usual exhausted old upfront thespian, staggering about the stage under the weight of his dead Cordelia, we get an almost Chekhovian revelation, as though the whole play has been leading up to this moment and not counting down towards it; similarly, Hawthorne plays the post-Dover scene with John Carlisle's equally brilliant Gloucester as if they were the tramps from *Godot*, adrift in a bleak landscape of the broken mind and awaiting they know not what. (Morley, 1999: 66)

Hawthorne had seen Sanada Hiroyuki play Hamlet at the Barbican in 1998 and suggested that he might be an appropriate choice to play Lear's Fool. Thelma Holt had arranged for dozens of actors to audition for Ninagawa during the previous summer, but none had sparked his interest. Sanada was eventually chosen and set about the arduous task of getting his English to a standard acceptable for the RSC. His achievements in this regard were met with a varied response: some critics found him unintelligible (Edwards, 1999), but he was also awarded an honorary MBE for his performance. His playing the role could be seen as a revision of the idea of casting Yung-Biau Lin in *A Midsummer Night's Dream* – a foreign actor, noted for his athleticism, joining the company to play a trickster licensed to speak truth to power. There was no question of hiring an English-speaking actor to speak for Sanada – his excellent speaking voice alone would preclude the necessity of any such accommodations. His Fool was playful and energetic, and Hawthorne and Sanada developed a beautifully protective relationship on stage. Echoing the production's *noh* aesthetics, Sanada's belt was equipped with a variety of *noh* masks, which he used to entertain, to demonstrate, to mock or even hide behind. If this was a *King Lear* designed to echo the formality and philosophy of *noh*, then Sanada occupied the position of a *kyogen* actor. *Kyogen* interludes within a *noh* programme are designed to make the audience laugh, and commentators eager to make intercultural comparisons have likened *kyogen* to *commedia dell'arte* and ancient Greek satyr plays. The Fool's comic contributions are no match for the play's nihilism, and so unlike a *noh* programme, in this *King Lear* any palate-cleansing comedy ended with his disappearance. Hawthorne was particularly moving when he said 'my poor fool is hanged' in Act 5, Scene 1 – his relationship with the Fool had become a clear substitute for his banished Cordelia, and the conflation of both losses was beautifully observed.

Although surely cold comfort in the aftermath of such a critical mauling, it is worth noting that Ninagawa was not the first Japanese artist to suffer such an onslaught for his version of *King Lear*. As far back as 1955, Noguchi Isamu's designs for Herbert Devine's production starring John Gielgud were endlessly ridiculed. Decades later, Suzuki Tadashi's *Tale of Lear* was panned when it was programmed at the Barbican in 1994, and Suzuki was so angered by this reception that he never brought another show to the United Kingdom. After his version Ninagawa returned to Tokyo and to his busy schedule of creating productions for his Japanese audience. His first productions of the new millennium were new versions of *The Water Magician* and *Three Sisters* at the Theatre Cocoon, followed by back-to-back revivals of *A Midsummer Night's Dream* and *The Tempest* for the Sai no Kuni series. It was quite some time before he directed a new Shakespeare, but a major production at Bunkamura in July 2000 laid the groundwork for one of the most extraordinary productions of his career.

## *The Greeks*

Having had major successes with *Oedipus Rex* and *Medea*, Ninagawa wanted to end the twentieth century with a Greek tragedy commenting on war. Instead of a single play, he chose

Barton and Cavander's cycle *The Greeks*, created for the RSC in 1980. This ten-play marathon combines and condenses material by Homer, Euripides, Aeschylus and Sophocles, and is divided into three parts: *The War*, *The Murders* and *The Gods*. Ninagawa staged it in traverse, splitting the Cocoon audience in a spatial arrangement he would repeat in numerous future productions. The prologue began with several female company members dashing through the space, dressed in contemporary clothing and looking like latecomers. Their discussion morphed into the production's prologue, as they formed a bridge between contemporary Tokyo and the mythology of the plays to come.

The production starred many Ninagawa regulars. Hira Mikijiro played Agamemnon and Apollo, Shiraishi Kayoko was Clytemnestra and Rei Asami was Andromache. The film and television star Terajima Shinobu was cast as Electra, having worked with Ninagawa on a number of previous productions. Her real-life brother, the rising *onnagata* star Onoe Kikunosuke V, was cast as Orestes. As discussed, *kabuki* celebrates family lineage, and it is often a key selling point for a production to feature fathers and sons. Terajima, daughter of a leading *kabuki* family, had no chance of performing on stage with her father and brother at the Kabuki-za, but had achieved even greater fame as an independent actress. The stunt of casting these siblings from the Otowaya dynasty was available to Ninagawa in a way that was impossible in traditional theatre. This combination of actual family members and the juxtaposition of *kabuki* and contemporary performance led to some extraordinary moments within the show. Most noteworthy was the confrontation between Orestes and Clytemnestra in *Electra*. Ninagawa staged the scene in a manner deliberately reminiscent of Chikamatsu's *kabuki* play *The Woman Killer and the Hell of Oil*. In this play, a desperate man is driven to kill a woman for money, but as he tries to stab her in the oil shop where he finds her, a barrel is knocked over. The two struggle dramatically (and messily) in the spilled liquid before the climactic murder. Ninagawa incorporated this moment and had Orestes overturn an amphora in the scene, soaking the stage. Shiraishi and Kikunosuke's desperate struggle was rendered all the more dramatic by this evocation of the Chikamatsu play. In it, the murderer's guilt cripples him almost immediately after he commits his crime, and he is eventually destroyed by it. While the Sophocles play justifies the murder on the basis of Clytemnestra's previous crimes, Ninagawa's staging thus heavily inferred that Orestes would likewise be undone by his crime.

This combination of Japanese and ancient Greek traditions was a highlight within a very beautiful production. It was the first of many collaborations with Kikunosuke, and soon afterwards the actor made a fascinating proposal. He invited Ninagawa to direct a production of *Twelfth Night* at the Kabuki-za. After a quarter of a century of responding to *kabuki*, and countless shows that demonstrated its seminal influence on his work, it was extraordinary for Ninagawa to be given the chance to direct at the Kabuki-za. *Kabuki*'s structure is such that 'directing' has significantly less of a place in the artistic process than in other theatrical forms. Roles are learned by rote, and key patterns or interpretations called *kata* are passed down through generations. Only very senior actors are entitled to innovate. Rehearsal periods are short, since actors are generally familiar with the repertoire. It was a significant honour for Ninagawa to be invited into this world.

## *Ninagawa Twelfth Night*

The production necessitated a new translation of the play, since Odashima's 1970s version still sounded too contemporary for a *kabuki* interpretation. (By contrast, the early translation by Tsubouchi Shoyo sounded too arcane and complicated for modern audiences to understand.) Imai Toyoshige was hired to create a new, retro-fit *kabuki* adaptation. Imai's translation of the text was only a part of the relocation, since various elements of the Shakespeare story could not have made sense in the context of a *kabuki* world. For the first time in a Ninagawa Shakespeare, the characters' names were actually changed. Sebastian became Shuzennosuke, Olivia became Oribue and Orsino was renamed Oshino no Sadaijin. Malvolio's name was transformed to Maruo Bodaiyu, and charmingly Viola's name became Biwa, so that its musicality was retained in the name of a comparable Japanese musical instrument.

*Twelfth Night* was Kikunosuke's idea, and he was the production's star, playing both Biwa (Viola) and Shuzennosuke (Sebastian). The doubling allowed for a prolonged demonstration of the actor's skill both as an *onnagata* and a *wagoto* performer. Indeed, some of the production's biggest laughs came from his constant vocal alterations as he switched between male and female – even more amusingly when he was playing a woman playing a man. After the considerable success with *The Greeks* starring Kikunosuke's sister, Ninagawa now employed the 'calculated intimacy' of casting Kikunosuke's father, the Living National Treasure Onoe Kikugoro VII, as both Maruo Bodaiyu (Malvolio) and as Feste, here renamed Sutesuke.

The production's set was designed by Kanai Yoichiro, who had never designed for the Kabuki-za before Ninagawa hired him.[29] The design was a beautiful synthesis of Ninagawa's ideas and approaches to Shakespeare. Once the *jyoshikimaku*, the traditional *kabuki* curtain, was pulled back, the hybrid world of the production became apparent. Audiences gasped and applauded the first image, a huge mirror reflecting the entire Kabuki-za. It was in fact translucent, and an enormous cherry tree appeared behind it. Under its blooms three young boys sang a version of the Christmas carol 'O Come O Come Emmanuel' – a nod both to the title, *Twelfth Night*, and to the burgeoning influence of Christianity in Japan in the period during which the production was set. This being the Kabuki-za, Ninagawa could finally have characters enter and exit via a bona fide *hanamichi*, which he did with the flair of a real connoisseur.

In a nod to several previous productions, particularly *The Tempest*, Ninagawa (and Imai) added a storm scene after Shakespeare's Act 1, Scene 1. In this new scene, a ship appeared from the back of a totally bare stage, and the audience was introduced to Shuzennosuke and the ship's captain. With thanks to some trickery and the use of a *fukikae*, or dummy actor, Kikunosuke repeatedly went in and out of the ship's lower quarters, and each time he reappeared he had changed from Shuzennosuke to Biwa, or back again. As the father of fraternal twins, Shakespeare himself would have known that a twin brother and sister would never be identical, but this did not stop him from including it as a major plot point in *Twelfth Night*. Kikunosuke's prowess as an interpreter of young male *and* female characters made for a very nuanced performance. Since he was playing both siblings, they were literally identical, making unprecedented sense of the Shakespearean plot. By setting this introduction to both siblings on a boat, Ninagawa made Kikunosuke's *hayagawari* quick changes all the more impressive. It seemed as though there was nowhere to hide, let alone perform complete costume and wig changes in a matter of seconds. Throughout the production Ninagawa inserted little vignettes to fill in any time that might have been required for quick changes, for either Kikunosuke or his father. These were often scenes from *ukiyo-e* paintings, most notably a charming reproduction of the barrel-building scene at Fujimigahara, one of Hokusai's *Thirty Six Views of Mount Fuji*.[30]

The set design relied on a variety of mirrored walls. These echoed and enhanced the doubling inherent in the Shakespeare play (wherein Viola becomes the double of her twin brother when she 'becomes' a man) and the further doubling in the production (in which the two lead actors each played multiple characters). Having held a mirror up to nature in *Hamlet*, and indeed presented his *Tempest* as 'the interweaving reflections of a broken mirror', Ninagawa's *Twelfth Night* enhanced and extended a scenic element he particularly enjoyed.[31] In a particularly charming concession to the world of *kabuki*, wherein the exchange of rings would make little cultural sense,

Ninagawa chose to have Oribue send a hand-mirror to Biwa in Act 2, Scene 2. This small intercultural gesture made sense within the production's cultural context (and its set design) and also enhanced the Shakespeare text's own mirroring and doubling of identity.

Kanai designed an elegant house for Oribue, decorated with irises that owed as much to art nouveau as *kabuki* architecture, and created several vermilion bridges for the outdoor scenes in the latter half of the play. His most arresting image was for the garden, where Toin Kanemichi (Belch), Ando Eichiku (Aguecheek) and Maa (Maria) lay their trap for Maruo Bodaiyu. The design featured three large sand sculptures, directly reminiscent of the *kougetsudai* ('moon viewing platform') at Ginkakuji, Kyoto's Silver Pavilion. It is rumoured that, looking from the top floor of the Pavilion by moonlight, the surface of the sculpture looks like a reflection of the full moon. The design was also a very elegant reference to *A Midsummer Night's Dream*, which Ninagawa had fashioned after another of Kyoto's famous stone-and-sand gardens. Ninagawa put three *kougetsudai* in Oribue's garden, creating plenty of spaces for the conspirators to hide and observe the love-sick steward. It was a particularly striking scene (in an already beautiful production), made all the more impressive when one spotted the distant moon glowing overhead. Even within the structure of an authentic *kabuki* production, Ninagawa managed to present a great variety of visual flourishes, many of them resonant nods to his previous successes.[32]

Ninagawa might never have imagined in 1980 that *NINAGAWA Macbeth* could one day lead to a Shakespeare production at the Kabuki-za. It would never even have occurred to him as a possibility. Echoing the dynamic within the title of *NINAGAWA Macbeth*, the *kabuki* production was marketed as *Ninagawa Twelfth Night*. This time all the names were written in Japanese, suggesting that this was a meeting of equals. By now the foremost interpreter of Shakespeare in Japan, Ninagawa's contribution could be considered on an equal footing with everything that the *kabuki* company

FIGURE 2 Ninagawa Twelfth Night *(2005): the moon-viewing platforms designed by Kanai to replicate the famous sand sculpture at Ginkakuji, Kyoto. Photo © Donald Cooper/Photostage.*

brought to the table. If anything, *kabuki* needed Ninagawa more than he needed *kabuki* – the invitation had, after all, come from Kikunosuke, in the hope that Ninagawa and Shakespeare might make *kabuki* more accessible to Japanese audiences. An extraordinary change had come about in the twenty-five years since Ninagawa had started using the elements of *kabuki* that informed his own theatrical taste to bring Shakespeare to Japanese audiences. Now it was the other way around. After so many successful productions manipulating Japanese imagery to help local audiences appreciate Shakespeare, *Ninagawa Twelfth Night* was an exquisite synthesis of Ninagawa's passions, influences and talents.

# 3

# Hamlet

## *Hamlet* in Japan

The first references to Shakespeare came to Japan via texts translated from Chinese and Dutch in the mid-nineteenth century. During the Meiji Restoration, Japan became fascinated with Shakespeare's plays, and as English literature became more widely available it became increasingly popular. In the 1880s *Hamlet* captivated Japanese men of letters, who responded to its 'modernity' in their eagerness to promote a contemporary Japanese literary identity. Several writers attempted to translate the play, but very few completed it. Adaptations were popular, and the story of *Hamlet* became increasingly familiar to readers and audiences.[1] The first complete translation of the play was by Tsubouchi Shoyo. Tsubouchi was central to the introduction of Shakespeare to Japanese audiences, and the first person to translate the complete works into Japanese. His *Hamlet* was published in 1907 and staged in its entirety at the Imperial Theatre in 1911. Tsubouchi's text was indebted to the language and musicality of *kabuki*, and as a result it felt old-fashioned at a time when so much energy was devoted to creating a modern Japanese identity. It was also revolutionary, since it was an actual translation of the Shakespeare play rather than an adaptation of its themes or storyline. For decades

Tsubouchi's translation was the go-to choice for the majority of Japanese productions, despite the many others that had been produced.

After Tsubouchi finished his translation of Shakespeare's complete works, there was a period of what Takahashi Yasunari called 'reflective assimilation' (2002:108). A distinctly Japanese Shakespeare developed as more and more thinkers and writers translated and engaged with the plays. Shakespeare (and most other foreign writers) were suppressed during the period of the Second World War, but in its aftermath his popularity grew again. In the 1950s Fukuda Tsuneari emerged as a new voice in Shakespearean translation. Inspired by an Old Vic production he had seen in London, Fukuda translated and directed *Hamlet* for the Bungakuza company in 1955, in a highly influential *shingeki* production that aimed to present the play as a modern text, relevant to contemporary Japan. The next big turning point came at the end of the 1960s, a decade of remarkable innovation in Japanese theatre. The *angura* movement introduced key figures such as Terayama, Kara, Suzuki and others, all eagerly developing theatre practices aiming for a more resolutely Japanese mode of theatrical expression, no longer indebted to Western theatre or the imitative strictures of *shingeki*. During Ninagawa's early years with Gendaijin Gekijo there were no fewer than eighteen productions of *Hamlet* in Tokyo. While Ninagawa worked with Shimizu on plays that sought to reflect contemporary issues, another important collaboration was under way. Deguchi Norio directed a new translation of *Hamlet* by Odashima Yushi, again for the Bungakuza, in 1972. They had experimented initially with a combination of Fukuda's and Odashima's versions, but Deguchi preferred Odashima's translation. After Deguchi left the Bungakuza, he directed all of Shakespeare's plays, all in his distinctive 'jeans and T-shirts' style and all translated by Odashima, between 1975 and 1981. Their extraordinary achievement completely revitalized the possibilities for Shakespearean performance in Japan.

## Ninagawa and *Hamlet*

Ninagawa directed eight productions of *Hamlet* over the course of his career. Other productions (such as *Suicide for Love* or *Medea*) were revived more frequently, but no single play captured his imagination quite like *Hamlet*. He described the experience as being 'like climbing a very high mountain. Every time I am near the summit, I fall back a little' (Shilling, 2015). Even after so many different versions, he never felt fully finished with it, and invariably hinted after a production opened that he might try it again. He was not alone in this fascination. By 1978 *Hamlet* had kept theatre-makers, scholars and readers busy for over a century. *Hamlet* has been translated into Japanese well over a hundred times, and continues to be the subject of treatises, guides, studies and stage productions. A writer who produces a useful Japanese translation can hope to see it produced multiple times if the translation is published. Ninagawa's seven Japanese productions used four translations of the text. These were by Odashima Yushi, Tsubouchi Shoyo, Matsuoka Kazuko and Kawai Shoichiro. He also directed one production in English. This variety gives a sense of how mutable an entity 'Shakespeare' can be in Japan – written by a man or a woman, in translations from just about any point in the last 150 years. When a translation starts to feel old-fashioned, another can be commissioned to reflect the particular interests of a given production.

Ninagawa explored multiple ideas in his productions of *Hamlet*, and a number of key images appeared in repeated interpretations. He set the action in differing time periods, cast actors of different ages, played with different spatial arrangements and even juxtaposed different Japanese translations within the same production. This chapter examines all eight of Ninagawa's different productions, with reference to their translation, casting, design and music, and the context in which they were presented. The treatment of the Players and the theatricality of the play-within-the-play were also significant in each production. Ninagawa preferred not to cut the plays he directed, considering it a challenge to stage the entire text.

> I never make any cuts or revisions in a playwright's lines. The only reason I have anything to write home about is thanks to the words that someone else wrote on paper as a play. A director's work can exist only within such a framework. Therefore cutting and pasting a text goes entirely against my principles. [...] I feel that I never want to be outdone by Sophocles, Shakespeare, Namboku, or Chikamatsu. Unless one has the nerve never to be outdone, one may not succeed in doing this kind of work, expressing one's own life through another's words. (Ninagawa, 1993: 103–4, my translation)

*Hamlet*'s extraordinary length demanded some concessions, and certain scenes were frequently edited. (Polonius' servant Reynaldo was invariably cut.) Ninagawa always staged *The Murder of Gonzago* and the dumb show before it – the latter was usually an excuse to foreground the relationship between Claudius and Gertrude before the play was cancelled. Fortinbras was never cut from the play, because for Ninagawa he represented a critical contrast to Hamlet.

Ninagawa's initial approach to the play showed the influence of several critical ideas. In the late 1970s Japan was awash with Shakespearean activity, already parodied in Inoue's *Tenpo Juninen no Shakespeare*. Deguchi's ambitious project was well under way, there was a century's worth of textual criticism in print, and radical reinterpretations were happening at the hands of directors like Suzuki Tadashi. When Nakane Tadao first approached him to direct a Shakespeare play for Toho in 1974, Ninagawa had suggested *Hamlet*. Demoralized at the state of his own theatre company, Ninagawa was contemplating the radical idea of setting *Hamlet* on the night of the Doll Festival, and having Hamlet appear as a ghost, played by the rock singer Hagiwara Ken'ichi. The idea behind a casting stunt like this was not so much a desire to sell tickets, but rather an earnest hope that the production could reject Shakespeare's status as an educational figure and instead stage his work in an innovative, entertaining way.[2] Nakane explained that 'I wanted to work with Ninagawa to combine classical stylization and the pop culture embodied by Hagiwara within the framework of Shakespeare' (Ninagawa, 1995: 210). Although this particular *Hamlet* did not happen, its ideas haunted several of Ninagawa's later productions. They resurfaced when he directed his first production at the Imperial Theatre, four years after *Romeo and Juliet*.

Ninagawa's published notes on the 1978 *Hamlet* begin with a reference to 'Bottom's Descendants', an essay by Takahashi Yasunari, one of Japan's foremost literary critics. It came from an edited volume of academic essays about clowning in art and literature. Takahashi had also recently completed, with Kishi Tetsuo, the Japanese translation of Brook's *The Empty Space*. Ninagawa certainly read it, and Brook's was a recurring influence for decades. Ninagawa's approach to Shakespeare was also heavily inspired by Bakhtin's *Rabelais and his World*, translated into Japanese by Kawabata Kaori in 1974. Bakhtin's fascinating study of the exuberance of medieval life, celebrating carnival and the grotesque, encouraged the kind of revolutionary interpretation that Ninagawa wanted to bring to Shakespeare. What Ninagawa responded to in particular was the carnivalesque's power to challenge authority and the status quo, to celebrate the grotesque and the base, and Bakhtin's material bodily principle – his concept of grotesque realism.

> The material bodily principle, earth and real time become the relative centre of the new picture of the world. Not the ascent of the individual soul into the higher sphere but the movement forward of all mankind, along the horizontal of historic time, becomes the basic criterion of evaluations. Having done its part upon earth, the individual soul fades and dies together with the individual body; but the body of the people and of mankind, fertilized by the dead, is

eternally renewed and moves forever forward along the
historic path of progress. (Bakhtin, 1984: 404)

For Ninagawa, *Hamlet* was the ideal play to explore Bakhtin's
ideas; it depicts a kingdom on the brink of war, facing
repeated challenges to its leadership, and a prince determined
to upend the order of the court. The gravedigging scene is
certainly 'fertilized by the dead', featuring its two clowns
literally pulling human bodies apart as they laugh and sing
about life and death.[3] Although it is an iconic scene – so much
so that its grim realities can easily be overlooked – the scene
of Hamlet holding the rotting skull of a former acquaintance
and musing on the passage of time is as clear a depiction of
Bakhtin's material bodily principle as any in Shakespeare. All
these influences – Brook, Bakhtin, Takahashi and others –
converged in the 1978 *Hamlet*. The clowns, the play of space,
the carnivalesque and the Bakhtin-inspired evocation of
Renaissance life were all on full display.

# Imperial Theatre, 1978

Ninagawa's 1978 *Hamlet* was at the Imperial Theatre, where
Tsubouchi's influential production had been staged in 1911. The
theatre had been remodelled in 1966 and is predominantly a
receiving house for large musical theatre productions. Most of
Ninagawa's commercial productions since 1974 had been at
the nearby Nissay Theatre, but he had directed a production
of Brecht and Weill's *The Threepenny Opera* at the Imperial
the previous summer. Hira Mikijiro starred as Hamlet, in one
of their earliest collaborations. He had played the role before,
and was already famous from his work in theatre, film and
television. The 1978 *Hamlet* happened in August, a few months
after their spectacular production of *Medea* in February.[4] These
two 1978 productions were of major importance for the rest of
Ninagawa's career. *Medea* was the first of his productions to tour

internationally, and between its 1983 tour and 2019 there was no single calendar year that did not see a Ninagawa production performed outside Japan.[5] *Medea* toured for over twenty years, and was one of Ninagawa's most successful international productions. The 1978 *Hamlet* was not revived, but it marked the beginning of Ninagawa's lifelong dialogue with the play.

The set for this first *Hamlet* featured an enormous staircase, with playing areas on various levels throughout. The design was by Asakura Sestu, who was, amazingly, responsible for the design of Ninagawa's eighth *Hamlet* in 2015. The 1978 set presented challenges in the staging of more intimate scenes but was extremely effective for the larger scenes of court and particularly for the final tableau. Ninagawa cast a huge number of actors in this first Hamlet, eager as he was to populate the expansive set. The costumes were by Lily Komine and were an obvious continuation of the design experiments that had been so successful in *Medea*. Claudius and Gertrude wore exaggerated robes and headpieces, and the king even sported the stripes of *kumadori* make-up that indicate an evil character in *kabuki*. These designs, and the impressive robes worn by the crowds of lords, were juxtaposed with Hamlet's more contemporary clothes and his lack of extravagant headgear; by the end of the play Hira was wearing more contemporary trousers and a vest for the duel.

Scale was a major focus in this production. With an acting company of over seventy performers, this was easily achieved, and the sheer size of the Danish court was impressive. As in *King Lear* (with its crowd of unruly knights) and *Oedipus Rex* (which had featured an enormous chorus), this *Hamlet* showed Ninagawa's extraordinary talent for choreographing huge crowds. The influence of his youth in Saitama, the 'human slag heap', lasted throughout his life, and these early productions always placed their protagonists in a swirling morass of human bodies. The Danish court, as presented on this vast set of steps, was a vertical, top-down society, and by the end it had suffered a grotesque reversal. This *Hamlet* ended like Bakhtin's carnival, with 'everything inverted in relation to the outside world. All who are highest are debased, all who are lowest are crowned' (Bakhtin, 1984: 384).

The impressive staging owed more of a debt to modernist European designers such as Josef Svoboda than anything expressly Japanese, but the production achieved an astonishing coup by incorporating a very specific Japanese image. For *The Mousetrap*, Ninagawa created a large-scale version of a *hinadan*, the display-stand used to arrange the dolls associated with *hina-matsuri,* the Doll Festival. This is an integral part of the celebration of Girls' Day on 3 March. Before Western culture permeated Japan in the nineteenth century and individual birthdays began to be celebrated, girls were celebrated on Girls' Day (3 March) and boys on Boys' Day (5 May). The third day of the third month was sometimes called the Peach Blossom Festival,[6] since the peach trees tended to bloom at about that time. The adoption of the Gregorian calendar offset this somewhat, but Girls' Day is still celebrated on 3 March. The *hina-matsuri* focuses on the presentation and enjoyment of an intricate set of dolls. These are always displayed in a particular arrangement, on a tiered stand lined with red fabric. The stand is called a 'doll platform' or *hinadan* – and Ninagawa used this image in four of his eight *Hamlets*, more than any other interpretative idea.

The dolls on a traditional *hinadan* are arranged in a strict hierarchical order that represents levels of status within the Japanese imperial court. The top tier seats two 'imperial' dolls, representing the emperor and empress. They do not symbolize any particular historical rulers, so much as the general idea of the position. The next tier down holds three ladies-in-waiting and the third holds five musicians. The next presents the Minister of the Left and the Minister of the Right, both senior officials in the imperial court. The lowest level seats three drinkers, attendants to the emperor and empress. A traditional *hinadan* also features various items of furniture, food and foliage, all with distinct symbolism and meaning.

Originally the tradition was for the dolls to be displayed in the period leading up to the Girls' Festival and then ceremonially brought to a nearby river and washed away. As the tradition grew in popularity, it became increasingly expensive for a family to afford a set of dolls to display and discard every year. It became customary to keep the dolls, and families would wrap them carefully and store them when they were not on display. The whole festival was a time to pray for good luck for daughters and young women, the dolls representing a family's hopes for their daughter's happiness, in life and particularly in marriage. The arrangement of the dolls – and their careful unwrapping and rewrapping before and after the festival – was a particularly cherished occasion between mothers and daughters.

Ninagawa's first iteration of *Hamlet* (and this *hinadan* idea) presented a very clear image of a traditional hierarchy, deeply compromised by a figure not knowing his place. This made *The Mousetrap* instantly understandable – and shocking – to a Japanese audience, even one familiar with *Hamlet*. Here was a very strong provocation; the upward mobility of Lucianus, the villain, was made all the more intensely visible by having him move from the position of lower rank all the way up to 'emperor' on the now human-sized set of tiers on which the play was performed. Ninagawa always loved using stairs and staircases as a means of presenting the social hierarchy within a play, or indeed showing the relationships between large groups of people within a theatrical space. This first *Hamlet* did both. The story of a highly placed minister poisoning the ruler and moving up the ladder (or in this case up the *hinadan*) was physically presented in a way that would make sense to any viewer but had the extra resonance of this familiar Japanese image. With the large crowd gathered to watch *The Mousetrap*, the pressure on Claudius not to react was all the more intense. When he insisted that the play be stopped, the ensuing chaos was staggering. Ninagawa enhanced its theatricality by having the entire breakdown performed in slow-motion – a technique that he would repeat on numerous occasions throughout his career.

During Claudius' soliloquy, Ninagawa covered much of the stage with a red cross of light. Some reviewers found the image too heavy handed, but Ninagawa was eager to foreground the religious aspect of the king's turmoil.[7] This reading was a critical element in all Ninagawa's productions over the ensuing decades.

Ninagawa's early productions earned quite a reputation for his eclectic use of music, and this *Hamlet* featured Barber's *Adagio* and several of his favourite pieces by Bach. As in the 1974 *Romeo and Juliet*, he juxtaposed Western classical music with pop songs by Elton John. Ninagawa opened the show with the 1970 track 'The King Must Die', and it played again over the arresting image of Fortinbras atop the huge set of steps, while the massive chorus, like a Breughel painting, grovelled beneath him.

The production used Odashima's translation of the play. His translations had a virtual monopoly on the Japanese stage in the 1970s and 1980s. Odashima greatly popularized Shakespeare for Japanese readers and theatregoers, and he was only the second person ever to translate Shakespeare's complete works. Odashima's style liberated Shakespeare from the strictures of *shingeki* adaptations, creating a fluid, accessible language that tried to retain the humour and even the bawdy in Shakespeare's language. Ninagawa used his translations for the first twenty years of his career, and all of his early successes – *NINAGAWA Macbeth*, *The Tempest*, *A Midsummer Night's Dream* and *King Lear* – were based on translations by Odashima.

This first *Hamlet* laid down several markers for Ninagawa's future interpretations of the play. The steps, the crowds, the play with time periods, the visual and aural echoes of *kabuki*, the anachronistic non-Japanese music and particularly the *hinadan* would all reappear in subsequent productions.

# Spiral Hall, 1988

Ninagawa's next *Hamlet* was ten years later in 1988, at Tokyo's Spiral Hall, significantly smaller than the Imperial Theatre with only about 300 seats. This *Hamlet* starred Ken Watanabe, who went on to international fame with roles in *Batman Begins* and *Inception*. Watanabe first worked with Ninagawa in Kara's play *Shitaya Mannencho Monogatari* in 1981. In the 1988 *Hamlet* Ninagawa continued his vertical examination of the play, highlighting its importance even on the poster. The image was of Watanabe's face in front of a red, tiered set of steps – a clear evocation of the *hinadan* image, which was central to this production.

This production was more experimental than the 1978 version. The story was conceived as a fantasy happening on the night of the Doll Festival, as had been Ninagawa's original idea as far back as 1974. In a space dominated by the *hinadan*, the play began in the Sengoku Period (Japan's Warring States Period) and moved forward in time until the end of the play, where Fortinbras was a contemporary young man. The production also played with language and used two separate translations. One was the aforementioned version by Odashima and the second was the 'original' Japanese version by Tsubouchi Shoyo. Ninagawa's juxtaposition of these two tried to capitalize on their differences: 'Tsubouchi's old-fashioned Japanese for the older, established generation, and Odashima's modern and playful version for the young' (Ashizu, 2005). The translations came from separate eras and thereby gave a different sense of formality or intimacy depending on when each was used within the play. Alas, this was not successful because Ninagawa's audiences found it difficult to understand Tsubouchi's already antiquated Japanese.

The set design was by Nagakoshi Tsukasa. Nakagoshi began as a child actor, appearing in several early Ninagawa productions, and eventually moved into set design after university. *Hamlet* was among his earliest designs for Ninagawa, and their collaboration lasted right up until Ninagawa's death. Nakagoshi created almost every subsequent Ninagawa *Hamlet* – the 1995, 2001, 2003, 2004 and 2015 productions all featured his designs.[8]

In a space so much smaller than the Imperial Theatre, the production's scale was necessarily reduced, as was the cast – this time there were 'only' twenty in the chorus of nobles. Ninagawa again used the *hinadan* for the play-within-the-play, and the production was overall the most Japanese-looking of his *Hamlet*s. Although Watanabe's performance was praised for its athleticism, the press was critical of Ninagawa's approach. He was so angry at the 'arrogant' commentary of the Asahi Shimbun that he wrote and printed his own 'Ninagawa Newspaper', in which he replied to the review point by point.[9] Ironically, Ninagawa himself was ultimately dissatisfied with the production.

# Ginza Saison Theatre, 1995

A third production was created at the Ginza Saison Theatre in 1995. Operated by the Parco department store chain, the theatre had nearly 800 seats and was an important venue throughout its time in business, from 1987 to 2013. Ninagawa's third Hamlet was Sanada Hiroyuki, another popular film and television actor. His international career was launched by his appearance in *The Last Samurai*, alongside Ninagawa's previous Hamlet, Watanabe Ken. Sanada was already a big star in Japan, where he had made over forty films before he starred as the prince. Ophelia was played by Matsu Takako, also a well-established actress and, incidentally, the daughter of Ninagawa's first ever Romeo, Matsumoto Koshiro IX.

This production marked the first time Ninagawa worked with Matsuoka Kazuko and Kasamatsu Yasuhiro, both integral collaborators in the remaining decades of Ninagawa's career. Composer Kasamatsu has written operas and film scores and worked on almost all of Ninagawa's Shakespeare productions in the Sai no Kuni series. Matsuoka Kazuko is on course to become only the third writer – and the first woman – to translate all of Shakespeare's plays into Japanese. Her first Shakespeare translation was *The Comedy of Errors*, commissioned by the Tokyo Globe in 1993. Her *Hamlet* followed, and soon thereafter she was hired as the official translator for the Sai no Kuni Shakespeare Series. It is significant that Matsuoka is a female writer, since Japanese is a language wherein men and women have different vocabularies and modes of expression. Her translations are consistently praised for their accessibility and performability, and for her willingness to explore the more complicated areas of Japan's gendered language.

Dissatisfied with his two previous visual approaches to *Hamlet* – the exaggerated costumes of 1978 and the more restrictive historical designs of 1988 – Ninagawa chose a markedly different approach for the 1995 production. He had explored ways of dealing with the problematic tension of Japanese performers playing European characters as far back as 1987 in his production of *The Tempest*. In a way, all his productions, starting with his first *Romeo and Juliet* in 1974, had constituted a prolonged attempt to drag Shakespeare away from the artificiality of previous Japanese interpretations. The 1995 *Hamlet* revisited the pre-show induction that gave a glimpse of the theatre company, used so successfully in *The Tempest*. This time Ninagawa set the play in a two-tiered space full of dressing rooms. On the upper level were several private 'rooms', each closed off by a curtain and reserved for the principal characters. The lower level had a communal dressing area for the rest of the company. The actors were all on stage from the show's half-hour call, visible as the audience entered. Numerous subsequent productions started with variations of this pre-show presentation of the acting company getting ready, and it even featured in the Saitama *Timon of Athens* after Ninagawa's death. All artificiality was acknowledged up front – the audience saw the performers as a company, and then were immediately aware when the actors began acting.

> I often do this kind of style when I do Shakespeare. It gives it some distance. It shows that these are Japanese actors playing Shakespeare characters. It's difficult. It's a different language, different customs, different culture, different period. So that embarrassment, I hope I might be able to get

rid of. For a Japanese audience, it may convince them that this isn't such a distant thing. (Butler, 1998)

The play began in earnest when the curtains snapped shut and the theatre was plunged into darkness. The mirrors in the dressing rooms gave an eerie glow throughout the performance and were often cleverly manipulated to heighten the sense of eavesdropping. Small electric fans in the set made the curtains billow throughout the performance, creating a constant state of mutability and uncertainty. Hamlet's first appearance was lit by shafts of light reflected through several mirrors on stage – a physical manifestation of Ninagawa's earlier concept of *The Tempest* as a collection of images reflected in a broken mirror. *Hamlet* is the play that attempts to hold the mirror up to nature, and so this first appearance was particularly appropriate. The mirrored light appeared again later in the play, accompanying Ophelia's mad scene. Now it was Ophelia's mind that had been 'o'erthrown', and the fragmented light literally mirrored the scraps of songs and broken ideas crowding her mind.

In a production that thus began with the presentation of the company as actors, the role of the Players became doubly significant. Ninagawa dropped an actual *kabuki* curtain (in the traditional colours of black, brown and green) to mask the set-up of *The Mousetrap* on stage. The troupe of actors featured performers of various shapes and sizes, including a dwarf who introduced the dumb show. By all accounts this variety of physicalities owes as much to Ninagawa's admiration for Fellini as to Bakhtin's carnivalesque, but the exuberant appearance of so varied a group of people was welcome in the harsh, suspicious world of this production. Behind the shoddy *kabuki* drop, a revised version of the *hinadan* was being set up, employing Ninagawa's by now customary exaggeration of its traditional arrangement. This time, several of the life-size 'dolls' were in disrepair – one figure had a broken musical instrument, another appeared to be missing a limb. Many things, it seemed, were rotten in this state of Denmark.

Ninagawa greatly expanded the use of the *hinadan* in this production, relating its symbolism more specifically to Ophelia. The first scene between Ophelia and Laertes showed her arranging the dolls on a real, normal-sized *hinadan*. In her next scene with Polonius, she was wrapping the dolls and putting them away. Since this activity would usually be done by the women of the house, Ninagawa thereby managed to highlight the absence of Ophelia's mother without changing a word of the text. It was especially moving to see Ophelia putting away the trappings of this festival expressly celebrated to bring marital fortune to young women *at the same time* as she discussed Hamlet's strange behaviour towards her and their recent strained relations. Again, this gave a particular poignancy to the scene, prefiguring what was to come.

For her mad scene, Ninagawa had Ophelia bring in and distribute dolls instead of herbs. In her grief – at her father's death and at her loss of Hamlet – she literally gave away these tokens of lost hopes, the cherished dolls that should have symbolized future happiness. It was an extraordinary choice and gave even more resonance to her off-stage death. Traditionally the dolls were discarded and washed away in a river, and in *Hamlet* Ophelia dies by drowning. By associating her so closely with the *hina-matsuri* dolls, Ophelia's death was made all the more poignant to Japanese audiences familiar with the image. This was a master stroke from Ninagawa, superimposing such traditional imagery and using it in so many different ways throughout the story – to heart-breaking effect.

The *hinadan* appeared again in the final scene of the play. Claudius and Gertrude sat atop the large set of steps connecting the upper dressing-room level to the stage floor. Behind them stood a gold-leaf folding screen, leaving no doubt that this was the image Ninagawa was manipulating. Various courtiers sat below the king and queen on the steps, gathered to watch the duel between Hamlet and Laertes. By the end of the match, as the body count was rising, the queen fell most of the way down the steps, while Claudius died close to the top. In the shocking finale, however, the various lords left alive scrambled to pay obeisance to Fortinbras when he entered above, every inch the new 'emperor' of Denmark. One of the scrambling courtiers nudged the corpse of Claudius, and he tumbled awkwardly to the bottom of the heap. (This fall was so dramatic that the actor's entire costume was padded, to prevent serious injury during the stunt.) Ninagawa's first three *Hamlets* all ended with the image of the surviving Danish courtiers clambering up the steps towards Fortinbras, grovelling towards their new ruler. In this version, his men smashed all of the dressing-room mirrors when they entered, signalling that the time for acting or mirroring nature was well and truly over.

# Saitama Arts Theatre, Small Hall, 2001

Ninagawa's next *Hamlet* was the eleventh instalment of the Sai no Kuni Shakespeare Series. This new *Hamlet* starred Ichimura Masachika, previously a stalwart member of Shiki Theatre Company, where he made a name for himself starring in an extensive variety of musicals. After he left Shiki for an independent career, he worked on a variety of productions with Ninagawa, starring in *Richard III*, *Hamlet*, *Pericles* and the final revival of *NINAGAWA Macbeth*. Gertrude was played by Natsuki Mari, a popular stage and film actress known to Western audiences particularly for her voice acting. Natsuki is in fact six years younger than Ichimura, and this disparity gave a curious urgency to the Oedipal tensions underlying the mother–son relationship in the play.

A major stylistic shift happened in Ninagawa's approach to Shakespeare between the *Hamlets* of 1995 and 2001. The *King Lear* at the RSC was the last production in which he drew from specifically Japanese iconographies – in this case the various scenic elements derived from the visual language of *noh*. The 1995 *Hamlet* was a turning point in the way that Ninagawa manipulated Japanese imagery in his Shakespeare productions. Its framing device was theatrical rather than specifically Japanese, and the one expressly Japanese visual idea was the *hinadan*. The image was used throughout in astonishingly detailed ways, but it was a specific image rather than a framing device. Thereafter Ninagawa's Shakespeare productions began to employ specific images – still frequently Japanese – rather than the overarching concepts that had framed his earlier productions.

Ninagawa's approach to Shakespeare changed quite substantially when he began working on the Sai no Kuni Shakespeare Series, as discussed in Chapter Four. His early productions there tried a variety of new approaches, and the 2001 *Hamlet* was a major step forward. Gone were the extravagant designs, the play with scale and large choruses of actors. This *Hamlet* was created in Saitama's smaller performance space, set in promenade with the audience on both sides of the playing area. Ninagawa made very effective use of the space's overhead gantries for the early scenes on the battlements with the Ghost, and Ophelia's observation of Hamlet from above during 'To be or not to be'. The only piece of furniture was a tiered bank of bleachers. At one end of the space there was a large set of doors that opened and shut at key moments. The design consisted of a collection of exposed swaying lightbulbs and several lines of barbed wire stretched from floor to ceiling. These were lit in similar fashion to the streams of sand that trickled throughout *A Midsummer Night's Dream* (and even the falling rocks in *King Lear*), and again were a means of defining the physical and metaphorical space of the production.

In a production so concentrated on the actors, occupying what Kennedy (1994: 13) calls a 'shared present', unencumbered by any scenery other than the barbed wire, Lily Komine's costumes became a major signifier. The entire court was dressed in red floor-length robes – plush velvet for the king and queen, and Komine's signature textured fabric for the numerous attendant lords. Hamlet's first appearance within this sea of red (in his customary suit of solemn black) made him appear all the more isolated. As the play progressed from the public court scene of Act 1, Scene 2 towards more intimate, private and covert scenes, the costumes became more simplified. Polonius and his family took their farewells in shades of grey (and white for Ophelia) and Hamlet traded his robe for a simpler shirt and a pair of leather trousers – still, naturally, in black. When Rosencrantz and Guildenstern arrived, they were all in grey and black, but directly after they agreed to report on Hamlet's behaviour they changed to red scarves – a clear but subtle indication that they were now Claudius' agents.

Several striking moments were achieved simply by the placement of actors in the space. After Hamlet's rejection of Ophelia and the 'get thee to a nunnery' attack, Ophelia was left prone on the floor. Claudius and Polonius, both in red, circled her as they discussed what to do next in a very telling piece of stagecraft. Polonius was more interested in maintaining political status than dealing with the obvious distress of his daughter.

The arrival of the Players brought a burst of colour, as the motley crew of actors was dressed in a rainbow of different fabrics. The troupe was as multifaceted as ever, populated with a variety of different heights and body shapes. As in the 1998 production, Ninagawa cast a dwarf among the troupe, and indeed Narimiya Hiroki, who would appear as Fortinbras later in the show, appeared in the troupe in full (and convincing) female drag. Hamlet's attention focused on another actor, Tsukikawa Yuki, as the boy player who has become an adult since Hamlet last saw the company perform. Tsukikawa was also dressed as a woman and would later play the very androgynous Player Queen.

As Hamlet stage-managed *The Mousetrap*, cast-iron candlesticks were positioned throughout the space. Candles often accompanied Ninagawa's presentation of the play-within-the-play, since they are such a ready signifier of performance. Before electric light all performances were staged by candlelight, and many traditional *kabuki* theatres still feature them. Candles – the equivalent of footlights – were perhaps the only scenic element employed consistently through all eight of Ninagawa's *Hamlet*s. Although another set of tiered steps was used in this version for the presentation of the play-within-the-play, this time any connection to the *hinadan* was only an echo. Here it was 'just' a set of seats for those observing the play, and indeed Gertrude and Claudius were on the lowest seats, and in the centre, while all of the red-clad courtiers gathered on the cheaper seats at the back. Ophelia sat on the floor, with Hamlet in her lap.

As Ninagawa's career progressed, his versions of the dumb-show became more and more experimental. In 2001 it looked a little like a Balinese puppet play, but instead of puppets it was performed by actors in elaborate, sparkling two-dimensional costumes. Instead of performing in shadow behind a curtain, they lay on the floor, sliding around on wheels attached to the backs of their costumes. The effect – best viewed from Claudius and Gertrude's perspective on the bleachers – was akin to so many actors lying on skateboards. By contrast, and with little visible connection to what had gone before, the play was performed by two young shirtless actors. Tsukikawa played the queen, a startlingly androgynous blend of masculine and feminine. Lucianus appeared naked apart from a grossly exaggerated phallus that tapered to a sharp, dangerous-looking point. The character's transgressive intentions were thus foregrounded, and when he bent over and snatched the sleeping king's crown it was entirely clear why Claudius had had enough and stopped the play. Previous productions had moved into slow motion at this point, as Hamlet's suspicions were confirmed and he became the eye of the storm. This time things went at full speed – Claudius slapped the crown off the actor playing Lucianus, and his courtiers followed suit, attacking the other players. The whole court swooped down from the bleachers and across the full length of the space, while Hamlet stood still and observed the confusion.

Claudius' Act 3, Scene 3 soliloquy was staged particularly elegantly. The space was almost completely dark, lit by two shafts of light forming a cross that echoed Ando Tadao's Church of the Light. Ninagawa had used lighting to foreground Claudius' religious crisis as far back as the first *Hamlet* in 1978 – in this more intimate space the Ando reference, a syncretized Japanese and Christian image, was particularly effective.

One of the production's most interesting interpretations was the closet scene between Hamlet and Gertrude. With no furniture on stage, Hamlet stalked through the space, tying a long string of red thread to the columns of barbed wire like a spider weaving a giant web. Gertrude was trapped inside, and eventually he wrapped his remaining skein of thread like a noose around her neck. As he moved to choke his mother, Hamlet heard Polonius off stage and rushed to him. The violence of Hamlet's anger towards his mother was intensely performed, and it really felt as if the Ghost reappeared to Hamlet to prevent him from killing her. Natsuki's extraordinary performance in this scene and its aftermath made her perhaps the finest of all Ninagawa's Gertrudes. In the final scene she wore a necklace that looked like a tangled web of tiny rubies – her costume actively echoed her experience in the play. On a larger stage this would not have been visible, but here it was yet another telling detail in Komine's beautiful costume design.

The play's final scene showed Ninagawa's mastery of bodies in space even when operating in a 'stripped back' production. Gertrude and Claudius, both still in red, died opposite each other at the bottom of the bleachers from which they watched the duel, while Hamlet, now in white, looked down on them. He died at the other end of the long playing-space, leaving the steps clear for Fortinbras to ascend (literally) and speak the play's closing lines. This *Hamlet* was due to open three days after the 9/11 attack in New York. Ninagawa was so distressed by it that he changed the ending of the production. Fortinbras was already an obnoxious thug who careered through the tiny space on the back of a noisy motorbike. Ninagawa heightened his violence and had his henchmen gun down Horatio and all the surviving courtiers. Although reminiscent of the Ingmar Bergman *Hamlet* seen at the Tokyo Globe in the late 1980s, for Ninagawa it was a desperate comment on the seemingly hopeless state of world politics.

This was the first Ninagawa *Hamlet* wherein age and ageing became a semiotic component. The three decade age difference between Hamlet and Fortinbras gave a feeling not just of regime change but of generational change in the play. Ichimura's childless, ageing Hamlet had no offspring, and so his 'election' had no choice but to fall on Fortinbras, a substantially younger new ruler. Ichimura was Ninagawa's oldest ever Hamlet, and Narimiya was, at just nineteen, Ninagawa's youngest Fortinbras. Analysts have for decades been warning that Japan's very high life expectancy and low rates of childbirth would lead to substantial changes. Was this *Hamlet* something of a cautionary tale from Ninagawa? A lesson to be learned? That Japan would have to start incorporating foreign influence?

After ten productions, Ninagawa had developed an audience for Shakespeare in Saitama, and could rely on their understanding of how a Shakespeare play was different, say, from a Japanese text or a piece of contemporary drama. He no longer needed to bridge the gap between Shakespeare and Japan with a visual framing device. In this intimate setting there was no distance between Ichimura and the audience, and the production achieved a more conversational quality than had been possible in the more monumental spaces of Ninagawa's previous Elsinores. This was a dark, threatening space, suffused with shadows and studded with barbed wire, complementing Ninagawa's bleakest reading of the play.[10]

# Bunkamura Theatre Cocoon, 2003

The next *Hamlet* opened at the Theatre Cocoon at Bunkamura in November 2003, starring Fujiwara Tatsuya. Known to audiences from the *Battle Royale* film series, Fujiwara's professional debut was as the teenage lead in Ninagawa's spectacular *Shintokumaru* (Poison Boy). He was twenty-one in 2003, the youngest of Ninagawa's Hamlets to date – in fact the youngest Hamlet in Japanese history. This is notable in a theatre culture where Hamlet was still considered the preserve of more established actors. Hira was forty-five when he led the first production, but the comparative ages of Watanabe (twenty-eight), Sanada (thirty-five) and Ichimura (fifty-one) show Ninagawa's interest in approaching the play and its protagonist afresh with each collaboration. Fujiwara and Oguri Shun, who played Fortinbras, were both born in 1982, while Anne Suzuki, who played Ophelia, was even younger. Inoue Yoshio, as Laertes, was at twenty-four the oldest of the production's four young stars. Casting Fujiwara as such a young Hamlet raised some eyebrows, but his youth – and that of his co-stars – was the lens through which Ninagawa framed (and marketed) this version.

This production employed a new translation by Kawai Shoichiro, one of Japan's leading Shakespearean scholars. His version had been commissioned and developed for Jonathan Kent's production earlier the same year. Nomura Mansai played Hamlet and was heavily involved in the preparation of the script. Kawai's translation was published in May 2003 and has been used for multiple subsequent productions. Remarkably, from over 100 Japanese translations, Kawai's is the first to have been based exclusively on the Folio text. Kawai incorporated substantial feedback from Nomura, who had many suggestions as to how the play should sound as a spoken text. Kawai used traditional rhythms from Japanese poetry for the first Player's speech, and at Nomura's behest infused *The Murder of Gonzago* with the rhythms of *kabuki* dialogue, heightening the difference between regular and performed speech in the play. Emulating Tsubouchi's attempts to interpret Hamlet via *kabuki* a century earlier, Kawai managed to find a balance between style and intelligibility. Ninagawa so loved this version that he continued to use it for the rest of his career.

Ninagawa had seldom presented Shakespeare at the Theatre Cocoon in Shibuya. Unlike his work in Saitama, so clearly concentrated on the Sai no Kuni series, Ninagawa's Bunkamura programme was significantly more varied. Fujiwara's 2003 *Hamlet* played to audiences who had recently seen Ninagawa's *Shintokumaru*, *A Streetcar Named Desire*, *The Water Magician*, *The Cherry Orchard* and the brilliant *Oedipus Rex*. This new *Hamlet*, featuring a young star with an established relationship with Ninagawa and crafted especially for the space at Bunkamura, was a huge box office draw.

Ninagawa directed each new *Hamlet* with a different approach. As he had in *The Greeks*, he played the Bunkamura production in traverse, seating the Theatre Cocoon audience on either side of the stage. This production went even further than the barbed wire ropes of the 2001 design in its reading of 'Denmark's a prison', with a space closed off by a very high chain-link fence. Search lights flashed over the audience at the beginning and the end of the play, giving a real feeling of a police state. Nakagoshi's set design resembled an outdoor basketball court in a concrete housing project, or indeed a prison, as much reminiscent of New York as of the urban jungle of Shibuya outside the theatre. As in Saitama, the space was uncluttered, with all focus on the actors' performances. A catwalk ran around the outside of the fences, allowing actors to remain outside the action at key moments. While Hamlet stalked around inside the cage for 'To be or not to be', Ophelia knelt outside, praying. Unlike the same scene in 2001, in this version Polonius came directly to his daughter after Hamlet's outburst and held her until the end of the scene. This moment of parental care showed Polonius in a significantly more sympathetic light. Contrasting with the 1995 version that so emphasized the absence of Ophelia's mother, this production laid significant emphasis on missing fathers, since all four of the young lead characters have lost theirs.

Fujiwara's Hamlet was very energetic, railing like an animal in a cage. Kawai writes that he 'banged on the fences and threw himself against them as if to try to free his soul. He was a Hamlet with an entrancing tension, stoic but bewildered, manly but fragile' (Kawai, 2008: 280). The actor had already played complicated young men in Ninagawa's productions of *Shintokumaru* and *Yoroboshi*. His Hamlet was another smart and highly strung outsider passionately trying to find his place in a hostile world. Fujiwara showed almost inexhaustible energy throughout, giving vigorous performances of the soliloquies and still having reserves left for the impressive sword-fights in the final act. Fujiwara's stage combat abilities would be employed with equal flair in the 2015 *Hamlet*, and indeed they so impressed Inoue Hisashi that he wrote *Musashi*, about the famous swordsman-philosopher Miyamoto Musashi, with him in mind.

This production had costumes designed by Maeda Fumiko, simpler but not markedly different from those designed by Komine for the 1998 and 2001 productions. There was a reduction in scale, at least – the signature 'Ninagawa-esque' robes were reserved for the king and queen, while everyone else cut a leaner silhouette. Ninagawa replaced the sound effects from traditional Japanese theatre with songs and trumpet licks performed by Miles Davis. The trumpet featured in almost all the different styles of music used in the piece, encompassing pieces by Davis at the beginning of each act, marching band music for Fortinbras' first entrance and a surprisingly effective burst of the trumpet when the ghost appeared during the closet scene.

The dumb show was again presented as a kind of masked performance, this time even more reminiscent of Balinese drama. Most impressive was the startling green skull mask worn by Lucianus. While Claudius and Gertrude whispered their usual sweet nothings to each other, Hamlet sucked his thumb – the ultimate gesture of Shakespearean insolence, which starts the fighting in *Romeo and Juliet*. Fujiwara played Ninagawa's third Romeo the following year.

In the actual performance of *The Murder of Gonzago*, Tsukikawa Yuki appeared again as the Player Queen. This time the character wore a dress, and Tsukikawa appeared less androgynous. The actor's rather extraordinary femininity clearly fascinated Ninagawa, and the seeds of his all-male Shakespeare series within the Sai no Kuni programme can be traced to the 2001 and 2003 productions of *Hamlet*. Again Lucianus appeared in a tiny loincloth, this time with a seemingly bigger phallus attached. Candles were once again beautifully arranged around the space to light the performance, and courtiers all rushed to grab one when Claudius stood and asked for 'some light' as he stormed out. Ninagawa again returned to the slow-motion device for the end of this major set piece.

Fortinbras was presented significantly differently in this production. Ninagawa had spotted the young actor Oguri Shun on television and cast him as a foil to Fujiwara's Hamlet. Oguri went on to star in several Ninagawa productions and played Sasaki Koshiro opposite Fujiwara in the premiere of *Musashi*. Oguri was a martial, exuberant Fortinbras, in contrast to the murderous upstart played by Narimiya in Saitama and the disaffected interpretations still to come. At the end of the play he burst onto the scene with a streak of blood splashed across his space, suggesting that his access to the Danish throne had involved considerable fighting, but here the bloodshed stopped once he was in control. Rather than killing everyone, as in Saitama, this Fortinbras knelt down and kissed the dead Hamlet on the mouth, in a kind of acknowledgement, king to king, of the crown's passage from one to the other. This moment also played to the homoeroticism that is so modish in Japanese entertainment. Manga featuring *yaoi* 'boy's love' (love between young men) are particularly popular with young Japanese women. Ninagawa was canny enough to court commentary and attention from such fan bases by including this moment in the show and would refer to these manga aesthetics in numerous productions within the all-male series in Saitama.

# English tour, Barbican, 2004

After the onslaught of critical distaste for Ninagawa's *King Lear*, Ninagawa could have been justifiably hesitant about returning to London. This was not the case, and in 2001 he presented his double bill of Mishima's *Modern Noh Plays*, featuring Jo Haruhiko and Fujiwara Tatsuya. There was no English tour in 2002, but the following year Ninagawa returned with his magnificent *Pericles*. Almost eighteen months later, he came back to the UK to direct his sixth production of *Hamlet*, this time in English.

This was Ninagawa's third production of the play in less than five years, and featured many ideas reworked from the 2001 Saitama production. Komine's costumes were mostly the same, as was the minimalist set design of barbed wire and exposed lightbulbs. A major difference was that this production was conceived for a tour of several proscenium arch theatres in the UK, as opposed to the more intimate, immersive staging in Japan.[11] The production was performed by a company of British actors. Michael Maloney played Hamlet, with Peter Egan as Claudius and Frances Tomelty as Gertrude. This was certainly the least starry cast that Ninagawa had worked with in a very long time. Ninagawa opted for sensitive, sophisticated actors rather than the kind of fashionable stars that frequently populated his Japanese productions. Here was a solid company of reliable journeyman actors, hired to elucidate the text and perform to Ninagawa's specifications. There was one Japanese company member, Hira Takehiro, son of Hira Mikijiro, Ninagawa's first ever Hamlet. Hira Jr was the Player Queen, recreating Tsukikawa's performance, which Billington considered 'disturbingly androgynous' (Billington, 2004).

Ninagawa's replication of ideas extended to his casting of Michael Maloney, who was, at forty-seven, 'the oldest Hamlet in living memory' (Rees, 2004). Just as Ichimura's age had not been an issue in Saitama, so Ninagawa insisted that this was not a problem. Unlike Natsuki in Saitama, Frances Tomelty's Gertrude *was* older than her Hamlet, but certainly not by enough to have actually been his mother. There was a steeliness to the Irish actress's reading of the role, well matched in Maloney's particularly thoughtful performance as the prince. Maloney had played Edgar in Ninagawa's RSC *King Lear* and remained diplomatic about any difficulties he might have had with the experience, unlike many of his colleagues. Maloney had appeared in almost as many *Hamlets* as Ninagawa had directed. This was his second time playing the prince, and he had an impressive bedrock of experience (from Zeffirelli to Branagh) on which to draw.

The play was spoken at a terrific speed. Japanese can take longer than English to express complicated ideas like those in Shakespeare, and as a result it sometimes felt as though Ninagawa's Japanese actors were racing through their lines, eager to get to the end of a complicated sentence. It is entirely possible that Ninagawa encouraged a comparably swift reading of the play in English – trippingly on the tongue, as Hamlet himself insists – thanks to how his own ears were conditioned to hear Shakespeare performed.

True to form, London critics were unimpressed with what would be Ninagawa's final English-language production.[12] The lack of Japanese design elements (other than Komine's costumes) was a talking point, as was what was felt to be a generalized simplicity of approach. Charles Spencer called it 'punishingly dreary' (Spencer, 2004), while Michael Billington (always a champion of Ninagawa's work) endeavoured to identify some positive features, particularly Maloney's performance (Billington, 2004). The consensus was that Ninagawa, regardless of his previous success, was not entirely up to the task of directing actors in a language he did not speak. Any evolving subtlety that the director might have developed or earned through having created five previous versions of the play was overlooked, and Spencer's acerbic suggestion was that the production's visual simplicity stemmed from Thelma Holt having run out of money. This was not the case elsewhere around the country, where reviews were significantly more favourable, praising the acting, the stripped back yet impressive design and the limpid interpretation of the play.[13]

The 2004 *Hamlet* was the last to feature costumes by Lily Komine. She worked with Ninagawa for forty years, on five of his eight *Hamlets* and on productions of over seventy different plays. She was absolutely integral to the development of the signature look of Ninagawa's theatre. Komine and Ninagawa first collaborated on *Romeo and Juliet*, and their last production together was *Julius Caesar* in 2014. Born in 1947, Komine worked for Gekidan Shiki (like so many others) and also spent some time working in the costume department of the RSC in Stratford. Her productions with Ninagawa constitute an extraordinary body of work; the catalogue of plays she designed is too long to list, but her influence cannot be overestimated. The unforgettable costumes of *The Tempest*, *A Midsummer Night's Dream*, *Pericles* and *Titus Andronicus* were all hers, and she was responsible for over a third of the productions in the Sai no Kuni series. She died in 2017, a little over a year after Ninagawa.

## *Tenpo Juninen no Shakespeare*, 2005

Ninagawa returned to Japan after *Hamlet* to direct his new version of *Romeo and Juliet*. Marking thirty years since his first Shakespeare production, it starred his most recent Japanese Hamlet and Ophelia, Fujiwara Tatsuya and Anne Suzuki. Ninagawa's 2005 calendar included a surprisingly low number of Shakespeare-related projects in a year designed to highlight the many fascinations of his career. First was the magnificent *Ninagawa Twelfth Night* at the Kabuki-za, followed by his star-studded *Tenpo Juninen no Shakespeare* at the Theatre Cocoon. My association with Ninagawa began when I was invited to attend rehearsals for *Tenpo* in August 2005. The play combines elements from all thirty-seven canonical Shakespeare plays, with a cast of over forty characters. The Hamlet character (who is also the Romeo character) was performed, very appropriately, by Fujiwara Tatsuya. Early in my time observing rehearsals, Fujiwara came and introduced himself, presumably having asked who this enthusiastic foreigner might be. Moments later, with a huge grin, Ninagawa told me to ignore him, since he was only being cheeky, trying to get on the cover of whatever book I might write.

Hamlet/Romeo has an extraordinary moment in the first half of the play, in which he performs twelve significant Japanese translations of the phrase 'To be or not to be, that is the question'. Inoue updated the script for the new production, incorporating the most significant translations made since he wrote the play in 1974. Fujiwara was accompanied by the play's narrator, Kiba Katsumi, who introduced the scene by speaking the soliloquy's opening line in humorously accented English. The narrator listed the names and dates of all the translations, while Fujiwara performed each Japanese rendition in turn. The result was a potted history of *Hamlet* in translation, ending with the first ever version, by Charles Wirgman, published in a cartoon in *The Japan Punch* in 1874.[14] Wirgman's translation was a joke, poking fun at contemporary efforts to render Shakespeare in Japanese. It is actually very bad, almost nonsensical Japanese, translating words rather than sense, and Fujiwara's performance of it got a very big laugh. The scene was Inoue's nod to Japan's long and rich history of engagement with the play. Its absurd litany of translations highlights the sheer variety of approaches and landmarks reached since *Hamlet* first captivated Japanese readers and performers.[15] The Japanese language expresses *being* in a way significantly different to English, and as such there are significant challenges to translating the soliloquy. Inoue has his character speak only a fraction of the extant translations of the play, but the scene highlights a very real issue faced in the interpretation and performance of Shakespeare in Japan. Ninagawa was the ideal director for Inoue's play, and the *Hamlet*-inspired scenes were especially entertaining.

Inoue's scene between Hamlet and the Ghost was also particularly memorable. In a reworking of *Hamlet* entirely in keeping with Ninagawa's devotion to Bakhtin's carnivalesque, the ghost appeared to Hamlet while he was on the brink of orgasm with a particularly voluptuous and jolly prostitute. The 'Ghost' – in fact an actor being side-coached by the Richard III character – was none too competent, and so the increasingly frustrated Richard had to keep feeding him his lines. Besides the entertainment inherent in the story, Ninagawa's regular viewers had the added intertextual pleasure of watching Fujiwara Tatsuya as Hamlet/Romeo (again) seeing the Ghost played by Nishioka Tokuma (who had played the Ghost/Claudius to Fujiwara's Hamlet) being directed by Karasawa Toshiaki, Ninagawa's most recent Macbeth. By the end of the play, this Richard III was forced to hold a mirror up to his own deformed nature, and when it smashed, the Cordelia/Juliet/Helena/Lady Anne character (played by Shinohara Ryoko) killed herself with one of its broken shards. Shinohara had played Ophelia in the 2001 Saitama production, and actually married her Hamlet, Ichimura Masachika, in 2005. This kind of blurred, polysemic casting was part of the production's excitement – as was seeing Ninagawa's Titania, Shiraishi Kayoko, as a Witch, or his most recent Macduff, Katsumura Masanobu, recast as a particularly villainous Macbeth, all narrated by Kiba, who had played Iago for him a decade earlier. Ninagawa had directed so many productions that his regular actors brought with them multiple layers of intertextuality, as may well have been the case within Shakespeare's own company; this, added to the already complicated layers of Inoue's play, created a feast of inferences for Ninagawa's regular audiences.

# Saitama Next Theatre, 2012

Apart from the witty echoes in *Tenpo*, Ninagawa waited almost eight years before directing another *Hamlet*. The years following the English production were among his most prolific, and he directed over fifty other productions between his sixth and seventh *Hamlets*. In 2012, he created a completely new production with the actors of his newest company, Saitama

Next Theatre. It was retitled *Hamlet Performed by the Pale Boys and Girls* in reference to the company's youthful membership. The production was notable for the rather remarkable participation of the Komadori Sisters, twin chanteuses from Hokkaido. Born in the 1930s, like Ninagawa, the sisters Eiko and Tomiko were born into extreme poverty, and their rise to success in the 1960s mirrored Japan's recovery from the destruction of the Second World War. The Komadori Sisters sing *enka*, the same kind of sentimental ballads Ninagawa had so successfully woven into *Suicide for Love*. Their style of music is nostalgic and old-fashioned but represented for Ninagawa the lived experience of ordinary Japanese people. He had long considered what it might be like to include them in one of his productions, as he discussed in an interview in 2009:

> It is a fear of what the older people (who don't express their opinions and have lived normal lives) might think if they saw my plays. Would my plays be meaningful in light of the personal histories they have lived? I have feared that if the elderly or people who don't usually get to share their opinions saw our plays they might think, 'These things have been made by these people who just went to school and studied – they are superficial, lacking in substance.' That is a very real concern, and I have had it for a long time.
>
> An example I sometimes use when trying to explain this idea is this: if the Komadori Sisters suddenly crossed my stage, the whole play would have to freeze and come to a halt. I even thought seriously about creating a production wherein Hamlet is saying his 'To be or not to be' lines and suddenly the Komadori Sisters would appear. If the Komadori Sisters suddenly appeared in the midst of one of the classic plays I direct in translation, and they crossed the stage in their long-sleeved kimonos, playing their shamisen, the play would be destroyed in an instant. In other words, I have thought that in the face of the actual lived experience of ordinary Japanese people in the post-war era, exemplified

by the popular, nostalgic music of the Komadori Sisters, my productions, which are based on what I have learned from European drama, would likely seize up immediately. It is because of this long-held complex that I started the Saitama Gold Theatre project, so I would be working with the very people of that older generation whose lives have that meaning for me – even if it is not actually the Komadori Sisters themselves. (Ninagawa, 2009)

Three years after this interview, after several projects with the Saitama Gold and Next Theatres, Ninagawa created a *Hamlet* that was indeed interrupted by the Komadori Sisters. Many of Ninagawa's standard tropes were in evidence in the production, particularly in its costumes – Claudius and Gertrude in red, the Ghost in grey, Ophelia in white, Hamlet in black. Ninagawa again used Kawai Shoichiro's translation, and the set was designed by Nakanishi Noriyuki. This time the production was created with audience and action all on the main stage of the Saitama Arts Theatre. The playing space was made of Perspex, and the area below the stage was clearly visible, in an inversion of Ninagawa's earlier approaches to the play. The audience was now built into the vertical articulation of the space. So, for example, while Hamlet performed 'To be or not to be' on the main playing area, the audience could also see Ophelia praying below.

Ninagawa also reworked his preferred pre-show device of introducing the company as actors before the play began, this time appearing in it himself. He chatted with the actors on the lower level while they prepared for the show and cleared away the tables and chairs that had been laid out underneath. Again, he had Fortinbras massacre all the Danish survivors at the end of the play, this time with a woman as his right-hand man. The production's primary innovation – apart from its beautifully sleek design – was the appearance of the singing twins. Just as he had suggested in the 2009 interview, Ninagawa had them appear quite jarringly at key moments in the play. Having songs such as the hit 'I want to be happy', performed by these senior citizens in brightly coloured kimono, appear throughout a play like *Hamlet* was an impressively avant-garde choice for Ninagawa. The juxtaposition of this nostalgic music in the voices of these older women, opposite Kawaguchi Satoru's angry, rebellious Hamlet, struck a significant chord with audiences, and the production won the prestigious Yomiuri Prize for Drama in 2012.

The following year, Saitama Next Theatre performed a project based on the works of Wolfgang Borchert, echoing Ninagawa's first ever directing project in 1967. Borchert's works reflected his experience of the war, and Ninagawa's return to these themes – no more than his inclusion of the Komadori Sisters in *Hamlet* – signalled a new preoccupation towards the end of his life. After *Hamlet* he directed the Saitama Next troupe in productions of *Oedipus Rex*, *Caligula* and *Richard II* – all plays in which there is something rotten in the state, whether Denmark, Thebes, Rome or England.

**FIGURE 3** Hamlet *(2015): the Players' performance on the* hinadan *ends as the entire company (led by Fujiwara Tatsuya) moves in slow motion. Photo by Robbie Jack/Corbis via Getty Images.*

Ninagawa never stopped interrogating the plight of young people versus society, as these four late productions attest.

## Saitama Arts Theatre, 2015

Ninagawa's eightieth birthday was in 2015. Ten years earlier he had celebrated a new decade with new approaches to Shakespeare, presenting, in quick succession, two radically different but entirely appropriate responses to his career-long dialogue with the playwright. In 2014, close to the fortieth anniversary of his first encounter with Shakespeare, Ninagawa returned to *Romeo and Juliet* and directed a new all-male production in Saitama. It was marketed as a supplementary instalment of the Sai no Kuni Shakespeare Series, with the extra title 'Ninagawa Shakespeare Legend'. To mark the start of his ninth decade the following year, he directed a second 'Ninagawa Shakespeare Legend', a new production of *Hamlet*. Even though it was Ninagawa's last *Hamlet*, it was by no means presented as his 'final' statement on the play; discussions were afoot for a ninth production before he died in 2016. Although the production featured recognizable elements from earlier iterations, it also presented a variety of startling new ideas.

Twelve years after his first *Hamlet* with Ninagawa, this production starred Fujiwara Tatsuya, now in his thirties and one of Japan's most popular stage and screen actors. Fujiwara was so impressed by the Saitama Next production that he begged Ninagawa to let him return to the role. He was joined by Hira Mikijiro as Claudius, and Yokota Eiji as Horatio. Ophelia and Laertes were played by actual siblings, Mitsushima Hikari and Mitsushima Shinnosuke, and Ninagawa cast Saitama Next Theatre's Uchida Kenji as Fortinbras.

The play began with the sound of Buddhist chanting off stage, accompanied by a projected announcement saying 'This production is set in the kind of houses where poor people lived in the nineteenth century, at the time when *Hamlet* was first introduced to Japan. In this place, the final rehearsal for the play *Hamlet* is about to start.'[16] The acting company then processed onto the stage, forming a line in their impressive robes, all in various shades and patterns of red (if this was a company of poor people, their theatre troupe was remarkably well funded...). A gong sounded, the company bowed to the audience and the 'rehearsal' began. This was the simplest ever version of Ninagawa's conceit of introducing the company as actors before the play started, and the framing device of the rehearsal was not mentioned again. The actors' entrance, coupled with the projected explanation of the design, sought to frame the production as a means of looking at contemporary Japanese identity. The play's first appearance in Japan coincided with a major shift in the way Japanese people thought about themselves, in a world shifting from the samurai period of the Tokugawa Shogunate into a time of imperialist expansion, in which Japan restored the Meiji emperor and waged successful wars against Russia and China. None of this was *because* of Shakespeare's play, but Ninagawa was eager to interrogate contemporary Japanese identity via this throwback to the nineteenth century. As he frequently proclaimed, the play begins with the words 'Who's there?' – and *Hamlet* is a great play for asking such questions.

The set design of small, cramped houses evoked several previous Ninagawa landscapes, particularly *Nigorie* and *Shitaya Mannencho Monogatari*, which had both evoked a nostalgia for the wooden buildings of pre-war Japanese architecture. The majority of Japanese cities were firebombed during the Second World War, and since a substantial quantity of buildings were still made of wood at the time they were especially vulnerable. While pockets of 'old' Japan do remain, the character of Tokyo was drastically altered by this destruction during the war. The design of this *Hamlet* recalled this older Tokyo, and the Japan of Tsubouchi and Shakespeare's first introduction in the nineteenth century. In contrast to this historically evocative set, the lighting was state of the art, with precisely programmed moving lights creating dramatic spotlights and patterns in the near-constant haze. Ninagawa's productions were always notable for the precision and flair of their lighting, and this final *Hamlet* was no exception.

The row-houses in the set for this *Hamlet* had sliding shoji screens as doors, lit from within in an echo of the curtained dressing rooms used in 1995. The Ghost first appeared on the balcony wrapped around the playing space, and his off-stage calls for Hamlet to 'swear' were accompanied by a dramatic glow behind all twelve of the doors. The space was particularly effective as the lobby for Act 2, Scene 2 and Act 3, Scene 1. Light streaming through the paper doors suggested multiple hiding places for anyone who might wish to eavesdrop. While Hamlet accosted Ophelia during his 'Get thee to a nunnery' scene, he ran frantically around the space, checking behind all of the screens as though he knew he was being watched. Polonius also hid behind one of the doors for the closet scene, and Hamlet stabbed him through the paper screen. The space was effective in meeting the demands of a production of *Hamlet*, but the late nineteenth-century architecture had little further connection to the well-dressed inhabitants of the Danish court. Rosencrantz and Guildenstern had matching costumes, as Ninagawa always preferred, in the kind of 'intercultural' dress characteristic of late nineteenth-century Japanese fashion. Their clothes were an amalgam of Japanese robes and Western topcoats, a recognizable hybrid popular at the time of Japan's opening up to outside influence.

This production reunited Ninagawa with Hira Mikijiro, his original Hamlet. Since their first collaborations in the 1970s, Hira had played leading roles in a huge number of Ninagawa's productions – more than any other actor. Even at eighty-one years of age he was a sonorous, authoritative Claudius, and played the Ghost more movingly than any of his predecessors. His was quite the most sympathetic Claudius that Ninagawa ever presented. While the means by which he came to power were far from honourable, Hira's Claudius had an innate nobility, and his performance of the Act 3, Scene 3 soliloquy was extraordinary. He stripped down to his underwear and doused himself in cold water, pumping it from the communal standpipe built in front of the row-houses. This act of purification is called *mizugori*,[17] performed in the hope of forgiveness. The pump was dressed with the kind of *shide* paper streamers that designate holy places in Japan – Claudius performed these ablutions with 'holy' water, hoping to atone for his sins. At the end of the play, when he had been stabbed and forced to drink poison, he tore off his bulky coat and fell to the ground dressed in a red robe reminiscent of the one he wore in *Medea*. This last collaboration between the two great artists contained a neat sartorial nod to one of their earliest, decades before.

The 2015 *Hamlet* also revived the *hinadan* idea, this time presented as a full-sized recreation of the traditional display. There were seven tiers, and the stand was decorated with the full complement of people and pieces, with the play's king and queen at the top in front of a gilded folding screen. The doorways of the set's row-houses were all decorated with the same kind of candle-lit lantern that flanked the king and queen, while three less-Japanese chandeliers bridged the gap between the more traditional Japanese aesthetic of the play and the looser interculturalism of the 'nineteenth-century' Danish court. *The Mousetrap* was accompanied by *sho* flutes, the uniquely Japanese sound of *gagaku* music. This perfectly complemented the Heian-Period costumes traditionally worn by the dolls in a *hinadan* display. Ninagawa juxtaposed the imagery and music of a particularly ancient Japan – one before *kabuki*, before Shakespeare, even before *noh* – with the contemporary politics of Claudius' court. As ever, the play-within-the-play was performed by an all-male company. For a Japanese audience, there was a humorous irony to Hamlet's brief exchange with Gertrude during the performance. Gertrude was played by Ohtori Ran, a former Takarazuka *otokoyaku*. It is a testament to the glorious elasticity of gender in Japanese theatre that here Ninagawa could have a woman (whose career was built on playing men) suggest that a male actor (playing a lady) 'did protest too much'! Dragging us back into the world of this *Hamlet*, a *ki* clapper sounded when Claudius broke up the performance, and this *kabuki* sound effect sent the entire company into slow-motion. While actors and courtiers made themselves scarce, Hamlet upended Claudius' throne, and as Horatio took Hamlet's hand the *ki* sounded again, snapping them back into real time. The interplay of this many sign-systems – traditional theatre sounds, pre-modern Japanese court music, slow-motion choreography familiar from Ninagawa's earlier work and Fujiwara's contemporary energy – typified Ninagawa's work at its most startlingly dramatic.

This *Hamlet* featured more furniture than Ninagawa had used in decades. The closet scene used an actual bed, framed within a huge green gauze that gave an intimacy to Gertrude's chamber. Polonius hid quite far off, behind one of the row-house sliding doors, and the Ghost reappeared on the balcony; both appearances made effective use of the show's established design. The bed itself stood squarely at the centre of the space and seemed almost unnecessary. When Hamlet attacked Gertrude (pushing aggressively between her legs) he did so on the ground. He eventually tore down the net, and it stayed where it fell until the end of the scene. Rather incongruously, Claudius led Gertrude off stage at the end of the scene, maybe to a different bedroom in the 'palace', or to her dressing room for a break in this 'rehearsal'. The scene was dramatically effective, and well performed, but its design and dramaturgy were the only weak points in what was otherwise a very powerful *Hamlet*.

Ninagawa's new interpretation of Fortinbras was the production's most startling new approach. In previous versions, Fortinbras had been a flower-bearing youngster (1978), an aggressively different new ruler (1988, 1995), a violent murderer (2001, 2012) and an apparent foreigner (2004). This time he was an emaciated young man, played by Uchida Kenji. He wandered laconically across the stage in Act 4, Scene 4, picking up a pebble and quietly contemplating the world to the strains of a Beethoven piano concerto. Gone were the exuberance and violence of previous incarnations. Fujiwara's

Hamlet seemed to envy Uchida's quiet demeanour, in such stark contrast to the hot-headed passions of nearly everyone in this Elsinore. At the end of the play, Fortinbras did not assume command with a hostile takeover, but announced his new regime with a bored, listless tone. This was a disaffected, passionless Fortinbras, representing the new generation of Saitama Next Theatre that Ninagawa was only just getting to know and understand. It was a startling, bleak ending to what would be his final *Hamlet* – simultaneously mysterious and challenging, as he had always found the play.

Ninagawa's eight productions give a brilliant overview of his directing career and represent a lifetime of evolving opinions about the play. Between his reading of Bakhtin (so integral to his approach to Shakespeare) and his own quest for an expression of a Japanese theatrical self, this play was a constant touchstone. His first production was a significant milestone in his developing approach to Shakespeare, and thereafter the play was nearly always a barometer for where Ninagawa's focus was heading. From the earliest production to the last, Ninagawa determinedly questioned his own method and his own madness. Key ideas and preoccupations figured across multiple productions, but he had no fixed directorial approach, preferring instead to adapt, revisit or reimagine his interpretations for each 'present push'. Few directors have ever directed the play as often, or have brought so much to it.

There were tentative plans in development at the time of Ninagawa's death to develop a ninth production of *Hamlet*, starring Oguri Shun. The actor had initially expressed interest in *Macbeth*, but since Ichimura Masachika was already due to lead a revival of *NINAGAWA Macbeth*, *Hamlet* was suggested instead. Ninagawa died in May 2016, and as a result these plans did not come to be.

# 4

# The Sai no Kuni Shakespeare Series

## The early phase

The Sai no Kuni Shakespeare Series was launched in 1998 at the Saitama Arts Theatre. It was the brainchild of the then artistic director Moroi Makoto, and the ambitious hope was to stage all of Shakespeare's plays, directed by Ninagawa, over a thirteen-year period (1998–2011). The series' advisory committee was initially chaired by Takahashi Yasunari, and more recently by Kawai Shoichiro. As the twenty-first century began, Ninagawa's directing schedule expanded continuously, and the series extended well beyond its proposed timeframe. There was still a handful of plays left to produce when Ninagawa died in 2016. The name Sai no Kuni is a popular alternative name for Saitama Prefecture, and was given to the publicly funded Shakespeare series at the Saitama Arts Theatre in acknowledgement of its deliberately local focus. Mere months before the turn of the millennium, the series was launched as a conscious new beginning, a renewed attempt to create Shakespeare productions that were relevant, accessible and entertaining for Ninagawa's Japanese audience.

If the 1980s and 1990s saw Ninagawa presenting foreign plays reframed with Japanese imagery to help his audiences to understand them, this new project took that work as already complete. Fittingly, Ninagawa launched the Saitama series with a new production of *Romeo and Juliet*, the first Shakespeare he had ever directed. His 1974 production had been an iconoclastic affair, an eager rejection of the trappings of *shingeki* acting and design. The new 1998 production had an abstract set design (by Horio Yukio) and a new text by Matsuoka Kazuko, the series' designated translator. Horio's design looked nothing like what an audience might have expected of a Ninagawa production. The walls of this Verona were built out of steel grids and metal cubes, moved and manipulated to frame and reframe the playing space of each consecutive scene. Ninagawa's emphasis on the story's speed and the youth and passion of its leading couple was as intense as it had been two decades before, but now he felt more confidence in Japanese actors tackling Shakespeare and no longer drowned them out with rock music.

Emphasizing the move away from any expectations derived from his previous productions, the second presentation in the Sai no Kuni series was a small-scale, intimate production of *Twelfth Night*. It was performed in the studio space at the Saitama Arts Theatre. This production felt almost unrecognizable from the director famous for opulent visual effects and bombastic sound and movement. It was performed almost in the round, with next to no furniture. A path lit by candles operated like a kind of *hashigakari*, giving actors access to and from the playing space, but there was no further reference to *noh* or any other traditional theatre. The most successful aspect of it was its immediacy, and the charm of Togashi Makoto's Viola, playing with the more malleable gender forms of the Japanese language to great comic effect. Her discomfort and quick corrections when she referred accidentally to herself as female were very effective, and made her patently false moustache seem all the sillier and sweeter. This clever interpretation of Viola laid some groundwork for Ninagawa's 2005 production at the Kabuki-za, this time with even more layers of gender confusion to manipulate.

Next came a production of *Richard III*, starring Ichimura Masachika. Saitama-native Ichimura, known primarily as a star of musical theatre and television dramas, was a clever choice for *Richard III*. His likeable stage presence – and his status as a local – exemplify Ninagawa's 'calculated intimacies'. Casting an actor as popular as Ichimura ensured that an audience would at least give the villainous Richard the benefit of the doubt – an important consideration for any anti-hero, but essential when staging *Richard III*. The production was a continuation of Ninagawa's experiments with abstract space, featuring another steel-cube set by Horio. It became notorious for its opening three minutes, during which Ninagawa had a horse run through the set before dropping another one from the ceiling. The effect was shocking, and jolted an audience into the world of the play. It was particularly effective as a support to Richard's ironic tone – audiences were hardly about to trust Richard's opening soliloquy describing this 'glorious summer' in the aftermath of such a violent display.

The Sai no Kuni series thus began with a variety of experiments; a new scenic approach in *Romeo and Juliet* and in *Richard III*, a stripped down audience arrangement reminiscent of Ninagawa's work at the Benisan Pit for *Twelfth Night*, and the collaborative English-language production of *King Lear* discussed in Chapter Two. Thereafter Ninagawa remounted two of his biggest Shakespearean successes, *A Midsummer Night's Dream* and *The Tempest*. The original productions are also discussed in Chapter Two, but the revivals were notable for bringing the likes of Shiraishi Kayoko, Terajima Shinobu and Hira Mikijiro into the fold at Saitama.[1] Apart from some casting changes, these revivals were ostensibly the same productions, but a significant difference was an update of the translations. The 1987 and 1994 originals were by Odashima Yushi, but the revised Saitama productions included contributions by Matsuoka Kazuko.[2]

Next came a new version of *Macbeth* – this time without Ninagawa's name in the title. The production starred Otake Shinobu and Karasawa Toshiaki, frequent Ninagawa collaborators who were very popular on stage and screen. The production looked substantially different from *NINAGAWA Macbeth* and had a much more modern setting; gone were the *butsudan* altar, the male witches and the cherry blossoms. This version took place in a mirrored box, and the opening battle scenes were fought in a field of oversized, desiccated lotus leaves. Lady Macbeth's first appearance echoed this, as she entered with her letter and a large fresh lotus blossom in her arms. This switch from cherry blossoms was not echoed in the representation of Birnam Wood, so beautifully achieved in the earlier production, and the lotus imagery was significantly less resonant throughout.

*NINAGAWA Macbeth* was an unmistakably Buddhist interpretation of the play, but the 2001 Saitama *Macbeth* had far less religious specificity. Ninagawa had used the lotus blossom, a symbol of purity and transcendence in Buddhism, to startling effect in *The Greeks* as a symbol for Iphigenia. In this *Macbeth* the field of decaying flowers suggested a world of corruption and political uncertainty. During the England scene, the lighting design again echoed Ando Tadao's Church of the Light near Osaka. This was substantially different from the setting filled with Buddhist *nio* statues in his earlier production, and it meant that much of the visual subtext of masculinity, power and anger was removed. Fauré and Brahms were replaced with music by Dead Can Dance, in another instance of the move from classical to contemporary, and from religious to secular. At almost every point, a new choice was made in how to present the play. Significantly, these choices all felt as if they were made within the same overall structure of *NINAGAWA Macbeth*. Each new item operated in exactly the same location as whatever it replaced, which made for a curiously hollow viewing experience. Just as the *butsudan* had been opened and closed by the vigilant old women, this new *Macbeth* began with sliding screens revealing the play, which once again closed while Malcolm delivered his final speech. Despite spirited performances and a variety of compelling images – particularly the mirrors, the lotus flowers and the chandelier beside which Macbeth gave his 'tomorrow and tomorrow' speech – the production lacked the impact of its predecessor. Of course, *NINAGAWA Macbeth* was a particularly tough act to follow, but this new iteration unfortunately felt like a faded black and white photocopy of a technicolour original.

Early in the Sai no Kuni series, Ninagawa's productions were supplemented by a number of visits from the Oxford University Dramatic Society. Productions of *The Winter's Tale* and *Love's Labour's Lost* travelled to Saitama under the patronage of Thelma Holt, and were a welcome means of presenting plays within the series that had yet to spark Ninagawa's directorial interest. A production of *The Merry Wives of Windsor* was directed by Kokami Shoji in 2001, with Ninagawa credited as an artistic 'supervisor' because he was unwell at the time. Ninagawa eventually directed his own versions of *The Winter's Tale* and *Love's Labour's Lost*, discussed later in this chapter.

The next production directed by Ninagawa himself was the 2001 *Hamlet* starring Ichimura and was his most radical interpretation to date. The first few years of the series featured experiments with form, space and design, alongside the various revivals and reinterpretations, all legitimate and necessary first steps as the Sai no Kuni series found its feet.

## *Pericles*

At the turn of the new millennium, Ninagawa's programme at the Theatre Cocoon focused squarely on bringing new life to plays he had interrogated in the past. In quick succession, he revisited *The Water Magician*, *Genroku Harbour Song*, *Hearty But Flippant*, *Suicide for Love*, *The Threepenny Opera* and *Yotsuya Kaidan*, plays that had brought him considerable early success. These productions, alongside the two major Shakespeare revivals in Saitama, might suggest an uncharacteristic lack of forward motion in Ninagawa's thinking, but they happened at the same time as several major new projects. These included *The Greeks*, *Oedipus Rex* and *Ninagawa Hi No Tori*, an enormous spectacle at the Saitama Super Arena. The negative critical response to *King Lear* may have contributed to the unusually long gap between Shakespeare presentations in London, but it did not dent Ninagawa's impressive touring schedule. A revised version of the *Modern Noh Plays* premiered in Saitama before visiting the Barbican, *A Midsummer Night's Dream* toured to Paris and *Macbeth* was remounted for the Next Wave Festival at Brooklyn Academy of Music. The original hope had been that *The Greeks* might visit Athens as part of the Cultural Olympiad, but the logistics proved impossible and *Oedipus Rex* was chosen instead.

Ninagawa's next production in the series was *Pericles*, chosen when Sir Trevor Nunn invited Ninagawa to present it towards the end of his tenure as Artistic Director of the National Theatre. Complicated even by Shakespearean standards, the story of *Pericles* meanders around the Mediterranean before its reunions at the Temple of Diana in Ephesus. Given the play's complex web of geographic, mythological and religious references, Ninagawa framed it in a more Japanese setting than he had employed for some time. Cynics might infer a feeling of his having had something to prove after *King Lear*, resulting in a return to his proven technique of making Shakespeare's plays look Japanese. Even if this were the case, the production was so inventive – and its approach so novel – that the response was overwhelmingly positive.[3]

The play's episodic, rambling nature poses many challenges, and Ninagawa understandably felt a greater need than usual to introduce the performance. Here he added a new layer to the familiar device of having the actors of his company present themselves before the story began. The set design was a cavernous space, with ten working standpipes arranged across it. Small piles of rubble sat around the edges, and a skull sat ominously in one corner. The show began with a cacophony of war sounds, while bells chimed and plaintive music sounded.

The company entered through the audience, staggering towards the running water of the standpipes. Some were injured, some were amputees, and their ragged clothes suggested refugees on the move. They rested, helped each other drink and lined up to bow to the audience. Ninagawa presented a community in distress, and *Pericles* became a story of solace and eventual hope.

The play is narrated by the medieval poet John Gower. *Pericles* travels all around the Eastern Mediterranean, to cities with names only recognizable to Shakespeare's audiences from the letters of St Paul. To a Japanese audience, they were all but meaningless. Countering this, Ninagawa split the role of Gower between a double act of storytellers, performed by Shiraishi Kayoko and Ichimura Masachika. Ichimura performed as a blind biwa player, while Shiraishi accompanied him with a *binzasara*, the distinctive snake-like percussion instrument associated with folk music and storytellers. As they introduced the first part of Pericles' adventure in the murderous court of King Antiochus, severed heads were suspended from above on grisly red ribbons. The first Gower speech led the theatre audience into the world of the play, and most of the subsequent interludes were accompanied by dumb-shows, as stipulated in the text. Ninagawa staged these as *ningyo-buri*, an unusual form of dance inspired by puppetry in which real-life actors are dressed as dolls and manipulated by black-clad *kuroko*. Heightening the effect, Ninagawa played these dumb-shows in front of a large folding mirror, while Ichimura and Shiraishi narrated from the side of the stage. The travails of the story's characters became more mythical by virtue of their presentation in these dumb-shows, before their 'real' enactment by the performers. Ninagawa infused the production with a theatricality that called attention to its artifice throughout. Pericles and several characters wore leg braces in the early scenes, referring to the injuries seen in the prologue, and a variety of tricks from traditional theatre suggested a makeshift theatricality. Painted cloths covered the stage apron to indicate the seashore of Pentapolis, after a funny scene using *kabuki*-style *naminuno* sea-cloths depicted the first of the play's storms. The standpipes remained on stage throughout, grounding the proceedings and insisting on the reality behind the storytelling. For the scene introducing Pericles' future wife Thaisa, each standpipe was decorated with an oversized lotus, again symbolizing female purity and grace.

Since the show was conceived as a performance by a community of people, Ninagawa had most actors play multiple roles. Shiraishi and Ichimura played several characters each, frequently whipping off their outer costumes and reverting to Gower when the script required it, echoing the quick changes of *kabuki*'s *hayagawari*. Scene changes were presented in view of the audience, so, for instance, the removal of the shore-cloth was visible while the cushions and lamps were laid out for the brothel scenes. As the story grew more mysterious in the final act, the staging became more ambitious, and during the final scene at Diana's temple in Ephesus, Ninagawa turned the story into an expressly Japanese fable. While Shiraishi gave Gower's introduction to the scene, young women in white processed formally onto the stage, now dominated by a huge pine tree clad with *shide* paper streamers. The temple maidens performed a solemn dance, reminiscent of *kagura*, the ancient dances performed at Shinto temples. The women's masks were also reminiscent of *noh*, itself partly derived from *kagura*. Helped by some clever staging, Tanaka Yuko, who played both Thaisa and her daughter Marina, was able to enter the scene as her younger character and then join the temple maidens to be revealed as the long-lost Thaisa. The family reunion (with a dummy actor playing Marina) was particularly moving, under a red sun glowing in the background. The scene's imagery deliberately evoked the great Shrine at Ise, Japan's holy of holies, home to the worship of the Sun Goddess herself. Conflating Diana with Amaterasu, Ninagawa turned the story into one of restoration for all Japanese people.[4] As Pericles and his family walked off into the sunset, Ichimura and Shiraishi reappeared as Gower, ending the story while the full company changed back into their refugee costumes and then repeated the opening sequence. *Pericles* thus became an interlude in the progress of this damaged community. As Gower's own introduction suggests, it was a tale of potential hope and redemption, told 'for restoratives', shared as a balm in troubled times. This version of Ninagawa's framing device turned an often-overlooked play into a breathtaking meditation on the importance of storytelling. As the lights faded at the end, the last thing heard was the sound of an aeroplane flying overhead. When I asked Ninagawa about this, he said it intimated just how necessary hope and stories had been 'when he was young' – a typically oblique reference to his own experience growing up during and after the Second World War.

*Pericles* was the only 2003 contribution to the Sai no Kuni series. Elsewhere during the year, Ninagawa directed his second film interpretation of the story of *Yotsuya Kaidan*, entitled *Warau Iemon*. At the Theatre Cocoon, he directed new productions of *Electra*, *The Cherry Orchard*, a revival of *Richard III* and the *Hamlet* starring Fujiwara Tatsuya. He ended the year in rehearsal for *Titus Andronicus*, which opened in Saitama in early 2004.

# Roman plays I

Ninagawa was indelibly inspired by the visit of Brook's *A Midsummer Night's Dream* to Tokyo in May 1973. He liked to challenge himself to outdo Brook, as he had with his own *Dream* in the 1990s. As discussed, it featured Ninagawa's interpretations of many elements from the Brook production. Brook had directed *Titus Andronicus* for the RSC in August 1955, and the production was noted for its total lack of blood. Instead, Brook used red silk scarves, creating a theatrical rather than a literal interpretation of the play's carnage. In Saitama, Ninagawa again endeavoured to out-Brook Brook.

As Titus he cast Yoshida Kohtaloh, who would prove to be one of the cornerstones of the Sai no Kuni project. The set, a nod to Brook's empty space, was a white box, whose doors and windows closed flush to create a projection surface when necessary. An impressive recreation of the statue of Romulus and Remus suckling the wolf dominated the design, replaced when necessary with a large tree and a field of lotus leaves for the hunt and a variety of long dinner tables for the various shared meals throughout the play. Everything was painted a sterile, surgical white. All the Roman politicians were dressed in expansive white robes, and even Titus and his returning army came home clad in white furs and armour. This white was broken up by the multiple red threads dangling from the soldiers' grubby costumes, which suggested the blood of vanquished enemies. The only other colours were in the costumes of Aaron, Tamora and her sons, and their bold colours made their foreignness immediately apparent. The bodies of Titus' deceased sons were carried in Perspex coffins, and the bodies themselves were fashioned out of clear plastic. When Titus dismembered Tamora's eldest son, the remains were likewise presented as clear, seemingly exsanguinated plastic, dripping with more streams of red thread. This set up the symbolism of how blood would be represented in this bloodiest of plays. Ninagawa and his company were no strangers to stage blood, of course (although Thelma Holt has wryly commented that it was the one thing the RSC could do better than the Japanese),[5] but this production was determined to match Brook's achievement of staging the play without spilling a drop.

The resulting stylization created some extraordinary images. One of the play's most appalling moments is the rape and dismemberment of Titus' daughter Lavinia. Tamora's sons attack her during a hunt, in the countryside outside Rome. Afterwards, Lavinia (Manaka Hitomi) staggered back on stage through the field of outsized white lotus leaves. By now well established in Ninagawa's visual vocabulary as a sign of purity, these white versions provided a particularly stark contrast for the scene that followed. Lavinia had stumps attached to each hand, bedecked with more ribbons than had yet been seen.

The effect was of fresh-flowing blood, compounded by extra ribbons pinned all over her dress. Further threads dripping from her mouth indicated the removal of her tongue. The shock was compounded by the appearance of her two attackers, who re-entered seemingly naked but covered with a large quantity of this 'blood' covering their genitals. The design insisted on showing both elements of the attack – rape and mutilation. The effect was unforgettably disturbing.

In the Shakespeare text, Chiron and Demetrius make a sequence of horrific jokes at Lavinia's expense, all centred on her lack of hands and her new inability to speak. The scene is troubling because it looks for humour in appalling circumstances. Ninagawa pushed it in a totally different direction, having the two men appear almost hysterical in the aftermath of their violence. The humour – even as a means of solidifying an audience's contempt for these villainous men and justifying Titus' later revenge – was underplayed. When Lavinia was brought to Titus after the attack, he tried to bandage her hand, and removed one of the threads of blood from her mouth with a kiss. The next grisly moment – Aaron cutting off Titus' hand as ransom for his other sons – was performed on stage. Although the effect was simple (Yoshida had the stump in a coat pocket, and the flash of red threads as he pulled it out concealed the sleight of hand used to hand over the amputated plastic prop) the violence was grisly. The punishing whiteness of the set meant that each increasing act of horror was shown in sharp relief.

Ninagawa's direction of Chiron and Demetrius in their final scene (before Titus kills them and bakes them in a pie) was particularly eye-opening during the rehearsals for the 2006 revival. It gave a concrete insight into his manipulation of the theatrical potential of *kabuki* and other Japanese styles of performance. As ever, this production was in no way *kabuki* – and indeed this scene was as close to a play-within-the-play as Shakespeare gets in *Titus Andronicus*. Tamora (Rei Asami) and her sons appeared at Titus' door dressed in the enormous kimono-inspired robes worn by all of Rome's men in the play.

Tamora was adorned with a headdress made of crow feathers, while the two sons had extravagant headdresses derived from other Asian iconographies. The brothers also wore punishingly high platform shoes, a cross between Japanese oversize *okobo* and the *kothurnoi* of ancient Greek tragedy. Rei gracefully manipulated her pseudo-kimono as she performed as 'Revenge', showing the vestigial glamour of her time as a Takarazuka star. The two young men, however, went through several versions before Ninagawa was satisfied. Early in rehearsals, when the two men introduced themselves to Titus as Rape and Murder, Ninagawa has them strike a pose, roll their heads and cross their eyes in a *mie* pose, derived from *aragoto kabuki*. Without the context, make-up or *ki* sound effects of *kabuki*, the poses looked cheap, despite various attempts to make it work. The actors (Suzuki Yutaka and Okawa Hiroki, both stalwart Ninagawa Company members) tried several iterations of the idea, even trying to declaim their lines like *kabuki* actors, but nothing satisfied Ninagawa. Perhaps since the revival had been invited to Stratford for the RSC Complete Works Festival, Ninagawa asked me (the only foreigner in the room) my opinion on the scene. I said that my eyes were fixed on Rei's Tamora throughout, and that maybe the sons should do less rather than more. This was the only influence I had on any of the eight productions I watched Ninagawa create, but he took it on board, and had the actors perform most of the scene with their backs to the audience instead. Rei dominated the scene entirely, and it was only when she left the young men in Titus' care that Chiron and Demetrius came into sharp focus. Their deliberately shoddy 'performance' as Rape and Murder fell apart as Titus' sons entered and saw them for who they were, at which point their voluminous costumes and unwieldy shoes became a life-threatening obstruction. Throughout the production, various characters had already worn elaborate neckwear as part of the look of the show, as a helpful set-up for the fact that the young men's scarves hid yet more ribbon; when Titus slit their throats in full view of the audience, new streams of 'blood' flowed out.

*Titus Andronicus* set the bar high for Ninagawa's subsequent productions of Shakespeare's Roman plays. In *Coriolanus*, Ninagawa perhaps found the story best suited to his particular directorial interests. Its dramatization of the rift between political classes in early Rome spoke immediately to the kind of 'struggle play' with which he and Shimizu Kunio made such an impact at the beginning of the 1970s. The struggles between personal integrity and societal honour, and between martial heroism and civic niceties, came into sharp focus in Ninagawa's athletic production. Unlike the almost mythological presentation of violence in *Titus*, in Coriolanus the blood was realistic. Both productions were energetic and passionate, but there was far less distance between Rome and Japan in *Coriolanus*. As the performance began, lights came up on the audience, immediately reflected in the mirror that covered the entire stage. The chorus came through the audience and climbed onto the stage to bow, in coats and hats that suggested the twentieth century rather than ancient Rome. As the company exited, a huge set of steps behind the mirror was revealed, and the last stages of the plebeians' riot literally tumbled down and across them. The ordinary people of this 'Rome' had come directly from the theatre audience, and Ninagawa attempted to bridge the gap between both communities with their anachronistic costumes. The contrast between the ordinary people and Rome's patrician class was significant – the aristocrats and politicians wore extravagant robes, looking significantly more like the cast of a Ninagawa production. For *Coriolanus*, Ninagawa undercut such familiar elements of his work in order to expose the political workings of the play. The Shakespeare text introduces the crowd with a stage direction – 'mutinous citizens' – but does not stipulate anything like the violence that Ninagawa staged. It was an arresting, clever start to this tragedy of a man for whom action proved more useful than dialogue, in a world where public support was critical to survival.

The set design, once again by Nakagoshi Tsukasa, was a combination of recognizable elements – the mirrored walls

FIGURE 4 Coriolanus *(2007): the Roman mob atop Nakagoshi's impressive set of steps. Photo © Donald Cooper/Photostage.*

reflecting the audience, Buddhist statues imparting a renewed martial energy and the enormous set of steps, perhaps the largest seen since Ninagawa's first *Hamlet* in 1978. To differentiate between Roman and Volscian scenes, Nakagoshi topped the staircase with an impressive set of sliding panels, opening on successive designs and vistas. They created a dynamic sense of movement in a very limited amount of space.

Lily Komine's costumes returned to the kind of pan-Asian vocabulary that had been evolving throughout the 2000s – the silhouettes were familiar, with long robes for those of high or military status among the Romans and Volscians. These were embellished with Chinese, Mongolian and Japanese influences in the hair, jewellery and accessory design. The Romans wore black and the Volscians wore white, a simple, effective delineation with so much else going on. By contrast, the Roman plebeians were dressed in a considerably less unified manner, suggesting a rabble of thrown-together garments on a hungry populace who could not afford to dress as elegantly. The jumble of time periods was another manifestation of Ninagawa's concern about real Japanese people and what they might think of his work. Dressing the ordinary people in mid-twentieth-century clothes made them look like the ordinary community of the Saitama in which he grew up; they were at once historical but recognizable. The choice would be repeated memorably for the crowds of the Jack Cade rebellion in *Henry VI* and for the plebeians in *Julius Caesar*.

Ninagawa's interest was always in the public side of a play, the unruly mob tensions swirling around and ready to erupt into violence at any moment. His lived experience of 1960s Tokyo had taught him just how volatile an angry populace could be. In *Coriolanus*, the crowd scenes were staged with great precision. Ninagawa choreographed the large company of actors to use every square inch of the staircase, often moving from the top to the bottom within a given scene. The importance of status and the distribution of power were presented with tremendous clarity, with the entire company often shifting positions over the course of a single speech. Ninagawa's response to this play was almost the opposite of *Titus Andronicus*. In the earlier production, he had refined and simplified the staging to mitigate the extreme violence of the story. In *Coriolanus*, he activated the mob to work as a chorus of witnesses and mirrors of the audience's attention, and the ordinary people became a visible manifestation of changing public opinion.

Coriolanus typifies the kind of diffident anti-hero central to so many of the plays Ninagawa chose to direct. He is an angry young man, more used to physical battle than the more personal and rhetorical sides of politics. He finds that he is not cut out for such machinations, and his personal integrity leads to his downfall. Ninagawa cast Karasawa Toshiaki as the troubled warrior, after their earlier work together on *Macbeth*, *Tenpo* and *Warau Iemon*. Ninagawa hired Karasawa's Macduff, Katsumura Masanobu, as Coriolanus' nemesis Aufidius. This comparable narrative dynamic (the lead character and his eventual killer) invited audiences unfamiliar with the play to wonder if the outcome of *Coriolanus* might be similar, and also gave the two excellent actors more sparring time than Shakespeare wrote for them in *Macbeth*. The production also featured Shiraishi Kayoko as an extraordinarily powerful Volumnia. Looking not unlike the Chinese Dowager Empress, it was immediately clear that Caius Martius had been groomed for greatness by this termagant, whose innate power radiated throughout. Shiraishi's implacable, stoic matriarch was a career highlight for the actress and her director, and the reading of the character made it very clear how a world full of such men might have come about.

The battle scenes were high octane and blood-soaked, all the more impressive for the athleticism required of the company as they ran up and down Nakagoshi's punishing set of steps. Of the production's many impressive moments, the most haunting image was Coriolanus' death, when he was set upon by Aufidius' men and executed for his betrayal. The character may not have been cut out to be a politician, but he showed himself to be a dyed-in-the-wool soldier, hacking and flailing even after the fatal blow had been struck against him. Karasawa's extraordinary performance was shockingly grim, a testament to a kind of Japanese martial energy that had all but been eradicated after the Second World War. As Coriolanus' body was borne aloft by Aufidius' soldiers, nearly thirty white-clad men watched and followed it up the steps. The mirrored doors closed on this extraordinary elegiac image of a warrior finally at peace.

# All-male Shakespeare

## *As You Like It* (2004)

Between the outright monopoly of male performers in *noh*, *kabuki* and *bunraku*, and the enduring popularity of the all-female Takarazuka (whose *otokoyaku*, performers of male characters, are its undisputed stars), theatrical play with gender is very familiar to Japanese audiences. Men playing women and women playing men have long been at the heart of the Japanese performing arts. In *kabuki* and Takarazuka, *onnagata* and *otokoyaku* performers present a kind of idealized version of the opposite sex. Their versions of 'female' and 'male' are both so exaggerated and stylized that it would be considered as impossible for a woman to act in *kabuki* as it would be for a man to perform in a Takarazuka performance.

Aware of the trend of single-sex casting in global Shakespeare presentation, Ninagawa chose to expand on his own cross-gender experiments with an all-male production of *As You Like It* in 2004. He had cast men in female roles in the *Modern Noh Plays* and in *Medea*, and as the witches in *NINAGAWA Macbeth*, and successive productions of *Hamlet* had had an all-male *Mousetrap*. The two most recent had featured Tsukikawa Yuki, sometimes even described as an *onnagata* of contemporary theatre.[6] Tsukikawa had also performed as the daughter of Antiochus in *Pericles* and would appear in nearly all of what became the Saitama all-male series. In *As You Like It* he played Celia, opposite the Rosalind of Narimiya Hiroki. Both had been part of the troupe of players in the 2001 *Hamlet*, in which both were dressed as women. Tsukikawa also played the Player Queen, while Narimiya played Ninagawa's nastiest Fortinbras to date. *As You Like It* starred another Fortinbras, Oguri Shun, as Orlando.

Oguri and Narimiya were both very popular with young women by the time they appeared in *As You Like It*. They were famous from television and film, and numerous magazines ranked them on their 'favourite male actors' lists. Both exemplify the type of slender, pretty young men represented by major talent agencies in Japan. Johnny & Associates is the most famous of these companies, responsible for the discovery and promotion of attractive young men for decades.[7] The trend is a modern manifestation of the aesthetic of *bishonen*, 'beautiful boys', which has featured in Japanese art and literature for over a millennium. The prefix *bi*, meaning beautiful, usually refers to feminine beauty, except when applied to *shonen* – young men. The term was essential to the description of the boy players of early *wakashu kabuki*, and the trope of a slender, delicate young man, usually with long, beautiful hair, remains indelibly popular. In a country where gender is historically rigid and prescribed, *bishonen* present a softer ideal of masculinity, made all the more attractive by their sensitivity. The *ne plus ultra* of the aesthetic was Genji, the Shining Prince, hero of *The Tale of Genji*, and indeed other literary characters such as Yoshitsune have been recast as *bishonen* in manga and other popular forms of literature.[8] *Bishonen* are an essential component of *shojo* manga. Shojo literally means 'young woman' and is an umbrella term for the huge industry of comic books marketed to female readers. A major branch of such manga is *yaoi*, stories focused on homoerotic relationships between men. *Bara* is a separate genre of homoerotic manga marketed to gay men, and the distinction is important. *Yaoi* stories focus on romances between idealized, beautiful young men, and are considerably less sexually explicit than *bara*. As in Takarazuka, *yaoi* portrays a softer and more romantic version of masculinity, untroubled by any bodily realities. Ninagawa tapped into all this with his first exploration of all-male Shakespearean performance. An awareness of international trends in Shakespeare production coincided with the availability of a very particular Japanese market, and the *As You Like It* experiment was a significant milestone.

The show began with a blast of rock music, echoing the Elton John music Ninagawa had used decades before. The full company entered through the auditorium, dressed in their own clothes and all presenting as male. This was not just an acting company acknowledging their Japanese identity, now they were also acknowledging their gender. The men all bowed and left, leaving Oguri Shun to change into his costume on stage, while two pantomime horses appeared. These horses featured in a great variety of Ninagawa productions over the years, sometimes fooling audiences into thinking that there were real animals on stage. With their substantial internal structure, these horses could support the weight of an actor and be 'ridden'. Ninagawa had never shown their mechanics on stage before, and this small revelation added to the initial sense of the company 'putting on' their costumes – and the play.

Kitamura Sai has argued that much of the viewing pleasure of this *As You Like It* was derived from the difference between Narimiya's Rosalind and Tsukikawa's Celia (Kitamura, 2012). While Tsukikawa made an utterly believable female – and presented as such throughout – Narimiya charmed precisely because he was not an especially convincing woman. The change to Ganymede was certainly in the actor's favour, as he looked considerably better in male rather than female clothing. The great humour of his performance is inherent in Shakespeare's play, since he wrote for the restrictions (or possibilities) of an all-male company. Ninagawa's work with beautiful young male actors put a distinctly Japanese spin on this. Things became more amusing and complicated when Phoebe (played by an older actor, by no means a *bishonen*) fell in love with Narimiya's 'male' form as Ganymede, and aped various *kabuki*-inspired gestures and back-bends as she tried to impress him.

At the end, Rosalind revealed her femininity before departing to put on her wedding dress. The costume design for *As You Like It* presented an indeterminate time and space, its relaxed style giving a sense of the Duke's woodland company without specifying too much of a location. The only expressly Japanese reference was Ninagawa's interpretation of Hymen. His text was delivered by voice alone, while three large banners representing Ebisu, the Japanese god of good luck, were unfurled behind the trees. Hymen, the Greek god of weddings, was considered an obscure enough cultural reference to merit a small Japanese equivalent. As the jolly images of Ebisu smiled through the trees and the god blessed the various couples, a Bach cantata played, the first in a sequence of Western classical pieces that underscored the end of the play. A choral interpretation of Pachelbel's Canon and the wedding march from Mendelssohn's *A Midsummer Night's Dream* both played during the final scene, echoing the kinds of music played at fashionable Japanese weddings, which themselves attempt to replicate the format (if not the religious content) of European and American wedding ceremonies. Rosalind and Celia wore exaggerated white wedding dresses, with their grooms in fashionable formal wear. These costumes all owed a debt to the kinds of wedding-wear drawn in manga fantasies.

The production's romp through the vagaries of gendered performance ended with the entire company frozen in silhouette, while Narimiya-as-Rosalind spoke the epilogue. Without any of the attempts towards feminine delivery he had used throughout the play, his final lines came into sharper relief. Narimiya simply modified (or, more accurately, *stopped* modifying) his voice. He ended the epilogue with a graceful bow, slightly sweetening his tone for his final words, before lights came back up on the full company and 'Rosalind' stepped back into the play. This ending may have been the only time that Ninagawa ever *renewed* the conceit of an actor acknowledging his performance to the audience. For the most part, these acknowledgements were used at the start of a play to draw an audience *in* – it was seldom necessary by the end, because Ninagawa felt that by then the audience would have 'crossed the bridge' and engaged with the story, so he could allow it to end on its own terms. Epilogues such as Puck's, or Prospero's, have a neat finality to them, and bring their stories to a natural conclusion. Rosalind's is more complicated. Marriage is the typical, idealized end to a Shakespearean comedy – often with the more couples the better. Narimiya stepped out of this heteronormative image to acknowledge his masculine identity, and by extension the queerness of the entire enterprise. Before this extra layer of meaning became unbearably complicated (a troupe of male actors staging four weddings that were at once heterosexual and same sex), s/he stepped back into the frame, bowing with appropriately feminine grace throughout the curtain call.

## *The Comedy of Errors* (2006)

Two years later, in early 2006, Ninagawa returned to the all-male idea for *The Comedy of Errors*. It was a fascinatingly polysemic, multi-referential production. Its multiple sign systems and references were drawn from theatre, history and the assumed preconceptions of the Saitama audience. The play is set in Ephesus, on the Mediterranean coast of Turkey. Shakespeare took the plot from Plautus' *Menaechmi*, and its dramatis personae is a familiar list of the usual stock characters from a Roman comedy. It includes a domineering wife, a financial parasite, a funny prostitute and a quack doctor. Plautus' plot concerned one set of twins, but Shakespeare's innovation was to add a second pair; now there were two comical put-upon servants instead of one. Although Turkey was the heart of the Ottoman Empire by the time Shakespeare was writing, in Plautus' day Ephesus was a Greek city. Ninagawa's production was an intricately constructed millefeuille of perspectives: a Japanese director staging an Elizabethan playwright's adaptation of a Roman comedy set in a Greek city in the Turkish Empire. Impressively, these seemingly conflicting ideas were all woven into the production's design.

As the audience entered the theatre in Saitama, the set was immediately visible. Unlike the *kabuki Twelfth Night*, there was no pre-show curtain to hide the surprise that the set featured another enormous mirror. Both stories are built around the mistaken identities of identical twins, although *Comedy* has the complication of a second set of twins to confuse. The mirror backdrop was an appropriate repetition of a successful idea, visibly doubling the play's already manifold confusions. Unlike the Kabuki-za version, this mirror was not translucent. The proscenium was actually a simplified (but faithful) recreation of the Teatro Olimpico in Vicenza, Italy, built in 1570 for a performance of *Oedipus Rex*. The set also evoked the façade of the Library of Celsus, one of the most impressive remaining structures at the archaeological site of Ephesus.

By setting the play on a stage that evoked its literal setting in Ephesus *and* the Teatro Olimpico, Ninagawa called to mind several histories at once. The production thus acknowledged the play's ancient and medieval inspirations as well as its cultural provenance as a distinctly Renaissance play. Ninagawa's depiction of the Renaissance (filtered, as ever, via Bakhtin) was brash, cheeky and loud. Within the ribald physical comedy of the play, there were also charming moments of contemplation and genuine reflection. Ninagawa spent a lot of time with Oguri Shun (Antipholus) on his little soliloquy in Act 1, Scene 2:

> I to the world am like a drop of water
> That in the ocean seeks another drop;
> Who, falling there to find his fellow forth,
> Unseen, inquisitive, confounds himself.
> So I, to find a mother and a brother,
> In quest of them, unhappy, lose myself.

For Ninagawa, this beautiful moment summed up the story. Each twin was missing a part of himself and would not feel complete until his family was restored. Ninagawa spoke movingly about how much of his theatre revolved around his own desire to explore a Japanese sense of self, and how poignant he found this particular little speech. The mirrored wall, which had already featured in several Ninagawa productions (and would again), allowed Oguri a very endearing moment contemplating his own reflection, clearly missing his own lost twin – his reflection, or his other self.

During the rehearsal process, Ninagawa made frequent reference to *commedia dell'arte*, insisting that it was the bridge between Shakespeare and Plautus. With this in mind, Dromio (Takahashi Yo) was dressed in a diamond-patterned costume that forced the comparison with Arlecchino, the servant character central to *commedia*. The Italianness of the characters was important – these were hot-blooded, passionate people, and Ninagawa insisted that the Renaissance should come to life in their exuberant, carnivalesque performance, which began with a parade and ended with a dance.

Images of the multiple inspirations woven into the set design (Ephesus, Vicenza, *commedia dell'arte*) were posted on the wall behind the designer Nakagoshi's desk in the rehearsal studio. The costumes, meanwhile, drew on a different set of references. Designed by Miyamoto Noriko, they looked like a Japanese designer's idea of what Shakespeare's idea of Turkey might have been. For *The Comedy of Errors*, Miyamoto blended Elizabethan doublets and capes (for Antipholus) with Harlequin motley (for Dromio), while creating a variety of witty pastiches of 'Turkish' costumes, including Fez hats, turbans, exaggerated moustaches and wide trousers. The play's female characters were dressed in wide hoop skirts and boots, owing more to the eighteenth century than anything Shakespeare saw in his lifetime. Impressively, these multiple inspirations did not compete – rather, they fused to give a playful sense of 'dressing up', supporting rather than compromising the play's artificiality. Composer Kasamatsu Yasuhiro and his musicians were also costumed, as they were visible throughout the play. They sat on stage with various ensemble members, watching the story throughout. The playfully diverse costumes, visible musicians and on-stage observers constantly reminded the audience that this was a performance, in one of the simplest versions of Ninagawa's play-framing to date. These little details, reflected and refracted in the various mirrors, added a great deal to the play. Ninagawa staged an exuberant procession to start the show, but this time the company was introduced in full costume. This meant that there was no invited imaginative shift from contemporary Japanese (all-male) actors to the characters of the play.

The production starred Oguri Shun and Takahashi Yo, each playing a pair of twins. Takahashi had become a very regular Ninagawa performer, a major discovery from the Ninagawa Studio. Oguri had already appeared in several Ninagawa Shakespeares, including the 2003 *Hamlet* and *As You Like It*.

Ninagawa again featured the 'feminine' charms of Tsukikawa Yuki, this time opposite the hilariously waspish Uchida Shige as Adriana.

For all of it being a sweet, silly comedy, the manner in which Ninagawa presented *The Comedy of Errors* was fascinatingly complex. A design like this might elsewhere be dismissed as outrageously Orientalist, but where exactly is the 'Orient' when the transaction consists of one side of Asia interpolating designs from another? The costumes presented a rather naïve, generalized interpretation of 'Turkey', but there was no mockery implied. As if to celebrate rather than apologize for the distance between Turkey and Japan in the production, Ninagawa ended with a final surprise. The three reunited couples entered, seemed to kiss, and as they parted a red ribbon stretched between their mouths. This was a startling echo of the device used so memorably in *Medea* – but this time the ribbons showed a loving connection between partners rather than the loss of one. As the couples danced, still connected by the red ribbons in their mouths, the rest of the company joined them on the stage. The final moments combined this distinctly Ninagawa image with a final nod to Turkey, as all of the other actors raised their hands in the air and slowly twirled, the costumes of their skirts billowing like so many whirling dervishes. After the play's frenetic comedy, this delicate dance was hypnotically beautiful, and a surprisingly elegant end to the play.

## *Love's Labour's Lost* (2007)

By the time that he was developing this third all-male production, *Love's Labour's Lost*, Ninagawa was well aware that his audience for the burgeoning 'all-male series' (as it was now being called) was predominantly female, made up of the kinds of viewers who enjoy manga and Takarazuka musicals. The boys'-love stories depicted in *yaoi* manga are attractive precisely because they display a kind of romance totally removed from the female reader's real-life relationship experience. The fantasy is attractive because it is completely inaccessible. The all-male Shakespeare productions offered a poetic, live experience with about as much sex as might be implied in the romantic boys'-love comic books. *Love's Labour's Lost* is seldom performed even in English, because its extensive poetic allusions and bittersweet ending have not aged as well as some of Shakespeare's more effervescent comedies. For his production Ninagawa used a set of very specific references tailored to his Japanese audience.

*The Rose of Versailles* began as a *shojo* manga in the early 1970s and was a record-breaking success. It tells the story of Oscar, the daughter of a palace guard at Versailles, who is raised as a boy and becomes a personal guard to Marie Antoinette. The story was ideal material for adaptation as a Takarazuka musical, and the company first staged it in 1974. It is the most successful Takarazuka show ever produced and was responsible for the emergence of the company's 'top star' system. The majority of the Takarazuka graduates who worked with Ninagawa had played Oscar during their careers, among them Rei Asami, Ohtori Ran and Aran Kei. The show was so successful that it led to a boom in French lessons in Japan and Japanese tourism to Versailles. The manga's author, Ikeda Riyoko, was awarded the Légion d'Honneur for her promotion of French culture in Japan.

Within *The Rose of Versailles*, Oscar has a man's job and dresses like a man, but is entirely up front about her female identity. Her blurred gender is attractive to both men and women, to the extent that even Marie Antoinette falls for her. As the 1780s progress, Oscar becomes aware of the impending revolution and gets involved with the burgeoning resistance to royal authority. On the march to the Bastille, Oscar is shot and dies a hero(ine) while the Bastille falls. The Takarazuka musical version, true to its own unique form, ends with a spectacular finale that has nothing to do with the story's narrative. When Ninagawa was trying to imagine a suitable bridge to a story featuring a French princess, thwarted romance, spirited commoners and a bittersweet ending, all to be performed by a single-sex company of beautiful young people, he needed to look no further. Even just by dressing his *Love's Labour's Lost* in costumes reminiscent of pre-revolutionary France, the leap was made, although subtle nods to Takarazuka appeared throughout.

The set was simple but effective – an enormous willow tree dominated the entire stage, leaving a comparatively shallow playing space in front of it. As Ninagawa's experiments with Shakespearean comedy developed, his set designs relied less on spectacle and more on the creation of a versatile performance space.

With Bakhtin and comic subversion never far from his mind, Ninagawa focused just as much energy on the other inhabitants of Navarre as he did on the four pairs of lovers. In contrast with those eight tall, attractive men, the rest of the company was tall and short, fat and thin, old and young. Interviewed by Akishima Yuriko, Ninagawa explained his particular interest in the 'indispensable subordinate characters', in particular their masque towards the end of the play.[9] Their performance – *Love's Labour's Lost*'s version of a play-within-the-play – was exuberantly performed with huge masks for everyone but Don Armado, who had cast himself as the star of the show. When the news came that the King of France had died, forcing the separation of the four couples, Armado insisted that they perform the outstanding 'Dialogue of the Owl and the Cuckoo', bringing the show to its beautiful conclusion. In a final nod to Takarazuka, the villagers returned to the stage for the final song. They were all dressed in black, with headdresses made to look like cherry trees in bloom. The shape of these was reminiscent of the kinds of extravagant, feathered costumes worn by company members in the finales of all Takarazuka performances. The Ninagawa version was deliberately rustic, maintaining the endearing simplicity of the villagers' performance. As the song moved from spring to winter, a simple trick made the blossoms disappear, leaving the branches bare. In one of the most amazing feats of lighting of any Ninagawa production, the colour seemed to drain from the entire willow, leaching it from green to grey as the couples prepared to separate.

The inherent queerness of this all-male romantic performance was mitigated by another formal dance at the end, which led directly into the curtain call and obviated the need for any kissing between the couples. The story sat squarely in the world of *yaoi* and Takarazuka – idealized, romantic characters with little connection to the real male bodies underneath their costumes. This *Love's Labour's Lost* was elegiac and exquisitely beautiful, but it was not particularly sexual.

## *Much Ado About Nothing* (2008)

Following the trilogy of beautiful settings for the Forest of Arden, Ephesus and Navarre, Nakagoshi Tsukasa created another distinctive design for *Much Ado About Nothing*, the next production in the all-male series. The play was staged entirely in Leonato's garden, on a large tiered platform decorated with classical (European) statues. An immediate evocation of Italy's romance with its own past, this forest of statues provided a tremendous range of hiding places for the scene's multiple scenes of eavesdropping.

The all-male concept was by now well-enough established that Ninagawa did not stage any kind of an induction or prologue to the play. The performance began with a soldier running through the audience with the news that the war was over. Leonato came out to hear the news, accompanied by Beatrice and Hero, already recognizable 'women' in the respective bodies of Uchida Shige and Tsukikawa Yuki. Uchida had played extensively with the distance between his male body and Luciana's female character in *The Comedy of Errors*, and had been a sunburned, awkward Rosaline to contrast with Narimiya Hiroki's Princess of France in *Love's Labour's Lost*. For *Much Ado About Nothing*, he all but dispensed with any acknowledgement of his masculinity. His Beatrice was clever, funny and presented as thoroughly female. After the three earlier productions, there was comparatively little comedy left to mine in the presentation of boys playing girls, so Uchida and Tsukikawa played both parts 'straight'.

Bucking the trend of casting Beatrice and Benedick older than Claudio and Hero, Ninagawa presented Koide Keisuke and Uchida as the comic *and* romantic leads. Koide's was a charming, frequently bemused Benedick, who seemed to grow up over the course of the play. At its conclusion, Benedick ends his war of words with Beatrice by 'stopping her mouth' with a kiss. Public displays of affection are generally avoided in Japan even between heterosexual couples, and seldom represented on stage. The previous Saitama all-male productions had coyly avoided any kissing by ending with various kinds of jigs and dances, but since kissing is expressly mandated in the text, there was no way to avoid it. In *Much Ado*, the relationships between Don Pedro and his men were made substantially more intimate, with Don Pedro frequently kissing Claudio and others on the mouth. Ninagawa all but filled the play with kisses between men. Yoshida Kohtaloh's Don Pedro was a kind of bisexual romantic, whose upfront flirtations with everyone – including Leonato, Hero, Claudio and obviously Beatrice – belied the character's loneliness. His repeated attentions were harmless and never reciprocated; by the end of the play he was even attempting to flirt with members of the audience. These light-hearted flirtations served to throw the Hero subplot into sharper relief – it was all very well for this older man to try his luck, but the mere suspicion of Hero's virtue was enough to become a matter of life and death. Instead of ending with a kiss, her wedding was destroyed. The extreme heteronormative structure of Shakespearean comedy was at once foregrounded and undermined in this *Much Ado* – all of the female characters were played sincerely as women, with hardly any humour derived from the efforts of the male actors playing them. By playing the women straight and maintaining the play's focus on the importance of women's virtue (and the insistence that men should eventually get married), the audience all but forgot that the actors were all men. When the story did end with a prolonged kiss between Beatrice and Benedick, the actors' gender was entirely secondary to those of their characters. For all that, it was still a provocatively long kiss between two men, who had just agreed to get married in a country where same-sex marriage is still not legally recognized.

For Dogberry and his Watch, Ninagawa continued to display his taste for the ridiculous. Dogberry appeared in a fat suit, and his three henchmen looked tiny beside him. When they overheard Borachio and Conrad in the garden, they stripped almost naked and covered themselves in white paint, attempting to pose like the various statues in what looked like a hilarious pastiche of the world-famous *butoh* company Sankai Juku. Within the carnivalesque celebration at the end, in which the entire company danced around the garden while red flowers rained down on them, one of the Watch took Don Pedro's hand. With order restored and the couples happily (re)matched, there was a hint that the play's happy ending was broad enough to accommodate even some more unconventional romances.

## *The Taming of the Shrew* (2010)

Soon after *Much Ado About Nothing*, *Ninagawa Twelfth Night* returned for a third run at the Kabuki-za. The remount was very successful and it also toured to the Barbican in London. Although the whole project had been Onoe Kikunosuke's idea, the show was all but stolen by Ichikawa Kamejiro, who played the mischievous Maa (Maria). A very popular interpreter of both male and female roles, Kamejiro has appeared regularly in his uncle Ichikawa Ennosuke III's 'super kabuki'. The term was first used to describe Ennosuke's *Yamato Takeru*, a 1986 production that combined traditional *kabuki* staging with contemporary sets, music and lighting technology.[10] Kamejiro's performance impressed Ninagawa immensely, and as he began to plan his production of *The Taming of the Shrew*, the young actor struck him as a perfect link between his all-male experiments at Saitama and the Kabuki-za.

*The Taming of the Shrew* is unique among Shakespeare's plays in that it contains its own induction, the gulling of Christopher Sly. Ninagawa staged it in its entirety, with a pretty exterior designed for the inn and a lavishly appointed bedroom for the drunken man when he is put to bed. When Sly's 'wife' (the page Bartholomew, in rather unconvincing drag) was presented, it took all of 'her' efforts to convince Sly that he would need to wait for several nights before they could share a bed again, for fear of a relapse of his madness. Once he was convinced, Sly and Bartholomew left the stage and took their seats in the auditorium for the 'performance' designed for their entertainment. In an unusual revision of the presentation of the company, long employed to mitigate the artificiality of Japanese actors playing Shakespeare, Ninagawa staged a parade that was already part of the show. The remainder of *The Taming of the Shrew* was presented as a play-within-a-play.

There was a deliberate artificiality to the design once the action moved from the Sly scenes to the story of the Minola family in Padua. The playing space was kept clear, with a backdrop simply emblazoned with an oversized print of Botticelli's *La Primavera*. Chairs and tables were provided when necessary, but the set was kept bare to focus all attention on the actors' performances. Since the story had already been established as a company's performance in an inn, Ninagawa had no desire to complicate the layers of meaning and reality any further. The actors *were* the story.

The Minola sisters presented another intriguing blend of Ninagawa's experiments with gender. Tsukikawa Yuki played Bianca with the kind of quiet grace that had been a foil for a variety of sisters, cousins and rivals to date. Although it would never work for a female character in an actual *kabuki* play, Kamejiro played Kate almost like an *aragoto* character. He employed a variety of *mie* poses, acrobatic moves and vocalizations conventionally reserved for masculine *kabuki* characters. When Kate was upset, he would bite a handkerchief like a winsome maiden, and in moments of great anger or frustration he would cross his eyes and pose like a warrior about to attack an enemy. The last time Ninagawa employed so many aspects of *kabuki* to present a complicated female character had been in *Medea*. The effect again created a figure who felt as if she was at odds with the world around her, refusing to submit to the limited role she was allowed to play. Kamejiro's blend of innate talent and *kabuki* flourishes created an extraordinary character, simultaneously dignified and deranged, and quite unlike any Kate seen before.

Such a complicated Kate required a Petruchio that might have a hope of 'taming' her, and the role was played by Kakei Toshio. His Petruchio was even more extravagant than Kamejiro's Kate, swaggering about the stage demanding his audience's attention. He was not a bully or a misanthrope, so much as a man with a gleeful awareness of the ridiculousness of human life and a determination never to subscribe to it. His dreadful treatment of Kate throughout the play emerged as a kind of refusal to be ordinary, and a challenge to her to try his perspective. When they eventually began to see eye to eye as they returned from their monstrous honeymoon, Petruchio's 'kiss me, Kate' elicited a big laugh from the audience, who would very seldom have seen the *kabuki* star kissing anyone on stage. In the lead-up to the kiss Kamejiro knelt and posed demurely like a 'real' *onnagata* but stayed playfully coy and kissed Petruchio behind a large fan.

Kate's final speech continues to generate comment and controversy, and Kamejiro's interpretation was fascinating. This Kate had learned to play the role she had been given on her own terms, blending masculinity and femininity as was her nature. Even Kamejiro's voice modulated between an expressly effeminate, *onnagata* tone and a considerably more masculine register. On the lines 'I am ashamed that women are so simple/to offer war when they should sue for peace', Kate knelt demurely before Petruchio, but immediately grabbed his sword and moved back downstage centre for the remainder of the speech, planting the sword in the stage 'in token of which duty' at its conclusion. Kamejiro's masculine identity combined with the obsequious femininity instilled by his *kabuki* training to create a Kate of almost defiantly indeterminate gender – at once feminine, but not really female, and male, but not really masculine. While it brought little new to the debate over the play's gender politics, this was a fascinating *theatrical* presentation of the character.

## *Troilus and Cressida* (2012)

Ninagawa could fairly safely assume that Japanese audiences were unfamiliar with *Troilus and Cressida*, even if some resolute fans remembered the narrative of the Trojan War from *The Greeks*. To frame it for the Saitama audience, Ninagawa had Nakagoshi fill the entire set with sunflowers. Besides the obvious evocation of Troy's sunny climate, the text of *Troilus and Cressida* itself refers to the young soldiers as 'the flowers of Troy'. The flowers also had a very specific resonance in Japan in 2012. In the aftermath of the Fukushima nuclear disaster the previous year, sunflowers had been planted widely because they are known to soak up certain radioactive isotopes from contaminated soil. This visual reference to a destroyed community was a powerful frame for the play. The image also called to mind Basho's famous haiku about warriors' dreams in the tall summer growth,[11] and even the Kajii Motojiro quotation that so haunted *NINAGAWA Macbeth* – 'there are corpses under the cherry blossoms!'.

There was also a deliberate return to the *yaoi* manga aesthetics of the earlier all-male productions. Not finding the romance between Troilus and Cressida particularly satisfying, since they are quickly separated when she is given to the Greeks, Ninagawa made much more of the relationship between Achilles and Patroclus. The latter's death motivates Achilles to rejoin the war and eventually kill Hector, and Ninagawa was not coy about the nature of their relationship. In Act 2, Scene 3, both men appeared completely naked and even kissed in front of Thersites while he mocked them. While men (and women) had shown skin in Ninagawa productions for decades, there had never been quite so much of it on display. The scene was brief, but the kiss was deliberate, leaving no doubt about the nature of the relationship.[12] While the romantic love between the two soldiers was perfectly presentable within this kind of boys'-love manga presentation, and was entirely plausible in the context of Ancient Greece, Thersites' grim list of the perceived results of sex between men was excised. This would have shown too much of the real physical implications of such a relationship; its exclusion maintained the kind of theatrical (and predominantly sexless) filter that shimmered over the all-male project as a whole. In Ninagawa's version, the relationships between its men are significantly more interesting than the love between the title characters. The Achilles–Patroclus relationship provided a thread of doomed romance through the play, giving the audience an appealing story to follow, while the reconciliation between Ajax and Hector was an all-too-brief glimmer of hope.

The most striking of the play's four women was Cassandra, played by Uchida Shige. Having charmed and amused audiences as Luciana, Rosaline and Beatrice, his performance as the prophetess was startling. He had shown an occasional capacity for anger and lunacy in his previous female roles, but the force of his rage and terror was a highlight of the production. Lest there be any doubt of where the character's powers of divination had come from, the insides of Uchida's legs were stained red. While the potential results of sex between men were deemed too unpleasant, the after-effects of Apollo's rape were made visible, generating sympathy for the female character.

The play's prologue was simply performed – Thersites walked in through the audience, holding a sunflower, and spoke the play's own introduction. Ninagawa had by now used such entrances so many times that the idea came as much from him as from *kabuki*'s *hanamichi*. The costumes, again by Lily Komine, made a very clear delineation between

Trojan and Greek, using the same silhouettes and juxtaposed materials that had become the hallmark of Ninagawa's work. The dark-haired Trojans wore white clothes and silver armour, while the Greeks wore blue, with leather armour and blonde hair. The hairstyles owed the production's most significant debt to manga. A further comic book design was reserved for Helen, who was dressed in gold and made unusually buxom (particularly for an all-male production). This was a direct reminder that her venality had been the cause of the entire war. The manga aesthetics helped audiences to digest this problematic, confusing play, in a clever, memorable production.

## *The Merchant of Venice* (2013)

Ninagawa and Kamejiro reunited three years after *The Taming of the Shrew* for a production of *The Merchant of Venice*. In the mid-1990s Ninagawa had intimated that he had no interest in directing this play, because he could find no way to interpret it and present it 'his way' for a Japanese audience (Ninagawa, 1995: 218). Despite Ninagawa's feelings, *The Merchant of Venice* has had one of the longest performance histories of any Shakespeare play in Japan. It was the first play to be given a full performance, being presented in 1885 as a *kabuki* play entitled *A Time of Cherry Blossoms, A World of Money*.[13] This *kabuki* adaptation took many liberties, excising everything that might not easily be understood by a Japanese audience. It was not until 1908 that anything close to a translation of the play was presented, when Tsubouchi Shoyo's translation of the trial scene was staged at the Meiji-za. This production starred the *kabuki* actor Ichikawa Sadanji II, who had studied the play while training in Europe. Although he worked primarily in *kabuki*, Sadanji was especially eager to explore new modes of expression on the Japanese stage. The 1908 performance is also notable for having featured Japan's first professional actresses. *The Merchant of Venice* was the most popular Shakespeare play in Japan until the end of the Second World War.

Inspired by his forebear Sadanji, Kamejiro (another Ichikawa with an interest in theatrical innovation) convinced Ninagawa to direct the play and cast him as Shylock. There was still the issue of making the play speak to a Japanese audience. The play's tension between Christian and Jewish characters is less relatable in Japan, but as Matsuoka Kazuko wrote in the programme, Ninagawa focused on exploring the difficulties of being an outsider in a community: 'Ninagawa ... thought of Shylock as a foreigner in this society, and here depicts the social dynamics of a foreigner fighting back against a society that refuses to allow him any access to power' (Matsuoka, 2013, my translation).

According to his own programme note, Ninagawa's focus was also on the religious: 'I think this is a play about differing religious beliefs being suppressed by the orthodoxy. To me, Shylock appears to be fighting alone against a hundred opponents' (Ninagawa, 2013a, my translation).

Despite his concerns about bridging the gap between Shakespeare's Venice and his Saitama audience, Ninagawa did not stage any kind of introduction for the play. The performance began in darkness, as a voice sang the introduction to the *Vespers* of that most Venetian composer, Monteverdi. As the music swelled, the lights came up on a revised version of the set used for *The Comedy of Errors*, the recreation of the Teatro Olimpico in Vicenza. Enhancing the Venetian setting, numerous striped poles were installed at the downstage edge of the stage, as though ready for gondolas to moor. Antonio opened a door and ambled into the playing space, not knowing, in sooth, why he was so sad. While Solerio and Solanio tried to comfort him, a procession of monks in black robes passed behind them, further highlighting Venice's Catholic identity. This was also reflected in the costumes; all of the city's men wore white clothes with a cross around their necks.

Delineating Shylock's cultural otherness via these elements of the production design could only achieve so much, and so Ninagawa and Kamejiro hit upon a further solution, using Kamejiro's *kabuki* expertise as a further means of othering the character. Speaking and behaving in a manner more suited to *kabuki* than a contemporary Shakespearean translation, Kamejiro presented a Shylock who was linguistically, behaviourally and even emotionally at odds with his surroundings. This deft interpretation guaranteed that Shylock did not speak with a 'foreign' accent or risk being a caricature of Jewishness. Instead, the feeling was of a character literally from a different world. Kamejiro's magnetic performance meant that at all points he was the most interesting character on the stage. His curiously intercultural, anachronistic Shylock was infinitely more compelling than the group of dull Christians against whom he was pitted. The juxtaposition of his *kabuki*-derived acting against the more conventional performances of the other characters made for an interpretation that was acceptable to Ninagawa – uniquely Japanese, and a very clear way of showing a Shylock 'suppressed by the orthodoxy' and 'fighting alone', as he had described it.

Swimming somewhat against the tide of contemporary interpretation, Kamejiro was not interested in portraying Shylock as a sympathetic character. In the programme, he insisted that he had 'no intention of playing Shylock as an innocent victim', and was considerably more interested in playing the character's villainous side (Ichikawa, 2013, *my translation*). If the integrity of his approach eventually made an audience sympathize with the character, that was fine, but he did not want to avoid Shylock's active malice. Central to his reading was the idea that Shylock would 'better the instruction' of the horrible way that he was treated by his fellow Venetians; even as an outsider, he is very much a product of his surroundings. A quintessential Japanese proverb – one that all foreigners who move to Japan soon learn – is that 'the nail that sticks up will be hammered down'. Even though there was no direct reference to the phrase within the play or the staging, its meaning resonated throughout Shylock's story in the relentlessly Catholic universe of this production.

As has become almost standard for the play, in which Shylock disappears rather too early for most directors' taste, Ninagawa gave Shylock one extra scene at the very end. After the various happy couples had departed, Shylock appeared through the same door as Antonio had at the very beginning, clutching the cross that he had been forced to wear. Defiantly refusing to wear it around his neck, he held it so tightly that blood started to trickle between his fingers. This final image compounded Ninagawa's reading of the play as the story of one man defiant against his oppressors, and gave a glimmer of hope that this fascinating, difficult and uncompromising character had not been destroyed entirely.

*Troilus and Cressida* and *The Merchant of Venice* brought a darker mood to the all-male series. *Merchant* is technically designated a comedy, since the various lovers are granted a happy ending and the play ends in several marriages. The final image of Shylock muddied the generic water and deliberately complicated the audience's response to the play. *Troilus and Cressida* is among the most difficult of Shakespeare's plays to classify. Its blend of sardonic humour and biting commentary mitigates the deaths of several important characters by the story's end. Between the deliberately *kabuki*-infused performances by Kamejiro and the queer and manga aesthetics used to unpack this 'problem' play, Ninagawa was testing the limits of what the all-male concept might accommodate.

## *Romeo and Juliet* (2014)

In 2014, Ninagawa directed a new production of *Romeo and Juliet*, marking four decades since his first production of the play. This was a supplementary episode in the all-male series, not counted in the Sai no Kuni series proper but billed as 'Ninagawa Shakespeare Legend'. It was the first Shakespeare play he had ever directed and was second only to *Hamlet* in the number of times he had staged it. Performances took place in the small space at Saitama, which had been used primarily for the experimental productions of Saitama Gold Theatre.

The structure of *Romeo and Juliet* owes more to comedy than tragedy. Shakespeare had experimented with both forms by the time he wrote it, and indeed by 2014 Ninagawa had directed almost all of the plays that commentators believe predate it. If Shakespeare wanted, in *Romeo and Juliet*, to make a move towards storylines more startling and moving than the earlier comedies, Ninagawa was reaching a comparable point of curiosity with his own all-male experiment. This *Romeo and Juliet* was only possible as a result of the previous successes of the all-male series, which had cultivated a new audience for Ninagawa's brand of Shakespeare. His take on this particular play had always foregrounded the youth and passionate energy of the two central characters, and this return to the play was the most intimate production to date. Previous versions had all been for large theatres, for instance the Nissay Theatre or the main hall in Saitama, so the 2014 version was a chance to serve up the play in more microscopic detail. At its heart was the performance of Tsukikawa Yuki as Juliet. Besides his impressive résumé of Shakespearean young ladies, Tsukikawa had also played Paris in the 2004 production at the Nissay Theatre. Ten years later he was well over twice Juliet's stated age in the text, but the conceit of the all-male company (and the actor's extraordinary ability to play young women) allowed for this distinctly Ninagawa-style piece of casting. This production replicated Shakespeare's own graduation from his earliest plays; both experiments relied on the experience of regular actors and a seasoned audience, and both subverted the expectations of previously established forms.[14]

## *The Two Gentlemen of Verona* (2015)

By 2015, the Sai no Kuni series had produced almost all Shakespeare's cross-dressing comedies, virtually all within the 'all-male series'. The one remaining play, *The Two Gentlemen of Verona*, was the last of four Shakespeare productions in Ninagawa's eightieth year, after *Hamlet*, *Richard II* and the revival of *NINAGAWA Macbeth*. Ninagawa chose to infuse the play with several echoes of previous productions. The new set, by Nakagoshi as usual, presented an updated interpretation of the architectural *scaenae frons* idea featured in both *The Comedy of Errors* and *The Merchant of Venice*, now conflated with the forced-perspective corridors previously seen in *Richard III*. The entire wall was again mirrored, now highlighting both the differences and similarities between Proteus and Valentine.

Although his shows were filled with music, Ninagawa very seldom featured live singing in his Shakespeare productions. *Two Gentlemen* describes Proteus singing at Silvia's window, however, and this made for something quite new within the all-male series, and indeed the Sai no Kuni series overall. As the young suitor, Ninagawa cast the popular young performer Miura Ryosuke, who had previously appeared in his adaptation of *Never Let Me Go* and the 2012 version of *Yotsuya Kaidan*. Miura is best known to Japanese audiences as a character on the popular television series *Kamen Rider*, in which he played a complicated antagonist who loves and hates his best friend, another handsome young man. In the end, Miura's *Kamen Rider* character proves himself essentially good, and Ninagawa again relied on the 'calculated intimacy' of this previous performance. Since Proteus can appear capricious and even dangerous as his passions shift during *Two Gentlemen*, Miura's casting guaranteed a kind of sympathetic predisposition towards the character. Tsukikawa Yuki returned for this final all-male comedy, playing a Silvia who was as serene as 'she' was wise. In an unusual choice for a director who so reliably cast great numbers of actors, Ninagawa cast Yokota Eiji as both of the play's older men. Yokota had been a very recognizable presence in Ninagawa productions since the revival of *Hamlet* in 1998. Trained at the Bungakuza, Yokota played significant roles in more Ninagawa productions than almost any other actor.

Comedy was often the site of the most interesting (and untranslatable) interweavings of Japanese and Shakespearean influence in Ninagawa's work. Japanese comedy is as varied as its other performing art forms, with a rich history dating back at least as far as the *kyogen* pieces interspersed within traditional *noh* programmes. A key influence was the dynamic of *manzai* stand-up comedy duos (comprised of a straight man, or *tsukkomi*, and a funny man, *boke*). *Manzai* comedy relies on the *tsukkomi* correcting the *boke*'s inane suggestions, often with a smack on the head with a paper fan. Ninagawa conflated this dynamic with the *commedia dell'arte*, replacing the fan with a slap-stick. The figure of the comic servant emerged as a highlight to watch out for throughout his all-male comedies, in a distinctive combination of the Japanese *boke* and reconstructed European clowning. Ninagawa's interpretation of these Shakespearean clowns – Dromio, Tranio, Gobbo, Speed and Lance, in particular – also owed a visual debt to *commedia*, since they were almost all dressed in a version of Harlequin's motley, sometimes with enlarged shoes, a hat and, very memorably in *Two Gentlemen*, accompanied by a particularly adorable puppy. Ninagawa had blended Japan's unique kinds of comedy with Shakespeare's lighter characters as far back as the Porter in *NINAGAWA Macbeth*. Discoveries made during *The Tempest* and *A Midsummer Night's Dream* were instrumental to the formation of the comic style that Ninagawa developed across these multiple productions – always allowing for the play's own humour to inform the comedy of a given show. Whenever possible, Ninagawa relished the opportunity to exploit the juxtaposition of characters from different social strata – perhaps most memorably in the bizarre physical performances of the villagers in *Love's Labour's Lost*, whose antics so curiously undercut the romantic endeavours of the young lovers.

*The Two Gentlemen of Verona*, like *As You Like It*, features a community of outcasts who have rebelled against society and chosen to live by their own rules. If Ninagawa felt any residual echoes of the desperate measures taken by the United Red Army (another revolutionary community), they had little influence on the production. Indeed, Valentine and Speed first encountered the rebels when it turned out that a bush into which they were relieving themselves was actually a group of men in elaborate camouflage. In this otherwise elegant, even stately interpretation of the play, this silly, funny moment dragged the play back towards a more Bakhtinian, earthy presentation, insisting on a more dangerous world outside the pretty romances of the city. The play's conclusion sees its wayward young men forgiven their trespasses and invited to return to civic life, and Ninagawa's late career production was quite bittersweet. His career began with stories of angry, passionate young men trying to find their way in the world, and in this context Proteus and Valentine's resolution felt all the more romantic. Contemporary productions tend not to be quite as forgiving towards the *Two Gentlemen*'s bad behaviour, but the *yaoi*-tinged storybook world of Ninagawa's version all but demanded its happy ending.

It is worth noting that none of Ninagawa's Saitama all-male productions was ever selected to perform outside Japan. Even though they were a major part of the Sai no Kuni series and made up over a quarter of his productions there, Ninagawa never chose them to tour. While previous all-male companies (*Medea*, *Sotoba Komachi* and *Ninagawa Twelfth Night*) had enjoyed substantial acclaim abroad, the distinctly Japanese character of the Saitama all-male Shakespeares – particularly their humour – precluded him from suggesting any overseas performances. The all-male series was nonetheless a fascinating experiment, interrogating and reconstructing the gender politics of Shakespearean comedy in increasingly sophisticated and provocative ways. It is intriguing to wonder if a non-Japanese audience might have laughed as much at *Love's Labour's Lost* or been as enthralled by Kamejiro's Kate, but Ninagawa chose to keep these particular performances for his Saitama audience alone.[15]

# Tragedies and Histories

Amid the all-male series' gently provocative experiments with gender and comedy – often far more intriguing than their outward appearances – Ninagawa also created robust productions of Shakespeare's histories and tragedies. The Sai no Kuni series did not proceed according to genre, nor did it reflect anything like the order in which Shakespeare may have written the plays. *Pericles* and *The Tempest* came early, while *The Two Gentlemen of Verona* and *Henry VI* were staged much later in the series. Directly after the joyful elegance of *Love's Labour's Lost*, Ninagawa directed back-to-back productions of *Othello* and *King Lear*.[16]

Ninagawa's first *Othello* was in 1994. It starred Matsumoto Koshiro as Othello and Kiba Katsumi as Iago. When he saw the production on television, he felt it was a failure because the attempt to present race in a Japanese context did not work.[17] Thirteen years later, he had built up a strong cohort of performers and was more confident in his own ability to wrestle with the play's challenges. Staging *Othello* in Japan raises issues comparable to those of *The Merchant of Venice*. There are very small numbers of Muslims in Japan, and comparably few people of colour.[18] The likelihood of finding an actor who is both ethnically appropriate for the role *and* sufficiently fluent in Japanese is remarkably slim. Unlike many other Japanese productions, Ninagawa did not resort to blackface; as with Aaron in *Titus Andronicus*, the actor was made to look suntanned, but was certainly not painted black.[19] Yoshida Kohtaloh's Othello had a shaved head and a variety of tattoos (again like Aaron) and his white clothes set him apart from the red brocade-clad citizens of Venice, but there was no intention of his being painted black. Ninagawa had made a career out of liberating Japanese performers from the habit of trying to alter their racial appearance – he certainly was not about to start encouraging it.

The production was quite grand. Impressive, chiaroscuro evocations of Venice for the early scenes gave way to an industrial-looking maze of staircases for the military compound of Cyprus. Matching Othello's own white robes, an enormous white bed dominated the final scenes, giving an impressive platform for the sequence of deaths that end the play. Of all the Saitama productions, this had the least 'Japanese' appearance.

Apart from the familiar silhouettes of the costumes, and the participation of recognizable performers, there was little to identify it as a Ninagawa production, other than it having been a clearly staged, well-acted and moving production of the play.

The *Othello* was almost optimistic when compared with the bleak Japanese-language *King Lear* that opened early in 2008. This time the king was played by Hira Mikijiro, with Yoshida Kohtaloh as Gloucester and Takahashi Yo as Edgar. It was visually comparable to the English-language version, with similar costumes and a similar stage space. The echoes of *noh* theatre appeared only in the sound design – there were no more masks or stage properties, apart from the pine tree reminiscent of *noh*'s *kagamiita* on the back wall of the playing space. This *Lear* was even further along the path towards minimalism and clarity that had begun with the English-language version at the turn of the millennium. The final scene was now staged extremely simply, with the company on their knees surrounding Lear and Cordelia, while a familiar red moon glowed above them. The red sun at the end of *Pericles* may have encouraged hope, but the nihilism of *King Lear* demanded a darker image, and so the moon glowed red instead in Ninagawa's Japanese reclamation of the play.

This *Lear* also featured the falling rocks (now stones) during the storm sequence. Ninagawa repeated and revised the effect since he could rely on his extraordinarily meticulous stage crew to drop them at the correct moments within every scene and every speech. They were nothing compared with the onslaught of items that fell from above during the most ambitious of all the Sai no Kuni Shakespeares, Ninagawa's 2010 production of *Henry VI*.

Working from Matsuoka Kazuko's translation of all three plays, Kawai Shoichiro edited them to two three-hour episodes. These opened mere weeks after Ninagawa's production of Tom Stoppard's Russian epic *The Coast of Utopia* at Bunkamura. Theatrical marathons had become something of a forte for Ninagawa since the success of *The Greeks*, and *Henry VI* brought a comparable theatrical event to Saitama.

The set design for *Henry VI* owed a debt to the 'empty space' of Brook's *A Midsummer Night's Dream*. The play was performed on the main stage of the Large Hall in Saitama's Arts Theatre, but presented as if it were in traverse. Nearly all of the action was focused on a narrow white catwalk that crossed the stage, with several rows of audience members upstage of it. The effect was reminiscent of the traverse set-up Ninagawa had used many times at the Theatre Cocoon, the difference in Saitama being that the audience was now literally sitting on the stage. Some scenes and entrances took place on an upper level behind the on-stage audience, but the majority of the action took place on the main catwalk. The space created a strong dynamic between the two doors at either side of the stage, and the various parleys and arguments between factions became as easy to follow as a sequence of tennis matches. Lily Komine's costumes were typically sumptuous, synthesizing a variety of time periods, with a careful use of colour ensuring that characters' allegiances were always clear. The cast included several of Ninagawa's most frequent collaborators – Yoshida Kohtaloh, Yokota Eiji, Sagawa Tetsuro and many others. Impressively, Otake Shinobu played both Joan of Arc and Queen Margaret, juxtaposing the two primary female characters in the trilogy.

The performance began with a group of older women in white aprons and rubber boots cleaning up the large pools of blood that lay splattered on the stage. The women arrived like professional cleaners at a hospital (or an abattoir) and worked swiftly and silently, as sirens blared in the distance. The women struggled to restore the stage to its pristine white, creating a fresh canvas for this new (Japanese) rewriting of history. After at least five minutes, just as the work seemed finished, a sound of planes overhead made the women move for shelter at either side of the stage, and large slabs of meat fell from above. To the sound of sporadic gunfire, the women quickly collected this sticky, frightening debris and cleared the stage, until a bell tolled and the funeral procession for King Henry V made its way onto the stage.

This opening gambit was remarkable – without a word, Ninagawa presented the very real, often gruesome consequences of war. He foregrounded the frequent experience of women – silenced, marginalized and left to clean up the mess. In a manner both stylized and relatable, he invited the audience to have in mind the more mundane consequences of war before the play began. This was something of a precursor to the radical inclusion of the Komadori Sisters in the 2012 *Hamlet*. It was an acknowledgement of the ordinary lived experience of Japanese people, always in the back of Ninagawa's mind while he directed these plays about England and Europe's remote past. The cleaning ladies reappeared throughout *Henry VI*, moving set pieces, removing further slabs of meat or clearing the huge quantities of red and white roses that dropped, fittingly, on the houses of Lancaster and York. There was a feeling that all of this play-acting (however spirited and well done) was only possible thanks to the resilience and indulgence of these older women. With this device Ninagawa quietly acknowledged Japan's wars during the twentieth century, allowing for the artifice of the Shakespeare trilogy to exist as a palimpsest writ large on top of his country's (and his own) real experience.

Including breaks, the entire performance lasted well over eight hours,[20] and ended with a dance celebrating the 'glorious summer' of the house of York. Performers marched happily out along all possible aisles through the audience, with the exception of Gloucester (who would become Richard III), who limped knowingly through the on-stage door – as if to indicate that he was certainly not going anywhere. Once the stage was clear, yet more of the grisly meat patties began to fall, the music turned cacophonous and the sound of guns returned as the lights faded. The falling items would have reminded perceptive audience members of the barrage of materials that fell from the sky at the start of his 1999 *Richard III*, the play that begins precisely where *Henry VI* ends, but Japanese audiences would hardly need a reminder that humans continued fighting and dying long after the demise of the houses of York and Lancaster.

Presenting *Henry VI* as a single theatrical event worked so well that Ninagawa repeated the approach for *Henry IV*. The translation was by Matsuoka Kazuko, and again the plays were edited by Kawai Shoichiro. The prologue and epilogue that frame *Henry IV Part 2* were removed completely, within an editorial approach that sought to make the two plays as cohesive as possible.

Given Bakhtin's influence on Ninagawa's interpretation of Shakespeare, it was always going to be fascinating to see how he would approach Falstaff. The Fat Knight epitomizes so much of what Bakhtin identified and explored: his grotesque body, his deliberate, carnivalesque inversion of language and society, and his exuberant laughter. Ninagawa had presented two very different versions of Shakespeare's medieval history in the Saitama productions of *Richard III* and *Henry VI*, and *Henry IV* was different again. Here there was no framing device – no falling meat, flowers or animal corpses. Henry IV (played by Kiba Katsumi) marched on with an enormous retinue, and the play began in earnest with no attempt to bridge the gap between its world and that of the audience. Instead, the second scene established how the story would unfold. In a bathetic echo of how the king had entered, Prince Hal and Falstaff ran on in the same light from the same upstage entrance. Here was an energetic young man whose only retinue, in direct contrast with his father's established court, was Falstaff. *Henry IV* is all about Prince Hal's development, and his journey from youthful dalliance to the responsibility of being King Henry V. Elegantly, the double bill ended with Hal's procession to his coronation, attended by the same retinue of knights that first entered with his father. Hal's rejection of Falstaff was cruelly absolute, and the show's final image was the old man being dragged off to prison at Lancaster's behest, in exactly the same light that introduced him several hours before. The prince had become king, and the knight could no longer be part of his narrative. In Japan, young people are shown particular indulgence before they reach the point of adulthood when they get jobs and start contributing meaningfully to society. Ninagawa's *Henry IV* dramatized this in Hal's transition to Henry, and thus the young king's rejection of Falstaff was a recognizably necessary farewell to the exuberant freedom of youth.

Falstaff was played by Yoshida Kohtaloh in one of his most impressive performances in the entire series. He brought his usual passion and commitment to the role, playing Falstaff in a fat suit that gave him substantial but not ridiculous heft. Hal was played by Matsuzaka Tori, and both actors reunited for *Henry V* in 2019. Matsuzaka reprised his role as Henry V, while Yoshida played the Chorus and directed the production.

For a non-Japanese admirer of Ninagawa's work, and particularly of his Japanese rewritings of foreign plays, the *Henry IV* might seem disappointingly un-Japanese or even traditional. As in the recent *Othello* and *King Lear*, there was no attempt to reframe the story or to devise a particularly Japanese context for it. To be disappointed in this is to overlook Ninagawa's achievement with the Sai no Kuni series. *Henry IV* was the twenty-seventh production in the series, which had developed an extraordinarily knowledgeable audience for Shakespeare in suburban Japan. There was no longer as much need for elaborate inductions or reimagined contexts, because Ninagawa's audience was now so much more familiar with the world of the plays. There was something to be celebrated in the fact that Ninagawa had reached the point of being able to present a stately, handsome production of the play without worrying that his audience would not understand it. Yoshida's Falstaff and Kiba's wonderful Henry IV were performances by actors at the height of their powers, leading a company of Ninagawa regulars who had all honed their skills across multiple productions. There were still distinctly Japanese resonances and surprises, but *Henry IV* was the kind of production that Ninagawa could only approach after several decades and countless productions that opened his audiences' minds to the world of medieval Europe.

# Romances

While Ninagawa's personal life has been very seldom discussed in connection to his work, it is significant that he, like Shakespeare, was the father of two daughters, and that in all of the so-called 'romances' – *The Tempest*, *Pericles*, *The Winter's Tale* and *Cymbeline* (all plays that reunite fathers with their daughters) – Ninagawa cast female performers. In three of these four, he cast the popular actress Tanaka Yuko as the female lead, and indeed she played the mother *and* daughter roles in *Pericles* and *The Winter's Tale*. Tanaka rose to prominence in the monumentally popular television drama *Oshin*, charting the life of a Japanese woman from the late Meiji period until the 1980s. At its peak, over 60 per cent of the population watched the show, and it has become synonymous with perseverance and forbearance. It is no accident that Ninagawa cast Tanaka as the female leads in his interpretations of the plays that deal with dogged survival and eventual redemption. Employing an actress with such a powerful emotional resonance for the Japanese public was a particularly successful instance of Ninagawa's strategy of 'calculated intimacy'. The invited assumption was that Tanaka's character – however long suffering – would surely be rewarded in the end. This was very effective for both *Pericles* and *The Winter's Tale*, whose female characters (Marina, Thaisa, Hermione and Perdita) all go through extensive trials before their families are restored. Tanaka's particular brand of stoicism brought a great dignity to these plays, a kind of cynosure throughout the sprawling narratives of both.

Ninagawa saw Sir Trevor Nunn's production of *The Winter's Tale* when it visited Japan early in his career, and it, like Brook's *Dream*, had a profound effect on how he approached Shakespeare. Although Ninagawa tried to outdo the latter production with his own white-clad acrobatic fantasy in the 1990s, it was not until 2009 that he approached *The Winter's Tale*. Ninagawa staged the piece as a European fairy tale, depicted in comparatively bright primary colours – red for Sicily and blue for Bohemia. The play took place on an almost bare stage, a formal space walled only with massive recreations of classical Roman frescoes in the contrasting colours of the two locations. As in *The Taming of the Shrew*, set design elements were very minimal, again allowing for all focus to remain on the actors.

Ninagawa bookended the performance with a charming – if anachronistic – image of paper aeroplanes in flight, symbolizing the lost innocence of the friendship between Leontes and Polixenes. The men first appeared on stage chasing planes with Leontes' young son while Hermione looked on, and the final image of the production was of two planes circling above the empty stage to the sound of a young boy's laughter. The planes gave an immediate sense of the boys the two kings used to be, and whenever the action switched between their kingdoms, one of them entered holding a paper plane. There was no introduction. The play itself begins with a conversation between a Sicilian and a Bohemian, establishing the relationship between the two locations, and Ninagawa did not add to it.

The Bohemia scenes gave Ninagawa an opportunity for the kind of carnival, peasant celebration he had always enjoyed. The Shepherd, his Clown son and Autolycus were played by some of Ninagawa's favourite comic actors, and their scenes were filled with bodies, dancing and noise. This contrasted sharply with Ninagawa's monochromatic, oppressive Sicily, where only Paulina seemed capable of speaking out against the miserable vice-like grip of Karasawa Toshiaki's Leontes. Perhaps as a sign of hope for the future (and matching the colour of the paper planes), the young lovers Perdita and Florizel were dressed in white when they came to Bohemia, as was Hermione when she was 'resurrected'. As in *Pericles*, Ninagawa employed some careful staging and judicious lighting to manage Tanaka's switch from Perdita to Hermione for the play's conclusion. The production's very broad pictorial strokes and calculated casting made for a charming but rather austere reading of the play. Those who might have hoped for a spectacular Ninagawa response to the challenge of staging the bear that pursues Antigonus were disappointed – the famous attack was depicted with sound alone. The one significant theatrical stunt was Ninagawa's interpretation of the interlude performed by Time. This was performed by a masked actor in a nod to Chinese *bian lian* or face-changing, wherein the performer rapidly replaces a set of masks in quick succession. Ninagawa's Time moved through seven stages of a human life, each presented by a different mask, indebted as much to Jacques in *As You Like It* as to *The Winter's Tale*. As an anachronistic nod both to Japanese history and his own visual metaphor of the paper planes, the sound of a real plane flying overhead was played as the scene shifted back to Bohemia, several years later, where an earnest Polixenes (the excellent Yokota Eiji) flew yet another paper plane, evidently still hoping for reconciliation with Leontes.

While *The Winter's Tale* was presented rather generally as a fairy tale, with very few Japanese visual references, Ninagawa's last romance, *Cymbeline*, was substantially more specific. Staged in the aftermath of the devastating tsunami in March 2011, he turned the play into another parable of reunion and hope. *Cymbeline* is no more familiar to a Japanese audience than a production of the *kabuki* play *Yoshitsune Senbon Zakura* would be in London. Both plays have stories set in the distant past, and feature dead brothers, severed heads and divine intervention, but have not quite reached the level of global recognition of, say, *Hamlet* or *The Tale of Genji*. The production featured many of Ninagawa's favourite devices and approaches, the better to help his local audience access the story. *Cymbeline* has an unusual variety of theatrical demands – depictions of ancient Britain and Rome, battles, decapitated bodies, improbable reunions and even a *deus ex machina*. Ninagawa chose not to present it as a fairy tale, as he had *The Winter's Tale*, or even as a folk story, as he had *Pericles*. This was presented as a theatrical performance, featuring the most elaborate iteration to date of his pre-show introduction. Once again, Ninagawa acknowledged the sense of 'shame' he felt at presenting such foreign material, stating in the programme that 'Whenever I direct a Shakespeare, I always feel a small sense of shame. What occasions this emotion? I believe it is attributable to a recurring worry and fear: do I really understand a culture that is so very different from my own?' (Ninagawa, 2012).

The full company was visible as the audience entered, at mirrored dressing-room tables on the stage. At showtime, the company lined up and bowed to the audience, whipping off their contemporary clothes to reveal their actual costumes underneath. Thereafter the dressing-room set-up was broken apart and wheeled off, fading into the shifting darkness of the play. With a knowing wink, Ninagawa hinted that, yes, this was as ever a Japanese company performing a Shakespeare play, but there were still a few theatrical surprises in store. Nakagoshi's set featured images from ink-paintings and illustrations of *The Tale of Genji* that seemed to shimmer and hover in the darkness while the painted set pieces were moved and rearranged. The illusion was so delicate that it appeared as though it must have been projected, but it was in fact a carefully choreographed piece of live stage management.

Otake Shinobu starred as Innogen. Matsuoka's new translation insisted on using the modern revision of the name – a valid choice in its own right, but all the more necessary here because 'imo' is the Japanese word for potato, and would not have sounded good to Japanese ears. Innogen's time spent dressed as the boy Fidele might have suggested the play as a suitable candidate for an all-male production, but the play's sprawling story and unusual demands on an audience's credulity led to a more 'traditional' approach. As Posthumus, Ninagawa cast Abe Hiroshi, previously seen in *Suicide for Love*, *Dogen's Adventures* and in *The Coast of Utopia*, all at Bunkamura. Abe is a major film and television star in Japan, and his involvement was a coup for the series.

The company featured a strong cohort of Ninagawa regulars, with Yoshida Kohtaloh as Cymbeline, Sagawa Tetsuro as Belarius and Katsumura Masanobu as Cloten. As Saitama audiences became familiar with Shakespearean drama and began to recognize how the plays were structured, Ninagawa capitalized increasingly on this familiarity. Just as Shakespeare had written roles with the talents of individual actors in mind, the Sai no Kuni series cast several actors repeatedly in similar roles. The aforementioned contributions of Tsukikawa Yuki are an obvious example, as are those of Sagawa Tetsuro, who frequently gave great life to characters such as Belarius, Autolycus, Leonato and Duncan. As the series progressed, Ninagawa could rely on calculated intimacies not just from an actor's work elsewhere, but now even from within his earlier productions. In *Cymbeline*, the villain Iachimo was a direct descendant of Aaron in *Titus Andronicus* – comparably dressed, comparably malignant and comparably subversive. While Kubozuka Yosuke played Iachimo's malice for real, Ninagawa encouraged Katsumura Masanobu towards a more comic reading of Cloten, playing significantly more into the ridiculous than the outright evil elements of his character. Katsumura's Cloten mocked himself, his world and even the conventions of the production; while other characters had doors paged as they approached them to exit, he was often left on the stage, hilariously waiting for an opening to appear in the smooth walls of the set. His performance was so good that it led to a rare instance of this objectionable character being missed once he had his head cut off.

An alternating red and blue moon had featured prominently in *NINAGAWA Macbeth*, and an updated version appeared in *Cymbeline*, this time much larger and better defined. As in *Macbeth*, it hovered menacingly over fights and battle scenes, symbolizing a world out of joint. Ninagawa also employed his other long-running experimental technique of slow motion, again for the battle scenes but also for the final moments of the play. After the various emotional reunions, the entire company made their way upstage into the light. The moon was gone, and the only scenic element to remain was a large pine tree. The pine that appeared at the end of *Pericles* had been a painted one, reminiscent of a symbolic Japan. In *Cymbeline* the featured tree was not just realistic, but a depiction of a very specific tree, the 'Kashima single pine tree'. In the aftermath of the 2011 earthquake and tsunami, a forest stretching about 3 kilometres along the coast was completely washed away, with the exception of this one tree. It became a symbol of resilience and hope for the local communities as they rebuilt their lives in the aftermath of the disaster, and Ninagawa used the image very memorably. Ninagawa wrote an almost apologetic programme note to explain that he changed the words of the play, replacing 'cedar' with 'pine' as the stately tree under whose branches the play ends. This was hardly an egregious edit, even for a director so committed to keeping the plays intact, but it made for a particularly moving ending.

*Cymbeline* employed almost all of Ninagawa's most recognizable techniques and interpretative choices, chief among them the casting of several star performers, a theatrical framing device and the use of slow motion and dramatic sound effects. Apart from the pine tree, there was very little expressly Japanese imagery in the show, with the exception of

**FIGURE 5** Cymbeline *(2012): the replica of the Kashima single pine tree. Photo by Robbie Jack/Corbis via Getty Images.*

Act 1, Scene 4, set in Philario's house in 'Rome'. Here the design jumbled a startling variety of Japanese and Roman images. The walls were decorated with scenes from *The Tale of Genji*, while this Roman space was dominated by the large statue of Romulus and Remus suckling the wolf. Philario's kimono-clad guests sat on the floor amid lanterns and cushions, and Iachimo smoked a Japanese pipe. 'Rome' had already been memorably presented in the Sai no Kuni productions of *Titus* and *Coriolanus*, and here appeared in a happy conflation of countries and time periods. Ninagawa was far from finished with the statue of the suckling wolf, which reappeared soon afterwards in *Antony and Cleopatra*.

# Roman plays II

Among Shakespeare's female characters, Cleopatra is one of the most difficult to cast, since even from the stage she laments a future in which she might be played by 'squeaking' boys. Finding an actress who might embody her 'infinite variety' and her exotic foreignness *and* deliver three hours of eloquent Shakespeare in Japanese was no small feat. The role went to an ethnically Korean Takarazuka *otokoyaku* called Aran Kei, capitalizing on her popularity, stage presence and beauty. In stark contrast, Cleopatra's eunuch Mardian was played with simpering femininity by Okada Tadashi. Aran's queen, drawing on all of her Takarazuka tricks and training to present a Cleopatra with rather masculine manners, was constantly aware of how she presented herself and her gender.[21] Her Antony was Yoshida Kohtaloh, great veteran of the Shakespeare series.

Intriguingly, *Antony and Cleopatra* began with the opening of a *kabuki* curtain, in the traditional colours of black, green and brown, emblazoned with a portrait of Shakespeare. It opened to a mix of contemporary music and *ki* clappers (the sound design mirroring the curtain's blend of Japanese and foreign) and revealed another white box set, this time filled with statues from ancient Rome and Egypt. The company emerged from behind them and bowed to the audience, and then the actors and the scenic elements all moved smoothly into the darkness and the play began. If audiences had expectations of any *kabuki* influence within the production, they were disappointed; the curtain and the recognizable sound effects punctuating key dramatic moments, and a blue cloth used to indicate the seashore, were the only elements that appeared to have been derived from traditional theatre. This was more of a combination of ancient and modern, best exemplified in the use of lotus blossoms throughout Cleopatra's early Egyptian scenes. An essential symbol of ancient Egyptian iconography, it was also a conveniently familiar image in Ninagawa's theatrical vocabulary.

The Korean academic Im Yeeyon has frequently suggested that Ninagawa's theatrical approach was as Victorian as it was avant-garde, making particular reference to his proclivity for sentiment, spectacle and pageantry (Im, 2004). *Antony and Cleopatra* corroborated this reading, swirling as it did through a dizzying array of locations and set pieces. As in *The Comedy of Errors* and its evocation of Ephesus, this show presented a multitude of versions of 'Egypt' – contemporary, Shakespearean and ancient.

*Antony and Cleopatra* was the first Ninagawa production to perform in Korea, after several years of negotiations and planning.[22] In a perceptive review of the Seoul performance, Im lamented the lack of political engagement, wondering whether the production might have been stronger if Ninagawa made more reference to Aran's Korean heritage. There was certainly an opportunity to interrogate the relationship between Japan and Korea, although Ninagawa avoided any overt political allusions, instead framing the performance as another version of the story of *Romeo and Juliet*. But, as Im writes, 'it never seemed to occur to Ninagawa that the political situation between Rome and Egypt may remind Koreans of their colonial past under Japanese rule, and thus, by casting

Aran as Cleopatra, he is risking an analogy in the mind of the audience: an Egyptian queen proudly displayed as Roman booty' (Im, 2012: 465).

The Korean presentation of this Japanese Shakespeare indicates an entirely different kind of intercultural negotiation – crucially, one that does not happen via English. Presentations of Ninagawa's work in Singapore and Malaysia happened more frequently towards the end of his career, but these could at least rely on some audience knowledge of the English language originals of the plays he presented. In Korea and in Taiwan there was no such filter, and so a new kind of intra-Asian reception of Shakespeare (or Inoue, or Murakami) began to develop.

Ninagawa's final foray into the world of ancient Rome was in *Julius Caesar*, presented in late 2014. This monumental production was a summation of everything that had been learned and achieved throughout the Sai no Kuni Shakespeare Series. As he celebrated forty years of working with Shakespeare, Ninagawa could afford a little retrospection in this production, the last of the major tragedies.

*Julius Caesar* was performed on another enormous set of steps. Nakagoshi, the designer, gave this spatial arrangement a new depth by adding a second set of steps leading up from behind. This allowed for a variety of dramatic entrances, particularly during the battle scenes within the play's final acts. For one final production, the impressive sculpture of the suckling she-wolf was given pride of place atop these steps, once again highlighting the martial, kill-or-be-killed energy of Ninagawa's Rome. As they had in productions from *Hearty but Flippant* to *Coriolanus*, the steps acted as a barometer for power and status within the play.

*Julius Caesar* is a sufficiently famous figure that the story of his assassination required little cultural translation. Unlike *Coriolanus*, which Ninagawa had transported to a substantially more Asian setting, or even the Rome of *Cymbeline* that conflated Japanese and European imagery, this Roman tragedy took place without much explicit evocation of the ancient city.

In Brutus' garden, the sculptures were exclusively European (leftovers, perhaps, from Leonato's house in *Much Ado About Nothing*). These did not convey the masculine, military energy imparted by the *nio* sculptures in *NINAGAWA Macbeth* and *Coriolanus*. Despite the story's fame, this was still a thoroughly Japanese production, and Matsuoka's limpid, accessible translation was very clear. She even elided the play's most famous Latin line ('et tu, Brute?') in favour of a completely Japanese rendition.

*Julius Caesar* was the final collaboration between Ninagawa and costume designer Lily Komine, who created a new update of the kinds of robes and armour that had become the signature silhouette of their work together. For *Titus Andronicus* the costumes had been predominantly white and for *Coriolanus* they were black. In *Julius Caesar* the men's robes were mostly white and red, while different colours of metal clearly denoted the armour of opposing factions.

Ninagawa chose many of his favourite actors for the lead roles – Fujiwara Tatsuya as Antony, Yoshida Kohtaloh as Cassius and Yokota Eiji as Julius Caesar. In an amusing professional coincidence, Abe Hiroshi had recently starred in the sequel to *Thermae Romae*, based on a witty manga in which an ancient Roman architect travels in time and brings Japanese bathing innovations to Hadrian's Rome. It was a funny coincidence that Ninagawa cast Abe, Japan's most famous 'Roman' as Brutus, 'the noblest Roman of them all'. Abe had already appeared in Ninagawa productions of various kinds, and the loose connection to the hit films was a convenient, if unplanned, bonus.

Fujiwara performed with blond hair and a beard as Antony, symbolizing the character's upstart youth. During the several decades since Ninagawa's first efforts to make Shakespeare look less like slavish *shingeki* imitations of European theatre, Japanese fashion changed radically. Nowadays young people with black (undyed) hair can sometimes feel like the exception rather than the rule. Fujiwara had previously bleached his hair for his first performance as Toshinori in the *Modern Noh Plays*, evoking the convention of manga characters with supernatural abilities or who have been exposed to terrible violence. In *Julius Caesar*, it was more an acknowledgement of Antony's 'golden boy' status than any return to *shingeki* or manga.

After the surprising efficacy of Yoshida Kohtaloh's bisexual Don Pedro in *Much Ado About Nothing*, Ninagawa did not shy away from the frequently inferred homoerotic undertones between Cassius and Brutus. Yoshida was a passionate but amusing Cassius; part political firebrand and part clingy admirer to Abe's Brutus. Abe is a supermodel in Japan, and so the admittedly one-way attraction was understandable, eliciting sympathetic laughter from the mostly female audience.

The production began with yet another variation of Ninagawa's induction. Here the full company gathered on stage in costumes more reminiscent of the early twentieth century than ancient Rome. It could have been a snapshot of the 'slag-heap' world of the Saitama in which Ninagawa grew up, or indeed of the morning in October 1960 when the Japanese politician Asanuma Inejiro was assassinated with a sword during a political debate. As a gong sounded, the company bowed to the audience before whipping off their coats and hats, revealing the brighter Roman robes underneath. Echoing his earlier, more political work, Ninagawa staged the opening scene as a play for status between the plebeians and the aristocracy. As the tribunes browbeat the celebrating commoners, the latter were inched slowly off the stage, relegated to the three low steps that connected the stage and the auditorium before they were finally sent home. The play's interrogation of tyranny and leadership was made remarkably clear on Nakagoshi's stepped set. Ninagawa's talent for the arrangement of bodies in space was a skill honed over several decades, put to superb use in the presentation of this play's shifting alliances.

Unlike *Titus Andronicus*, the Rome of *Julius Caesar* ran red with realistic blood. The assassination scene was dutifully grisly, and the conspirators got blood on their pristine white robes, which provided a very clear canvas for these spatters and stains. The battle scenes were particularly violent and featured a memorable entrance for Cassius with an arrow stuck in his face. The fight sequences in *Julius Caesar* were less stylized than other productions and moved at a faster pace. Gone were the adaptation of *kabuki*'s *tachimawari*, and Ninagawa's slow motion, in favour of a more dynamically choreographed series of fights.

*Thermae Romae*'s bathing parallel notwithstanding, a major similarity between the cultures of ancient Rome and historical Japan was an understanding of and even a respect for honourable suicide. *Julius Caesar* acknowledges this 'antique Roman' trait more than any other Shakespeare play. Significantly, Ninagawa staged all of the play's deaths in the manner suggested by the Shakespeare text, without any attempt to echo more traditionally Japanese forms of suicide such as *seppuku*. The production deliberately avoided any Japanese elements in the design or presentation, so it would have been unseemly or indulgent to try to force any suicide parallels so late in the play. Another enormous red moon shone over the final scenes, echoing *Macbeth* and the inevitability of death for all warriors. Finally, as Antony mourned Brutus' suicide, the moon again turned blue to denote the end of the hero's life.

## *Measure for Measure*

After *Julius Caesar*, Ninagawa directed his eighth *Hamlet* and a revival of *NINAGAWA Macbeth*, both programmed in honour of his eightieth birthday. In their respective ways, *Julius Caesar* and *Hamlet* each represented some of the greatest features of Ninagawa's work, and reviving *Macbeth* was an attempt to revisit his early masterpiece to see whether it still held its own.

The last of the Sai no Kuni Shakespeare series to be directed by Ninagawa was a production of *Measure for Measure*, which opened two weeks after the director's death in May 2016. The production was supervised by Ninagawa's excellent long-time associate Inoue Shonsho, since Ninagawa's own health was in serious decline. It featured a variety of recognizable choices – first among them sight of the entire company warming up and dressing on stage before bowing to the audience as the play began.

Ninagawa's death cast a pall over the proceedings, and the production design was itself rather sombre. The sumptuous robes – a hallmark of so many of Ninagawa's Shakespearean courts and communities – were black rather than red, and the overall look was significantly gloomier than any other Shakespeare comedy in the series. Despite *Measure for Measure*'s designation as a 'problem' play, Ninagawa's interpretation focused primarily on its comic aspects. Continuing the trend of incorporating European paintings into the scenic design, already seen in *The Winter's Tale* and *The Taming of the Shrew*, Nakagoshi's backdrop featured Giotto's *Seven Vices*, from the Capella Scrovegni in Padua. They are Desperation, Envy, Infidelity, Injustice, Wrath, Inconstancy and Foolishness. These monumental, elegant depictions of medieval vice provided a fascinating backdrop for a play so deeply concerned with the difference between idealistic and practical morality. At different moments, different vices were highlighted, with injustice dominant throughout. After the scenes of forgiveness and redemption that end the play, the Giotto images were removed to reveal a bright blue sky.

In keeping with the mood suggested by the Giotto reproductions, the Vienna of this production looked distinctly Christian. Processions of monks and nuns filed through various scenes, quietly insisting on the city's heavily religious character and contrasting with Mistress Overdone's community of male and female prostitutes. In a world so filled with adult sexuality, Isabella's zealous chastity appeared simultaneously heroic and naïve. At her first entrance she released a (mechanical) dove, a curious image for a young woman training to be a nun. The image was repeated in a coda added to the end of the play, this time symbolizing her own release from the strictures of her earlier choices. Tabe Mikako's baby face and cream-coloured costume set her Isabella in stark contrast to the rest of the characters, and Ninagawa's version turned the narrative into her journey from zealous teenager into a more worldly adult woman.

*Measure for Measure* had a variety of features that a Saitama audience might expect from a Ninagawa Shakespeare – actors recognizable from film and television (and previous productions), entrances and exits through the audience, percussive sound effects, an impressive design, lavish costumes and spirited acting. In this final production, Ninagawa even managed to include a joke at the expense of his signature slow-motion technique. During the early court scene, he had several actors move in and out of it, for once even *speaking* in slow motion, and joking about how poorly they did so. Inspired by Bakthin to the last, Ninagawa's production was a very human comedy, insisting on the truth that human nature will always compromise zealously held beliefs – both positive and negative. Throughout, he poked fun at anything too serious – religion, chastity, death and even himself. After the emotional scenes of forgiveness (and acceptance) that conclude the play, Isabella's coda had a feeling of a spirit released – as much Ninagawa's as the heroine's.

The Sai no Kuni Shakespeare Series has turned Saitama into a major hub of Shakespearean interpretation, with a committed local audience and a global reach, thanks to the extraordinary ambition of its artists, its steering committee and its visionary director. Ninagawa's commitment to his Saitama audience was understandable. The theatre is in Yonohonmachi, where Ninagawa grew up, and the project gave him the opportunity to bring world-class Shakespeare productions to his hometown, telling these stories to his own people. The thirty Shakespeare productions were only a part of Ninagawa's contribution to Saitama's cultural life; he was also passionately committed to the two acting companies he developed and participated in a vigorous programme of talks and outreach events. By the time of Ninagawa's death, the Sai no Kuni series had presented all but five of the thirty-seven canonical Shakespeare plays. In 2017 it was announced that Yoshida Kohtaloh would take over as artistic director, and he directed and starred in all five outstanding Shakespeare plays. He began with *Timon of Athens* and *Henry V*, but the final performances of *Henry VIII* and the entire run of *King John* were cancelled because of the coronavirus pandemic. Rather fittingly, the series concluded in May 2021 with *All's Well That Ends Well*.

# 5

# Conclusion

The last time I spoke with Ninagawa was in the summer of 2009, soon after his latest production of Shimizu Kunio's *In That Rainy Summer, Thirty Juliets Came Back*. The play was revived to celebrate the twentieth anniversary of Bunkamura and also marked forty years since his first collaboration with Shimizu. He asked if I had finished 'the book' – my study of his work – and joked that maybe I should wait until he finished the Saitama Shakespeare series. I chose to do so, although he died before it was complete. During the same brief conversation, I asked him what he felt might be the most important thing to consider as an overall theme or approach in his work. He acknowledged that this was a difficult question, but having thought about it, he suggested that memory was critical. His own memory? Japanese people's collective memory? The idea of memory? I tried to get a more concrete response. He smiled and said, 'Yes. All of them.'

In an excellent 1995 interview between Ninagawa, producer Nakane Tadao, translator Matsuoka Kazuko and others, there is an extended discussion of memory and its central place in Ninagawa's approach to his work. Collective memory emerges as a key point, and in particular its evocation via familiar Japanese images. Ninagawa insisted that his response to the past was not academic or intellectual, so much as that of 'just an ordinary human being'. The desire was always to create work that was accessible, and the manipulation and representation of collective memories was a tried and tested means of bridging the gap between audience and (foreign) text. Ninagawa's continued interest in memory echoes Jean Jacques Roubine's discussion of postmodernism from as far back as the 1990 book *The Dramatic Touch of Difference* – 'postmodernism looks for the future through past and foreign experiments, and for novelty through memory' (Roubine, 1990: 73). As Matsuoka elegantly described it, Ninagawa's work cross-fertilizes the past with the present (Ninagawa, 1995: 217).

Elsewhere in the 1995 interview, Ninagawa described a zeal to put *everything* on the stage, in his desire 'to reflect life!'. Just as *NINAGAWA Macbeth* was a kind of requiem for the lost idealism of the 1960s, and *The Tempest* was a response to his own midlife crisis, he approached his 2015 *Richard II* as a play about ageing and power. Its opening image featured an entire phalanx of elderly actors (the company of his Saitama Gold Theatre) wheeling onto the stage en masse as the English court. Ninagawa's weakening health confined him to a wheelchair in the final stages of his life, and on good days he found the limitation fascinating, seeing it as a new skill that had to be learned. He again reflected his own condition in the extraordinary scene of these wheelchair-bound elders of Richard's court. *Richard II* was a co-production between the Gold Theatre and Saitama Next Theatre, a collaboration of some sixty actors, old and young. Even more startling than the noisy entrance of the elderly in their wheelchairs, all dressed in formal kimono, was the sequence that followed. The senior citizens left their wheelchairs and performed a tango. Old danced with young, male with female, Gold with Next, with the exception of Richard himself, who danced with Aumerle in an intimation of the power struggles ahead. The tango had been a music of great nostalgia in Ninagawa productions stretching back several decades. He used it in plays from *Shitaya Mannencho Monogatari* to *Doctor Faustus*, and it had been central to Shimizu's poetic *Tango at the End of Winter*. In *Richard II* it became a metaphor for the passage of time – its rhythms moved young and old, weak and strong, and at the very end of the production the dance was repeated, pointing to the cyclical natures of time and history.

*Richard II* was an extraordinary late-career achievement for Ninagawa. It featured echoes of previous productions in the kabuki-inspired wave-cloths that engulfed Richard as he returned from Ireland, and in the intersecting beams of light that formed the cross within which he was executed.[1] The production was staged in yet another new configuration of the main hall of the Saitama Arts Theatre, demonstrating Ninagawa's determination to continue finding new ways to present Shakespeare. It was presented at the Craiova Shakespeare Festival in April 2016 and was thus the last production to open before he died.

Throughout his career, Ninagawa courted nostalgia by marking anniversaries and landmark birthdays. This awareness of the passage of time – a kind of living in the present while acknowledging the past – was central not just to how his work was programmed but how his stories were told. His productions vibrated with memories, but were always contemporary, always experimenting with new approaches and ideas. His eight productions of *Hamlet* demonstrate his restless imagination, determined always to try again, or in the oft-cited Beckett phrase, 'fail better'. The sentiment behind the naming of his first company – the Contemporary People's Theatre – resonated throughout his career; it was always for contemporary Japanese people. Of course, three decades of international touring also indicate a desire to communicate with other audiences.

# Foreign readers

A kind of inconsistency plagues much of the existing English-language academic work on Ninagawa's output. Many articles are filled with errors, mistranslations and fanciful suggestions of tours or productions that never even happened.[2] Essays by close collaborators such as Matsuoka Kazuko and Kawai Shoichiro have appeared in various publications; these provide more reliable commentary on Ninagawa's work. Early responses to his output were generally enthusiastic about his interpretations of foreign classics, but a determined insistence that his work was pandering exclusively to global performance markets dominates much of the bibliography. Ninagawa was certainly a major figure on the world stage, but his home audience always came first.

One of the best-informed articles on Ninagawa was also the most critical. Kishi Tetsuo's 'Japanese Shakespeare and English Reviewers' (Sasayama et al., 1998) interrogated several reviews of Ninagawa's productions in the British press. By no means a fan of Ninagawa, Kishi at least understood the director's work from a Japanese perspective and offered a passionate rebuttal of the often extravagant praise for Ninagawa's productions by English critics, who, Kishi claimed, praised his work because they did not understand what they were watching. Foreign critics went to great lengths to discuss, for example, the 'spectacular' *noh* effects Ninagawa employed (Kishi, 1998: 112). *Noh* is famous for its austere refinement and artistic economy, and while Ninagawa's theatre was undoubtedly spectacular, its visual splendour certainly did not come from *noh*. Kishi articulates some of the major issues and vulnerabilities of interpreting Ninagawa's work outside Japan:

> What they do not seem to realise is that their criticism of Ninagawa is actually a reflection on themselves. [...] One is never free from the danger of showing oneself as essentially vulnerable even when one responds most positively. (Kishi, 1998: 123)

What particular orientalist compulsion made reviewers praise the versions they couldn't understand, and then turn sneeringly on [nearly every] English production, is left unstated, but Kishi and Bradshaw are alert to the ways in which Japanese cultural productions for an international audience occupy a mobius strip of prejudice and national stereotypes, shaped by Japanese assumptions of Western assumptions of what is authentically 'Japanese'. (Smith, 2006: 370–1)

## Other readings

Three of the most constructive recent pieces on Ninagawa's work, by Huang (2013), Im (2004) and Hamana (2017), present imaginative alternative ways to interpret Ninagawa's work. Huang's extended survey of Ninagawa's career in the Arden *Great Shakespeareans* is a helpful contribution, locating Ninagawa's work in the context of Japanese theatre history. Im has written several nuanced articles about Ninagawa's productions, including a very balanced discussion of 'The Pitfalls of Intercultural Discourse'. Her contention has frequently been that Ninagawa's work is best analysed for its Victorian affinities: 'traditional interpretations, love of spectacles (including the exotic and the Oriental), emphasis on star-performers and populist commercialism' (Im, 2004: 7–8). Although these affinities are clearly recognizable throughout Ninagawa's work, there is an irony to her suggestion that Ninagawa's spirit is Victorian, given the fraught relations between Victorian England and nineteenth-century Japan. For all that, it was also the period in which appropriation of Japanese culture became intensely fashionable overseas at precisely the same time as Japanese people were first becoming aware of Shakespeare. While it would be reductive to suggest that Ninagawa was no different from showmen who pre-dated him by a century, the analogy is helpful at least in its delineation of his major trademarks. Her conclusion is also particularly helpful with regard to the intercultural – or Orientalist – concerns regarding Ninagawa's work:

> The disturbance Ninagawa's productions have caused among Shakespeareans should be ascribed, not simply to his superficial Orientalism, but to the Victorian qualities of his

theatre, which are at odds with current 'post-' discourses. The critiques of Ninagawa's intercultural theatre have focused on its Orientalism, justly if perhaps too much, to eclipse the possibility for alternative criticisms. What Kishi wrote of English reviewers may be equally true of postcolonial criticism: the power of Orientalist discourse can cloud other equally interesting aspects of Ninagawa's intercultural theatre. (Im, 2004: 27–8)

Writing about Ninagawa's final Shakespeare productions, Hamana Emi takes as her interpretive lens the work of Stephen Greenblatt, citing his 1991 study *Marvellous Possessions: The Wonder of the New World*. Beautifully, she reframes Greenblatt's seminal definition of wonder in terms of how Ninagawa brought Shakespeare to his Japanese audience: 'Wonder – thrilling, potentially dangerous, momentarily immobilizing, charged at once with desire, ignorance and fear – is the quintessential human response to what Descartes calls a "first encounter"' (Greenblatt, 1991: 20). Hamana's excellent paper uses this quotation alone and does not further discuss the implications of the traffic between cultures at the heart of Greenblatt's book. This is perhaps a missed opportunity, since both journeys inherent in Ninagawa's work – bringing Shakespeare to Japanese audiences in a thoroughly new manner and bringing Japanese performances to other cultures – represent contemporary possibilities for the kind of 'wonder' Greenblatt articulates. Hamana's identification of the idea is still a fitting acknowledgement of the manner in which Ninagawa worked to provide arresting, unforgettable intercultural 'first encounters' with Shakespeare for Japanese spectators.

# Postmodern 'double functioning'

The film director Pedro Almodóvar 'views contemporary Spanish culture as an amalgam of conflicting influences which melt together' (Chin, 1991: 94). Almodóvar's is very much a

Spanish cinema, combining 'conflicting influences' to portray the exuberant multiplicities of contemporary Spanish life. Ninagawa's extended, eclectic use of signifiers from multiple aspects of *Japanese* cultural life suggest a similarity with the Spanish director:

> Almodóvar's signature ... is the synthesis of the melodramatic mode with a clash of quotations. This combination allows Almodóvar both a quasi-classical Hollywood narrative structure (which facilitates audience identification) and a very self-conscious narration (which normally produces a sense of alienation) ... Almodóvar drills a heart into the postmodern and fills it with an operatic range of feeling. (Arroyo, 1998: 493)

Arroyo could equally be discussing Ninagawa. His actors' passionate performances could easily be considered 'melodramatic', and while his strict adherence to the original text and his established commercial position might undermine his classification as a 'postmodern' theatre practitioner, his 'clash of quotations' and the method of interpretation this demands indicate that Ninagawa's was a theatre for a 'postmodern' audience.

Ninagawa personally enjoyed films far more than theatrical performances, and while he never formally studied directing he learned much from the cinema (Ninagawa, 1993: 11). Having started his career with late-night performances in an actual cinema, an affinity for end-on pictorial presentations persisted throughout his career. Although several of the Sai no Kuni Shakespeares were presented in unusual and creative configurations in the smaller spaces in Saitama, the majority of Ninagawa's works were directed for end-on theatrical configurations. Reading Ninagawa's productions as one might parse a film – in that they present a complete stage picture, utilizing multiple frames of reference, carefully constructed imagery and juxtaposing images to create an intertextual 'montage' – makes their novelty significantly clearer. Pearson's definition of 'postmodern' is helpful:

> Postmodern: a term used to describe many aspects of contemporary cultural production of the 1980s and 1990s. Among its many characteristics are an eclectic borrowing from earlier styles, an emphasis on stylish surface appearances rather than social realism or psychological depth, and a blurring of the dividing line between cultural forms, products and tastes, such as the division between 'high culture' and 'popular culture'. (Pearson and Simpson, 2001: 463)

Postmodernism has several other characteristics, but those listed for Pearson's definition of postmodern *film* are nearly all recognizable characteristics of Ninagawa's theatre. The finely woven webs of intertextuality, and aesthetic strategies such as synecdoche and bricolage (in Ninagawa's combinations of different elements of Japanese traditional theatre and cultural life) combine to form a densely polysemic, exuberantly eclectic art form. The more abrasive of Ninagawa's critics might argue that there was a focus more on 'stylish surface appearances' than on psychological depth, but this would do a disservice to the sophistication of Ninagawa's collaborations with some of Japan's finest actors.

Ninagawa's oeuvre may not exemplify the standard notion of what constitutes postmodern *theatre*, but its process of creation in the mind of both the director and the spectator (an equally important 'creator') is typical of postmodern art. Discussing interculturalism and postmodernism, Chin goes as far as discussing postmodern architecture, and his quotation from Robert Venturi is helpful:

> I like elements which are hybrid rather than 'pure', compromising rather than 'clean', distorted rather than 'straightforward', ambiguous rather than 'articulated', perverse as well as impersonal, boring as well as 'interesting', conventional rather than designed, accommodating rather than excluding, redundant rather than simple, vestigial as

well as innovating, inconsistent and equivocal rather than direct and clear. Venturi's theoretical proclamation of a postmodern ambition in architecture was defined through 'double-functioning'. (Chin, 1991: 84)

Similarly, Ninagawa recognized the 'double-functioning' capacities of his theatre in the eyes of his postmodern audiences, who could simultaneously digest the story of a foreign play by Shakespeare and enrich their experience by identifying the multiple intertextual references with which Ninagawa imbued it. He was determined to make Shakespeare accessible and enjoyable for *all* people:

Unfortunately, many people in Japan view Shakespeare as something that comes from an advanced culture to an inferior culture. The attitude is that they teach us – in a patronising way. In fact, I don't see it that way. I do Shakespeare because he is good. My aim, therefore, is to *degrade* Shakespeare in a sense; to emphasise that in fact he's for *all* classes of people both high and low. That is why I put Japanese pop music in these plays. It's for those University of Tokyo professors, to show them that Shakespeare is not only for academia. (Ninagawa, 1998a: 41–2)

While Ninagawa's 'recontextualizing' theatrical translations fulfilled somewhat the criteria of 'intercultural' theatre, his intended audience was unlikely to consider them thus. Rather, the *intra*cultural Japanese references operated at a more intertextual level, and ultimate meaning was produced in the mind of the spectator, whom Ubersfeld designated 'king of the feast'. *Richard II* was an illuminating example of Ninagawa's vibrant theatricality and his ability to make foreign plays relevant to his audience while simultaneously commenting on the society in which he lived and worked. The *Richard II*, a beautiful examination of power and time suffused with Ninagawa's personal experience of growing old, was '"double voiced," "double accented" and "double languaged," presenting "the collision between differing points of view on the world"' (Bhabha, 1998: 33–4).

Ninagawa's directorial process was something like a theatrical equivalent to Bakhtin's analysis of Rabelais' language, which

> contains mixed within it two utterances, two speech manners, two styles, two 'languages,' two semantic and axiological belief systems. We repeat, there is no formal – compositional and syntactic – boundary between these utterances, within the limits of a single syntactic whole, often within the limits of a single sentence. It frequently happens that even one and the same word will belong simultaneously to two languages, two belief systems that intersect in a hybrid construction – and, consequently, the word has two contradictory meanings, two accents. (Bakhtin, 1981: 39)

In 'The Third Meaning' (1977), Barthes proposed that alongside the informational and symbolic levels of communication, there exists a 'third meaning' created by the individual spectator. This is an elegant identification of what could be considered the *result* of Ninagawa's 'double-functioning', 'double-languaged' theatre: a complicated, personal meaning created in the individual imagination. Barthes formulated it as a response to his study of film montage, but the idea of this 'third meaning' is also applicable to Ninagawa's work. Without it, the quality of his productions was not diminished, but the particular richness of the viewing experience was severely reduced.

Ninagawa's 'single syntactic whole', a theatre that was consistently imaginative, evocative and rich, vibrating with the energy of two languages – Shakespeare and Japanese – was remarkable. There was such a breadth of imagination in his work that it could simultaneously be described as intercultural or intertextual, global or local, Victorian or postmodern, cinematic or immediate, nostalgic or contemporary. His visual poetry, attention to detail and narrative clarity meant that his productions could be understood even by non-Japanese audiences, while his home audiences had the added layers of associated references woven into their viewing experience. His marriages of different cultural sign-systems created a new, distinct theatrical world, uniquely situated within the Japanese theatrical landscape. To paraphrase Bakhtin, this world was filled with 'manifestations of life that referred to the collective ancestral body of his people'. They did not reflect the drabness of everyday existence. Instead, Ninagawa's theatre was based on a 'triumphant, festive principle' – a banquet for all the world.[3]

# APPENDIX

## Ninagawa's Shakespeare productions 1974–2016

*The majority of productions were given a single run of performances, very often ending with a tour to Osaka or other Japanese cities. For productions that were given a revival, the first and last years are given. Productions that were performed outside Japan are marked with an asterisk, and productions in the Sai no Kuni Shakespeare Series are labelled SnK.*

| Year | Play | Venue |
| --- | --- | --- |
| **1974, 1979** | *Romeo and Juliet* | Nissay Theatre |
| **1975** | *King Lear* | Nissay Theatre |
| **1978** | *Hamlet* | Imperial Theatre |
| **1980–2018** | *NINAGAWA Macbeth\** | Nissay Theatre |
| **1987–2000** | *The Tempest\** | Nissay Theatre, SnK No. 6 |
| **1988** | *Hamlet* | Spiral Hall |
| **1991** | *King Lear* | Tokyo Globe |
| **1994–2002** | *A Midsummer Night's Dream\** | Benisan Pit, SnK No. 5 |
| **1994** | *Othello* | Nissay Theatre |
| **1995, 1998** | *Hamlet\** | Ginza Saison Theatre |
| **1998** | *Romeo and Juliet* | SnK No. 1 |
| **1998** | *Twelfth Night* | SnK No. 2 |

| Year | Play | Venue |
|---|---|---|
| 1999 | *Richard III* | SnK No. 3 |
| 1999 | *King Lear\** | SnK No. 4 |
| 2001, 2002 | *Macbeth\** | SnK No. 8 |
| 2001 | *Hamlet* | SnK No. 11 |
| 2003 | *Pericles\** | SnK No. 12 |
| 2003 | *Hamlet* | Theatre Cocoon |
| 2004, 2006 | *Titus Andronicus\** | SnK No. 13 |
| 2004, 2007 | *As You Like It* | SnK No. 14/All Male No. 1 |
| 2004 | *Hamlet\** | UK Tour |
| 2004–2005 | *Romeo and Juliet* | Nissay Theatre |
| 2005–9 | *NINAGAWA Twelfth Night\** | Kabuki-Za |
| 2005 | *Tenpo Juninen no Shakespeare* | Theatre Cocoon |
| 2006 | *The Comedy of Errors* | SnK No. 15/All Male No. 2 |
| 2007 | *Coriolanus\** | SnK No. 16 |
| 2007 | *Love's Labour's Lost* | SnK No. 17/All Male No. 3 |
| 2007 | *Othello* | SnK No. 18 |
| 2008 | *King Lear* | SnK No. 19 |
| 2008 | *Much Ado About Nothing* | SnK No. 20/All Male No. 4 |
| 2009 | *A Winter's Tale* | SnK No. 21 |
| 2010 | *Henry VI* | SnK No. 22 |
| 2010 | *The Taming of the Shrew* | SnK No. 23/All Male No. 5 |
| 2011 | *Antony and Cleopatra\** | SnK No. 24 |

| Year | Play | Venue |
| --- | --- | --- |
| 2012 | *Hamlet: Performed by the Pale Boys and Girls* | Saitama Arts Theatre |
| 2012 | *Cymbeline\** | SnK No. 25 |
| 2012 | *Troilus and Cressida* | SnK No. 26/All Male No. 6 |
| 2013 | *Henry IV* | SnK No. 27 |
| 2013 | *The Merchant of Venice* | SnK No. 28/All Male No. 7 |
| 2014 | *Romeo and Juliet* | SnK Shakespeare Legend No. 1 |
| 2014 | *Julius Caesar* | SnK No. 29 |
| 2015 | *Hamlet\** | SnK Shakespeare Legend No. 2 |
| 2015, 2016 | *Richard II\** | SnK No. 30 |
| 2015 | *Two Gentlemen of Verona* | SnK No. 31/All Male No. 8 |
| 2016 | *Measure for Measure* | SnK No. 32 |

# NOTES

## Chapter 1

1. Ninagawa became artistic director of the Theatre Cocoon in the 1990s, and was appointed in Saitama in 2006.
2. The situation became so extreme that in 1723 love suicide plays were banned by the Shogunate (Nellhaus et al., 2016: 270).
3. *Medea* was performed over 250 times between 1978 and 1999. Even this pales in comparison with the success of *Suicide for Love*.
4. Pronko (1996) discusses many of the ways NINAGAWA *Macbeth* was inspired by the form but is not itself a *kabuki* production.
5. The confusion did not end here. London reviewers such as Lyn Gardner (2010) still called it a '*kabuki*-style' production, somehow overlooking the fact that this was the real thing.
6. These were the premiere, directed by Deguchi Norio in 1974, and a 2002 production by Inoue Hidenori.
7. Ninagawa directed *The Trojan Women* in 2012 with a company of Israeli, Palestinian and Japanese actresses, performed in Tokyo and the Middle East. He directed one further tragedy, another *Oedipus Rex*, for Saitama Next Theatre in 2013.
8. The full catalogue of Ninagawa's productions is beyond the word count of this book but is available in Japanese at ninagawayukio.com (accessed 23 May 2021).
9. In late 2006 Ninagawa launched the Saitama Gold Theatre, an acting company for senior citizens. It was Ninagawa's acknowledgement of his own ageing and an attempt to create

a new kind of theatre for his community. It led eventually to a very successful production of Shimizu's *Raven, We Will Load Bullets*.

10 It is particularly difficult to describe oneself in Japanese. There are at least twenty different words for 'I', dependent on status, age, gender, context and so on. With so many 'selves' in play, it is understandable that Ninagawa was for so long fascinated at the lack of a Japanese 'self'.

11 Tourists are frequently bemused to hear 'Auld Lang Syne' played at closing time in many Japanese department stores. Most Japanese people believe it to be a Japanese song and are often surprised to hear it anywhere else in the world.

12 Singleton (2003: 629) suggests that Ninagawa's audience is primarily 'the globalized community of high-art consumers'.

13 While it is certainly the case that the Sai no Kuni productions chosen for performance overseas – *Pericles*, *Coriolanus* and *Cymbeline* in particular – were more Japanese-looking than some of the others, they were conceived for performance in Saitama regardless. In a personal correspondence, Thelma Holt insisted that the shows that travelled abroad were always selected by Ninagawa himself.

14 These were *Timon of Athens*, *Henry V*, *Henry VIII*, *King John* and *All's Well That Ends Well*.

# Chapter 2

1 Although Western and non-Western remain in use as descriptions for European and Asian, respectively, I think it more useful to refer to non-Japanese texts as foreign. With the notable exception of 'Western music' this is how cultural materials from abroad are referred to in the Japanese language and is itself an indicator of how such culture is digested.

2 The National Bunraku Theatre is in Osaka.

3 For the history of *kabuki*'s development, see Ortolani (1990), Senelick (2000) and Kawatake (2003).

4  Inoue Yoshie's analysis of Shimizu's play *May Even Lunatics Die in Peace* (2003) gives an excellent insight into some of his early work with Ninagawa.

5  Horowitz (2004) mistranslates the same title twice and calls these early productions 'curiously insubstantial'.

6  These were *Summer of Demons* (1981) and *Warau Iemon* (2004).

7  The 1955 Bungakuza *Hamlet*, translated and directed by Fukuda Tsuneari, was a very close imitation of the Old Vic production he had seen the previous year.

8  Interviewed in 2003, Ninagawa acknowledged that he no longer threw chairs or ashtrays (Irvin, 2003: 90), but the force of his attention remained intense.

9  Miyashita (1987) describes the 1974 production in some detail.

10  In fact Zeffirelli had been Toho's first choice. Nakane approached Ninagawa when the Italian director was unavailable.

11  In a 2015 interview Ninagawa explained that the idea for the ribbons had come to him on the subway, when he was feeling so sick that he feared he might vomit blood (Aspden, 2015).

12  During rehearsal for *Titus Andronicus* I asked Ninagawa about the Handel piece, and he confirmed that the recording he used came from the soundtrack to the film *Barry Lyndon*, released in Japan in 1976.

13  Ninagawa spoke at length about this concern in an interview with Senda Akihiko (Ninagawa, 2009). Several of the ideas discussed led directly to his 2012 production of *Hamlet*.

14  The witches were the most *kabuki*-derived element of the production. All three were played by men; one of them was often performed by an actual *onnagata*, Arashi Tokusaburo, while the others were presented as increasingly removed from traditional *onnagata* performance, both in their vocal delivery and their physical appearance. The third witch had blonde hair and a distinctly masculine voice.

15  The (transliterated) Japanese reads: 'negawaku wa hana no shita nite haru shinan sono kisaragi no Mochizuki no koro'.

16  For an analysis of how Ninagawa's work could be read as occidentalist, see Kennedy (2001) and Lim (2019).

17  Brandon (1990), Mulryne (1992), Nouryeh (1993), Brown (1993) and Pronko (1996) all discuss the production in detail. Zarrilli et al. (2010) and Salz (2016) also offer case studies.

18  Brown (1993) gives a detailed survey of enthusiastic reviews of *NINAGAWA Macbeth*, rather making the point that language could be bypassed in favour of everything else on stage.

19  Ninagawa's *japonisme* is discussed in Kishi (1988), Mulryne (1992) and Im (2004).

20  Singleton (2003) ignores Ninagawa's commitment to his Japanese audience, implying that he was creating work exclusively for 'cultural tourists'.

21  Kishi (1998) discusses *NINAGAWA Macbeth*, while Kishi (1993) dissects *The Tempest*.

22  Horowitz (2004) includes an enthusiastic, detailed account, but it has occasional errors in translation and interpretation.

23  After both men died in 2016, the television channel WOWOW aired a series of their productions, celebrating the work of these two 'legendary' artists.

24  Kokami's 1994 *Waiting for Godot* featured Shiraishi and Mariya Tomoko as a female Vladimir and Estragon, with Maro Akaji, founder of *butoh* company Dairakudakan, as Pozzo. Amazingly, Ninagawa also directed a double bill of contrasting *Godots* during the same year; an all-male company and an all-female company alternated on the same set.

25  The company operated under several different names over the years, including The Ninagawa Company, Ninagawa Company Dash, and Gekidan Ninagawa Studio.

26  *Waiting 2017* was created and performed in Ninagawa's memory at the Saitama Arts Theatre.

27  A rather more sympathetic analysis of the production features in Riley (2005).

28  Coveney wrote a very positive introduction to *Suicide for Love* at the National Theatre in 1989, insisting that 'we witness not just the renewal of plays in Ninagawa, but wholesale regenerative acts of theatre' (Coveney, 1989).

29  Kanai had designed for 'Super Kabuki', a more contemporary version that combines *kabuki* with modern theatrical lighting and stage technology.

30  The image also appeared in *Tenpo Juninen no Shakespeare* later the same summer.

31  Ninagawa's 2002 *Oedipus Rex* and his 2007 *Coriolanus* also made impressive use of mirrored walls. When I was studying with him I suggested that my eventual book might be called *A World Reflected*, which he particularly liked.

32  Imai's ending included a short solo for Biwa, referring to the '*akaki ito*' or red thread of love and marriage. This at once recalled the red ribbons of *Medea* and prefigured those featured in *The Comedy of Errors* the following year.

# Chapter 3

1  For an excellent survey of *Hamlet*'s reception in Japan, see Ashizu (2005).

2  Decades later, Ninagawa cast a member of the popular boyband V6 as Orestes in his production of Sophocles' *Electra*.

3  For a fuller exploration, see Knowles (1998).

4  In Japan, ghost stories are particularly popular in August, since it is the season for the Japanese festival of the dead, O-bon. Ninagawa's first ideas about the play very much treated it as a ghost story.

5  After his death, *NINAGAWA Macbeth* was performed in the UK and Singapore in 2017 and in the USA in 2018, and *Kafka on the Shore* was presented in France in 2019.

6  A *hinadan* features beautifully in Kurosawa's *Dreams,* in 'The Peach Orchard'.

7  Field (1979) provides a thorough analysis of the production.

8  He shared credit for the 2015 production with Asakura Setsu.

9  The incident is described in Akishima (2015: 189–90).

10  The production was filmed before Ninagawa revised the ending, and the DVD shows Narimiya's Fortinbras declaiming

11  The production was seen in Plymouth, Norwich, Poole, Edinburgh, Salford, Nottingham, Bath and for a fortnight at the Barbican in London. It was not performed in Japan.

12  Reviews by Spencer, Billington and Shuttleworth (all 2004) range from disappointment to disgust.

13  Tatspaugh (2005) gives a thoughtful, thorough account of the production's strengths and weaknesses.

14  Ashizu (2005) includes the cartoon and a helpful explanation of its context.

15  The full list is as follows: Kawai Shoichiro, Matsuoka Kazuko, Odashima Yushi, Ozu Jiro, Kinoshita Junji, Fukuda Tsuneari, Uraguchi Bunji, Tsubouchi Shoyo, Dohi Shunsho, Toyama Masakazu, Yataba Ryokichi and the deliberately dreadful version by Charles Wirgman.

16  The English version read, 'This is the final rehearsal of the play "Hamlet". The production is set in the houses where the poor lived in the late nineteenth century, when the play "Hamlet" was introduced to Japan for the first time.'

17  Ritual ablutions are very common in Japanese religious observance, particularly at Shinto shrines. Kawai (2016) refers to this moment as *mizugori* (the Buddhist term) rather than *misogi* or *kessai*, the Shinto terms.

# Chapter 4

1  Some actors were initially wary of this earnest project so far from central Tokyo, but the success of the series turned Saitama into a major destination for Japanese Shakespeare production.

2  Gallimore (2012) compares four major translations of *A Midsummer Night's Dream*, including Odashima and Matsuoka, and refers to the Ninagawa production at length.

3  Some critics, among them Taylor (2003), could not resist patronizing phrases such as 'a return to form'. Regardless, the

consensus was overwhelmingly positive – Cavendish called it 'brilliant', Billington 'superlative' and Tanaka 'a miracle' (all 2003).

4 Sorgenfrei's reading of this scene (2004) is particularly illuminating.

5 Holt's diary from the rehearsal period of *King Lear* is very entertaining (1999).

6 Kitamura (2012) unpacks the gender play in this production.

7 Neither Oguri nor Narimiya were Johnny's clients, although Ninagawa did on occasion employ popular actors from its roster.

8 Buruma (2001) is an excellent resource for further information. The popular character Abe no Seimei, famous from Nomura Mansai's recent *Onmyouiji* films (called *The Yin Yang Master* in English), was reimagined as a beautiful young man in a popular manga that began in 1989.

9 Akishima (2015: 138–9) discusses Ninagawa's interest in the play's juxtaposition of the nobility and the lower classes.

10 When Kamejiro took the name Ichikawa Ennosuke IV in 2012, one of his first performances was an updated production of *Yamato Takeru*.

11 The original haiku reads 'natsukusa ya/tsuwamonodomo ga/ yume no ato' – something like 'the summer grasses – the aftermath of the brave soldiers' dreams'.

12 This was also specified in Matsuoka's translation. When Thersites had to explain his having called Patroclus Achilles' 'male varlet', the Japanese said 'okama', a contemporary slang word for a gay man.

13 I once mentioned this production at a conference in Greece, and an acerbic Athenian academic joked that this could be the title of my eventual book about Ninagawa.

14 Singleton (1997a) theorizes that Mnouchkine's intercultural signs became intertextual, reliant on repeat audiences. The all-male series operated in a somewhat similar fashion, albeit less politically.

15 All of the all-male productions are available on DVD, as are most of the Sai no Kuni Shakespeare series.

16  This being Ninagawa, these were consecutive only in that they followed each other in Saitama. In between, Ninagawa directed Camus' *Caligula* and *Snakes and Earrings*, a film based on the novel by Kanehara Hitomi.
17  Ninagawa discusses the production rather ruefully in Ninagawa (1995: 217).
18  According to the Japanese government, less than 2 per cent of Japan's population is not Japanese.
19  Ninagawa's 1994 production actually did use blackface. It is discussed in remarkably few essays or journals. Ninagawa went so far as to say that it was 'wrong' for a Japanese director to stage it (Tierney, 2011).
20  Charmingly, at the end of the curtain call the company applauded the audience for *their* contribution and stamina, acknowledging the shared experience of the trilogy.
21  Aran was an *otokoyaku* throughout her Takarazuka career, and by the time she became a top star she was among very few women to have played all three of the male lead roles in *The Rose of Versailles*.
22  In subsequent years *Musashi* and *Kafka on the Shore* were also presented at the LG Arts Centre.

# Chapter 5

1  These had featured in *The Tempest*, *Pericles* and *Twelfth Night* and *Hamlet* and *Macbeth*, respectively.
2  The erroneous determination to label anything Japanese-looking as '*noh*' or '*noh*-influenced' persists right up until the time of writing, as in McIvor and King (2019: 304). Huang's excellent contribution to Arden's *Great Shakespeareans* (2013) is marred by occasional references to, for example, Ninagawa's '*kabuki* Medea'. The various mistranslations of Shimizu's play titles and the subtitle to *The Tempest* in Horowitz (2004) are discussed elsewhere. Bliss (2010: 105) mentions a tour of *Coriolanus* to Peter Brook's Théâtre des Bouffes du Nord in Paris. Pleasing as this might have been given Brook's influence

on Ninagawa, the production visited London only. Lee's analysis of Renaissance culture in Asia (2018) is also marred by errors; she describes, for example, the Elton John music from *Romeo and Juliet* as having been in *Macbeth* and confuses the playwright Inoue Hisashi with the director Inoue Hidenori.

3   Iswolsky gives a charming note at the end of her translation, explaining that this comes from a popular Russian folk expression, meaning a great feast at the end of a long story.

# BIBLIOGRAPHY

Akishima Yuriko (2015) *Ninagawa Yukio & Shakespeare*. Tokyo, Kadokawa.

Antosa, Silvia, ed. (2012) *Queer Crossings: Theories, Bodies, Texts*. Milan, Mimesis International.

Arroyo, José (1998) 'Critical Approaches to World Cinema – Pedro Almodóvar,' in John Hill and Pamela Church Gibson, eds, *The Oxford Guide to Film Studies*. Oxford, Oxford University Press.

Ashizu Kaori (2005) 'What's Hamlet to Japan?' The Shakespeare Variorum Project. http://triggs.djvu.org/global-language.com/ENFOLDED/BIBL/___HamJap.htm (accessed 23 May 2021).

Aspden, Peter (2015) 'Yukio Ninagawa conquers Elsinore,' *Financial Times* 1 May.

Bakhtin, Mikhail (1981) *The Dialogic Imagination*, trans. C. Emerson and M. Holquist. Austin, Texas University Press.

Bakhtin, Mikhail (1984) [1965] *Rabelais and His World*, trans. H. Iswolsky. Bloomington, Indiana University Press.

Barnes, Peter (1992) 'Working with Yukio Ninagawa', *New Theatre Quarterly* 8.32, 389–91.

Barthes, Roland (1977) *Image Music Text*, trans. S. Heath. London, Fontana.

Barthes, Roland (1982) *Empire of Signs*, trans. R. Howard. London, Jonathan Cape.

Barthes, Roland (1985) 'How to Spend a Week in Paris', in M. Blonsky, ed., *On Signs*. Baltimore, MD, Johns Hopkins University Press.

Bate, Jonathan and Eric Rasmussen, eds (2011) *RSC Titus Andronicus and Timon of Athens*. London, Palgrave.

Bhabha, Homi K. (1998) 'Culture's in Between' in David Bennett, ed., *Multicultural States: Rethinking Difference and Identity*. London, Routledge.

Bharucha, Rustom (1996) 'Somebody's Other: Disorientations in the Cultural Politics of Our Times', in Patrice Pavis, ed., *The Intercultural Performance Reader*. London, Routledge.

Bharucha, Rustom (2004) 'Foreign Asia/Foreign Shakespeare: Dissenting Notes on New Asian Interculturality, Postcoloniality, and Recolonization', *Theatre Journal* 56, 1–28.
Bigliazzi, Silvia, Paola Ambrosi and Peter Kofler, eds (2012) *Theatre Translation in Performance*. London, Routledge.
Billington, Michael (1989) 'Fatal attractions', *The Guardian* 11 October.
Billington, Michael (2002) *One Night Stands*. London, Nick Hearn Books.
Billington, Michael (2003) 'Pericles', *The Guardian* 31 March.
Billington, Michael (2004) 'Hamlet', *The Guardian* 12 November.
Bliss, Lee, ed. (2010) *New Cambridge Shakespeare:* Coriolanus. Cambridge, Cambridge University Press.
Blonsky, Marshall, ed. (1985) *On Signs*. Baltimore, MD, Johns Hopkins University Press.
Borlik, Todd A. (2011) 'A Season in Intercultural Limbo: Ninagawa's *Doctor Faustus*', *Shakespeare Quarterly* 62.3, 444–56.
Borlik, Todd A. (2017) 'Measure for Measure at Saitama Arts Theatre', *Shakespeare Bulletin* 35, 135–42.
Bradby, David (2001) *Beckett, Waiting for Godot*. New York, Cambridge University Press.
Brandon, James R. (1990) 'Contemporary Japanese Theatre: Interculturalism and Intraculturalism', in E. Fischer-Lichte, J. Riley and M. Gissenwehrer, eds, *The Dramatic Touch of Difference – Theatre, Own and Foreign*. Tübingen, Gunter Narr Verlag, 89–97.
Brandon, James R. (1999) 'Kabuki and Shakespeare: Balancing Yin and Yang', *TDR* 43.2, 15–53.
Brandon, James R. (2009) *Kabuki's Forgotten War 1931–1945*. Honolulu, University of Hawaii Press.
Brokering, Jon Martin (2002) 'The Dramaturgy of Yukio Ninagawa and Tadashi Suzuki', PhD Thesis, Royal Holloway, University of London.
Brokering, Jon Martin (2007) 'Ninagawa Yukio's Intercultural *Hamlet*: Parsing Japanese Iconography', *Asian Theatre Journal* 24.2, 370–97.
Brook, Peter (1968) *The Empty Space*. London, Penguin Classics.
Brown, John Russell (1993) 'Foreign Shakespeare and English-speaking audiences', in Dennis Kennedy, ed., *Foreign Shakespeare: Contemporary Performance*. Cambridge, Cambridge University Press, 21–35.

Brown, John Russell, ed. (2008) *The Routledge Companion to Directors' Shakespeare*. London, Routledge.
Brown, Sarah Annes, Robert Lublin and Lynsey McCulloch, eds (2013) *Reinventing the Renaissance*. London, Palgrave.
Bulman, James C. (2017) *The Oxford Handbook of Shakespeare and Performance*. Oxford, Oxford University Press.
Buruma, Ian (2001) *A Japanese Mirror*. London, Phoenix.
Butler, Robert (1998) 'Get thee to the Barbican', *Independent* 30 August.
Carlson, Marvin (1990) *Theatre Semiotics: Signs of Life*. Bloomington, Indiana University Press.
Carlson, Marvin (1993) *Theories of Theatre: A Historical Survey, from the Greeks to the Present*. Ithaca, Cornell University Press.
Cavendish, Dominic (2003) 'Apocalypse now and then,' *Telegraph* 1 April.
Chin, Daryl (1991) 'Interculturalism, Postmodernism, Pluralism', in Bonnie Marranca and Gautam Dasgupta, eds, *Interculturalism and Performance: Writings from PAJ*. New York, PAJ Publications.
Coveney, Michael (1989) 'Ninagawa at the National', *Suicide for Love Programme*. London, National Theatre.
Coveney, Michael (1999) 'This woeful King Worzel', *Daily Mail* 5 November.
Croall, Jonathan (2015) *Performing King Lear*. London, The Arden Shakespeare.
Croall, Jonathan (2018) *Performing Hamlet*. London, The Arden Shakespeare.
Davis, Tony (2001) *Stage Design*. Mies, Rotovision SA.
Delgado, Maria M. and Paul Heritage, eds (1996) *In Contact with the Gods? – Directors Talk Theatre*. Manchester, Manchester University Press.
Dyer, Richard (1986) *Heavenly Bodies – Film Stars and Society*. London, Macmillan.
Edwards, Jane (1999) 'King Lear', *Time Out*, 3 November.
Field, B. S. (1979) 'A Tokyo Hamlet', *Shakespeare Quarterly* 30.2, 277–9.
Fielding, Rosalind (2017) 'Now Mark Me How I Will Undo Myself: Ninagawa's *Richard II*', Interdisciplinary Studies on Shakespeare Conference, Chungbuk National University. Cheongju.
Fischer-Lichte, Erika, Josephine Riley and Michael Gissenwehrer, eds (1990) *The Dramatic Touch of Difference – Theatre, Own and Foreign*. Tübingen, Gunter Narr Verlag.

Frank, Glenda (1991) 'Review: Ninagawa Macbeth', *Theatre Journal* 43.3, 397–9.

Fuery, Patrick (2000) *New Developments in Film Theory*. London, Macmillan.

Fujita Minoru and Leonard Pronko, eds (1996) *Shakespeare East and West*. London, Routledge.

Fukahori Etsuko (2014) 'Staging Cultural and Theatrical Heterogeneity: Ninagawa's 2013 Production of *The Merchant of Venice*', *The Kwassui Review*, 13–22.

Furuya Seiji (2013) 'Kabuki Shakespeare: The *NINAGAWA Twelfth Night*', in Sarah Annes Brown, Robert Lublin and Lynsey McCulloch, eds, *Reinventing the Renaissance*. London, Palgrave, 162–73.

Gallimore, Daniel (2012) *Sounding Like Shakespeare*. Hyogo, Kansei Gakuin University Press.

Gardner, Lyn (2009) 'Shochiku Grand Kabuki – Review', *Guardian* 25 March.

Gardner, Lyn (2010) 'Kabuki', *Guardian* 6 June.

Gillies, John, Minami Ryuta, Ruru Li and Poonam Trivedi (2006) 'Shakespeare on the Stages of Asia', in Stanley Wells and Sarah Stanton, eds, *The Cambridge Companion to Shakespeare on Stage*. Cambridge, Cambridge University Press, 259–83.

Greenblatt, Stephen (1991) *Marvellous Possessions*. Chicago, Chicago University Press.

Habicht, Wenner and Roger Pringle, eds (1988) *Images of Shakespeare*. Newark, University of Delaware Press.

Hamana, Emi (2017) 'Last Shakespeare Plays directed by Yukio Ninagawa: Possessed by the Power of Theatre', *Journal of Literature and Art Studies* 7.3, 269–77.

Harris, Timothy (2003) 'Ninagawa's Pericles – Review', *Plays International* (April), 41–2.

Harris, Timothy (2004) 'Ninagawa's Hamlet – Review', *Plays International* (December/January), 43–4.

Hill, John and Pamela Church Gibson, eds (1998) *The Oxford Guide to Film Studies*. Oxford, Oxford University Press.

Holland, Peter, ed. (2013) *Brook, Hall, Ninagawa, Lepage: Great Shakespeareans vol. 18*. London, Bloomsbury.

Holt, Thelma (1999) 'Triumph of a tragedy in Japan', *Telegraph* 31 October.

Horowitz, Arthur (2004) *Prospero's 'True Preservers': Brook, Ninagawa, and Strehler – Twentieth Century Directors Approach*

*Shakespeare's The Tempest*. Cranbury, NJ, Associated University Presses.
Huang, Alexa (2013) 'Yukio Ninagawa', in Peter Holland, ed., *Brook, Hall, Ninagawa, Lepage: Great Shakespeareans vol. 18*. London, Bloomsbury, 79–112.
Huang, Alexa and Charles S. Ross, eds. (2009) *Shakespeare in Hollywood, Asia and Cyberspace*. West Lafayette, Purdue University Press.
Ichikawa Kamejiro (2013) Programme note for *The Merchant of Venice*, SAF.
Im, Yeeyon (2004) 'The Pitfalls of Intercultural Discourse: The Case of Yukio Ninagawa', *Shakespeare Bulletin* 22.4, 7–30.
Im, Yeeyon (2012) 'Review of Shakespeare's *Antony and Cleopatra*', *Shakespeare* 8.4, 461–7.
Inoue Yoshie (2003) 'On Shimizu Kunio's Play: May Even Lunatics Die in Peace', trans. Mari Boyd, *Asian Theatre Journal* 20.1, 1–11.
Irvin, Polly (2003) *Directing for the Stage*. Mies, Rotovision SA.
Kawachi Yoshiko (2006) 'Shakespeare in a Japanese Context for the Page and the Stage', in *Shakespeare's World/World Shakespeares*. Brisbane, International Shakespeare Association, 330–41.
Kawai Shoichiro (2004) 'Translating the Rhythm of *Hamlet*'. http://cejsh.icm.edu.pl/cejsh/element/bwmeta1.element. hdl_11089_1495/c/04-kawai.pdf (accessed 23 May 2021).
Kawai Shoichiro (2008) 'Ninagawa Yukio', in John Russell Brown, ed., *The Routledge Companion to Directors' Shakespeare*. London, Routledge, 269–83.
Kawai Shoichiro (2009) 'More Japanized, casual and transgender Shakespeares', *Shakespeare Survey* 62, 261–72.
Kawai Shoichiro (2016) 'Some Japanese Shakespeare Productions in 2014–15', *Multicultural Shakespeares* 14.1, 13–28.
Kawatake Toshio (2003) *Kabuki*. Tokyo, I-House Press.
Kennan, Patricia and Mariangela Tempera, eds. (1992) *Shakespeare from Text to Stage*. Bologna, Editrice CLUEB.
Kennedy, Dennis, ed. (1993) *Foreign Shakespeare: Contemporary Performance*. Cambridge, Cambridge University Press.
Kennedy, Dennis (1994) 'Shakespeare Played Small: Three Speculations about the Body', *Shakespeare Survey* 47, 1–13.
Kennedy, Dennis (1995) 'Shakespeare and the Global Spectator', *Shakespeare Jarbuch Vol. 131*. Stuttgart, Alfred Kröner Verlag.
Kennedy, Dennis (2001) *Looking at Shakespeare*. Cambridge, Cambridge University Press.

Kennedy, Dennis, ed. (2003) *The Oxford Encyclopaedia of Theatre and Performance*. Oxford, Oxford University Press.

Kennedy, Dennis and Yong Li Lan (2010) *Shakespeare in Asia*. Cambridge, Cambridge University Press.

Kimata Fuyu (2018) *A Somatic Approach to Drama*. Tokyo, Tokuma Shoten.

Kishi, Tetsuo (1988) '"Bless Thee! Thou Art Translated!" Shakespeare in Japan', in Wenner Habicht and Roger Pringle, eds, *Images of Shakespeare*. Newark, University of Delaware Press, 245–50.

Kishi, Tetsuo (1998) 'Japanese Shakespeare and English Reviewers', in Sasayama Takashi, J. R. Mulryne and Margaret Shewring, eds, *Shakespeare and the Japanese Stage*. Cambridge, Cambridge University Press, 110–23.

Kitamura Sae (2012) 'Queens, Girls and Freaks: Men in Women's Clothes and Female Audiences in Japanese Cross-Dressing Productions', in Silvia Antosa, ed. *Queer Crossings: Theories, Bodies, Texts*. Milan, Mimesis International, 161–78.

Knowles, Ronald, ed. (1998) *Shakespeare and Carnival: After Bakhtin*. London, Palgrave Macmillan.

Kobayashi Kaori (2006) 'New Intercultural Shakespeare in East Asia', in *Shakespeare's World/World Shakespeares*. Brisbane, International Shakespeare Association, 247–59.

Kondo Hiroyuki (2010) 'Matsuoka's Japanese Translation of Shakespeare: A Feminist Revision', *Foreign Languages and Literature Bulletin* 39, 3–18.

Kott, Jan (1964) *Shakespeare Our Contemporary*. London, Methuen.

Lee, Adele (2018) *The English Renaissance and the Far East*. Madison, Fairleigh Dickinson University Press.

Levenson, Jill L. and Robert Ormsby, eds (2017) *The Shakespearean World*. London, Routledge.

Lim, A. E. H. (2019) 'Routes and Routers of Interculturalism: Islands, Theatres and Shakespeares', in Charlotte McIvor and Jason King, eds, *Interculturalism and Performance Now*. London, Routledge, 61–87.

McIvor, Charlotte and Jason King, eds (2019) *Interculturalism and Performance Now*. London, Routledge.

Marranca, Bonnie and Gautam Dasgupta, eds (1991) *Interculturalism and Performance: Writings from PAJ*. New York, PAJ Publications.

Matsuoka Kazuko (2002) 'In the Nihongo words of the Bard', *Japan Times* 13 March.

Matsuoka Kazuko (2013) Programme note for *The Merchant of Venice*, SAF.
Miller, Gemma (2015) 'Review: *Hamlet*', *Shakespeare Bulletin* 33.3, 512–16.
Minami Ryuta (2010) 'What, has this thing appear'd again tonight?' in Poonam Trivedi and Minami Ryuta, *Re-playing Shakespeare in Asia*. London, Routledge.
Minami Ryuta, Ian Carruthers and John Gillies, eds (2001) *Performing Shakespeare in Japan*. Cambridge, Cambridge University Press.
Mitter, Shomit and Maria Shevtsova (2005) *Fifty Key Theatre Directors*. London, Routledge.
Miyashita Nobuo (1987) 'Ninagawa Yukio, Theatrical Pacesetter', *Japan Quarterly* 34, 400–4.
Mori Mitsuya (1997) 'Noh, Kabuki and Western Theatre', *Theatre Research International* 22.1, 14–21.
Mori Mitsuya (2001) 'Thinking and Feeling: Characteristics of Intercultural Theatre', in Stanca Scholz-Cionca and Samuel L. Leiter, eds, *Japanese Theatre and the International Stage*. Leiden, Brill, 357–66.
Morley, Sheridan (1999) 'Japanese lessons', *The Spectator* 6 November.
Mulryne, R. (1992) 'From Text to Foreign Stage: Yukio Ninagawa's Cultural Translation of *Macbeth*', in Patricia Kennan and Mariangela Tempera, eds, *Shakespeare from Text to Stage*. Bologna, Editrice CLUEB, 131–43.
Mulryne, R. (2006) 'An Artist Between Cultures', Programme note for *Titus Andronicus*. RSC.
Mulryne, R. and Margaret Shewring (1995) 'Authenticity and Cultural Translation: Ninagawa's *The Tempest*', *Shakespeare Worldwide* 14/15, 287–98.
Nakagoshi Tsukasa (2014) Interviewed by Senda Akihiko for Performing Arts Network Japan.
Nakane Tadao (1999) Programme note for *King Lear*, RSC.
Nellhaus, Tobin, Bruce McConachie, Carol Fisher Sorgenfrei and Tamara Underiner (2016) *Theatre Histories*, 3rd ed. London, Routledge.
Nightingale, Benedict (1999) 'The sadness of this king is not enough', *Times* 29 October.
Ninagawa Yukio (1993) *A Thousand Knives, A Thousand Eyes*. Tokyo, Kinokuniya Shoten.

Ninagawa Yukio (1994) 'In Conversation with Michael Billington, 4 March', in Maria M. Delgado and Paul Heritage, eds, *In Contact with the Gods? – Directors Talk Theatre*. Manchester, Manchester University Press, 191–200.

Ninagawa Yukio (1995) Interviewed by Yasunari Takahashi, Anzai Tetsuo, Matsuoka Kazuko, Ted Motobashi, and Ian Carruthers, 4 July, in Minami Ryuta, Ian Carruthers and John Gillies, eds, *Performing Shakespeare in Japan*. Cambridge, Cambridge University Press, 208–19.

Ninagawa Yukio (1998a) *The Stage: A Magnetic Field That Spins Dreams*. Tokyo, NHK Shuppan.

Ninagawa Yukio (1998b) Interviewed by J. M. Brokering, August 1998, in Jon Martin Brokering, 'The Dramaturgy of Yukio Ninagawa and Tadashi Suzuki', PhD Thesis, Royal Holloway, University of London.

Ninagawa Yukio (1999) *Ninagawa Yukio: Tatakau Gekijo* (Yukio Ninagawa: A Theatre Engaged In Battle). Tokyo, NHK Shuppan.

Ninagawa Yukio (2002a) Interviewed by Ryoko Maria Nakamura, *Japan Times* 6 October.

Ninagawa Yukio (2002b) *Note 1969–2001*. Tokyo, NHK Shuppan.

Ninagawa Yukio (2002c) *Rebellion and Creation – Conversations with Ninagawa Yukio*. Tokyo, Kinokuniya Shoten.

Ninagawa Yukio (2003) Interviewed by Caroline Lewis, *On Japan Newsletter*. London, Embassy of Japan.

Ninagawa Yukio (2009) Interviewed by Senda Akihiko for Performing Arts Network Japan.

Ninagawa Yukio (2012) Programme note for *Cymbeline*. London, Barbican.

Ninagawa Yukio (2013a) Programme note for *The Merchant of Venice*. SAF.

Ninagawa Yukio (2013b) *The Power of Theatre*. Tokyo, Nihon Seizai.

Ninagawa Yukio and Hasebe Hiroshi (2002) *On Directing*. Tokyo, Kinokuniya Shoten.

Ninagawa Yukio and Yamaguchi Hiroko (2015) *Ninagawa Yukio's Work*. Tokyo, Shinchosha.

Nouryeh, Andrea J. (1993) 'Shakespeare and the Japanese Stage', in Dennis Kennedy, ed., *Foreign Shakespeare: Contemporary Performance*. Cambridge, Cambridge University Press, 254–69.

Oki-Siekierczak, Ayami (2013) 'Transforming Shakespeare into a Kabuki Piece for the Modern Audience', in Silvia Bigliazzi,

Paola Ambrosi and Peter Kofler, eds, *Theatre Translation in Performance*. London, Routledge, 223–240.
Ortolani, Benito (1990) *The Japanese Theatre – From Shamanistic Ritual to Contemporary Pluralism*. Princeton, NJ, Princeton University Press.
Parker, Helen S. E. (2001) 'The Men of Our Dreams: The Role of *Otokoyaku* in The Takarazuka Revue Company's "Fantasy Adventure"', in Stanca Scholz-Cionca and Samuel L. Leiter, eds, *Japanese Theatre and The International Stage*. Brill, Leiden, 241–54.
Parry, Robert Lloyd (1999) 'Pathetic, weak, but easy to love', *Highbury-Islington Express* 5 November.
Pavis, Patrice, (1992) *Theatre at the Crossroads of Culture* trans. L. Kruger. London, Routledge.
Pavis, Patrice, ed. (1996) *The Intercultural Performance Reader*. London, Routledge.
Pearson, Roberta E. and Philip Simpson (2001) *A Critical Dictionary of Film and Television Theory*. London and New York, Routledge.
Peter, John (1999) 'Review: *King Lear*', *The Sunday Times* 31 October.
Powell, Brian (2002) *Japan's Modern Theatre – A Century of Continuity of Change*. London, Japan Library.
Pronko, Leonard (1996) 'Approaching Shakespeare through Kabuki', in Fujita Minoru and Leonard Pronko, eds, *Shakespeare East and West*. London, Routledge, 23–40.
Reader, Keith A. (1990) 'Literature/Cinema/Television: Intertextuality in Jean Renoir's *Le Testament du Docteur Cordelier*' in Michael Worton and Judith Still, eds, *Intertextuality: Theories and Practices*. Manchester, Manchester University Press, 176–89.
Rees, Jasper (2004) 'Go east, sweet prince', *Telegraph* 20 October.
Riley, Kathleen (2005) *Nigel Hawthorne on Stage*. Hatfield, University of Hertfordshire Press.
Rivkin, Julie and Michael Ryan (1998) *Literary Theory – An Anthology*. Oxford, Blackwell Publishing.
Roubine, Jean-Jacques (1990) 'The Theatre du Soleil: A French Postmodernist Itinerary', in Erika Fischer-Lichte, Josephine Riley and Michael Gissenwehrer, eds, *The Dramatic Touch of Difference – Theatre, Own and Foreign*. Tübingen, Gunter Narr Verlag, 73–82.
Said, Edward (1978) *Orientalism*. New York, Pantheon Books.
Salz, Jonah (2016) *A History of Japanese Theatre*. Cambridge, Cambridge University Press.

Sasayama Takashi, J. R. Mulryne and Margaret Shewring, eds (1998) *Shakespeare and the Japanese Stage*. Cambridge, Cambridge University Press.

Scholz-Cionca, Stanca, and Samuel L. Leiter, eds (2001) *Japanese Theatre and the International Stage*. Leiden, Brill.

Scholz-Cionca, Stanca, and Andreas Regelsberger, eds (2011) *Japanese Theatre Transcultural*. Munich, Iudicium Verlag.

Senda Akihiko (1997) *The Voyage of Contemporary Japanese Theatre*, trans. J. T. Rimer. Honolulu, University of Hawaii Press.

Senda Akihiko (2010) *The Theatrical World of Ninagawa Yukio*. Tokyo, Asahi Shinbun.

Senelick, Laurence (2000) *The Changing Room – Sex, Drag and Theatre*. London, Routledge.

Shevtsova, Maria (2016) 'The Craiova Shakespeare Festival and a Valediction for Yukio Ninagawa', *New Theatre Quarterly* 32.2, 276–82.

Shilling, Jane (2015) 'Moments of revelation', *Telegraph* 22 May.

Shuttleworth, Ian (2004) 'Hamlet', *Teletext* 10 November.

Singleton, Brian (1997a) 'Receiving Les Atrides Productively: Mnouchkine's Intercultural Signs as Intertexts', *Theatre Research International* 22.1, 19–23.

Singleton, Brian (1997b) 'The Pursuit of Otherness for the Investigation of Self', *Theatre Research International* 22.2, 93–7.

Singleton, Brian (2003) 'Interculturalism', in Dennis Kennedy, ed., *The Oxford Encyclopaedia of Theatre and Performance*. Oxford, Oxford University Press, 628–30.

Smethurst, Mae J. (2002) 'The Japanese Presence in Ninagawa's Medea', *American Journal of Philology* 123.1, 1–34.

Smith, Emma (2006) 'Shakespeare in Performance Reviewed', *Shakespeare Survey* 59, 368–74.

Sorgenfrei, Carol Fisher (2004) 'Performance Review: *Pericles, Prince of Tyre*', *Asian Theatre Journal* 21.1, 116–18.

Sorgenfrei, Carol Fisher (2005) *Unspeakable Acts*. Honolulu, University of Hawaii Press.

Spencer, Charles (1999) 'Sadness of King Lear lost in no-man's land', *Daily Telegraph* 29 October.

Spencer, Charles (2004) 'Shakespeare lost in translation', *The Telegraph* 13 November.

Suematsu Michiko (2003) 'The Cherry Tree and the Lotus: Ninagawa Yukio's Two *Macbeths*', *Journal of Social and Information Studies* 10, 15–23.

Suematsu Michiko (2017) 'Verbal and visual representations in modern Japanese productions', in James C. Bulman, ed., *The Oxford Handbook of Shakespeare and Performance*. Oxford, Oxford University Press.

Takahashi Yutaka (2001) *The Legend of Ninagawa Yukio*. Tokyo, Kawade Shobo Shinsha.

Takahashi Yasunari (2002) 'Hamlet and the Anxiety of Modern Japan', *Shakespeare Survey* 48, 99–112.

Tanaka Nobuko (2002a) 'Forsooth tis surely no great shakes', *Japan Times* 13 March.

Tanaka Nobuko (2002b) 'Ninagawa's *A Midsummer Night's Dream*', *Japan Times* 28 August.

Tanaka Nobuko (2003) 'Theatrical history in the making', *Japan Times* 23 February.

Tatlow, Antony (2001) *Shakespeare, Brecht and the Intercultural Sign*. Durham, NC, Duke University Press.

Tatspaugh, Patricia (2005) 'Shakespeare Performed', *Shakespeare Quarterly* 56.4, 448–78.

Taylor, Diana (1991) 'Transculturating Transculturation', in Bonnie Marranca and Gautam Dasgupta, eds, *Interculturalism and Performance: Writings from PAJ*. New York, PAJ Publications, 60–74.

Taylor, Paul (1992) 'Typhoon from the East', *Independent* 5 December.

Taylor, Paul (1999) '*King Lear* – Review', *Independent* 30 October.

Taylor, Paul (2003) '*Pericles* – Review', *Independent* 3 April.

Tierney, Robert (2011) '*Othello* in Tokyo', *Shakespeare Quarterly* 62.4, 514–540.

Trivedi, Poonam and Minami Ryuta (2010) *Re-playing Shakespeare in Asia*. London, Routledge.

Ubersfeld, Anne (1982) 'The Pleasure of the Spectator', trans. P. Bouillaguet and C. Jose, *Modern Drama* 25.1, 127–39.

Wells, Stanley and Sarah Stanton, eds (2006) *The Cambridge Companion to Shakespeare on Stage*. Cambridge, Cambridge University Press.

Worton, Michael and Judith Still, eds (1990) *Intertextuality: Theories and Practices*. Manchester, Manchester University Press.

Yamaguchi Takeshi, ed. (2001) *Ninagawa's Challenge: UK Tour Record*. Tokyo, Heibonsha.

Yoshihara Yukari (2007) 'Popular Shakespeare in Japan', *Shakespeare Survey* 60, 130–40.

Zarrilli, Phillip, Bruce McConachie, Gary Jay Williams and Carol Sorgenfrei (2010) *Theatre Histories*, 2nd ed. London, Routledge.

# INDEX

Abe Hiroshi 175, 181–2
Akimoto Matsuyo 4, 51, 61
   *Genroku Harbour Song* 5, 61, 129
   *Kaison – Priest of Hitachi* 5
   *Namboku Love Story* 5, 61
   *Suicide for Love* 4, 5, 50–1, 54, 70, 87, 115, 129, 175, 202 n.3, 205 n.28
all-male Shakespeare 3, 18, 33, 108, 109, 118, 140–65, 175, 208 n.15
Almodóvar, Pedro 192–193
Amaterasu 49, 132
Ando Tadao 103, 128
*angura* 6, 25, 36, 46, 54, 86
ANPO Security Treaty 6, 42, 57
*aragoto kabuki* 38–9, 40, 48, 136, 154
Aran Kei 149, 178–179, 180, 209 n.21
Arashi Tokusaburo 49, 204 n.14
Art Theatre Shinjuku Bunka 6, 7, 41
Asakura Setsu 51, 91, 206 n.8
Asanuma Inejiro assassination 182
Athens Cultural Olympiad 3, 130
Azuchi-Momoyama period 52, 58

Bakhtin, Mikhail, *Rabelais and His World* 15, 16, 33–4, 43, 74, 89–90, 91, 92, 98, 113, 123, 146, 150, 165, 170, 196, 197
Balinese drama 103, 108
*Bara* 142
Barber, Samuel, *Adagio for Strings* 48, 56, 94
Barthes, Roland 24, 29, 31, 196
*Battle Royale* 105
Beckett, Samuel 189
   *Waiting for Godot* 67, 76, 205 n.24
Benisan Pit 68, 127, 199
Bergman, Ingmar 104
*bian lian* (face-changing) 174
Billington, Michael 51, 110, 111, 207 n.12, 207 n.3
*bishonen* 141–2, 143
Brandon, James 26, 37, 205 n.17
Borchert, Wolfgang 117
Branagh, Kenneth 111
Brokering, Jon 29
Brook, Peter 27, 28, 43, 68–9, 72, 73, 74, 89, 90, 133, 134, 168, 172, 209 n.2
   *Empty Space, The* 43, 69, 72, 89, 134, 168
   *A Midsummer Night's Dream* (dir. 1968) 43, 68–9, 133, 168, 172

# INDEX

*Titus Andronicus* (dir. 1955) 133, 134
Buddhism 58–9, 118, 128, 138, 207 n.17
Bungakuza 2, 54, 86, 163, 204 n.7
Bunkamura Theatre Cocoon 1, 5–12, 15–23, 77, 105–9, 167, 175, 187
*bunraku* 4, 35, 36, 40, 50, 51, 140, 203 n.2
*butsudan* 52–5, 58, 59, 61, 128

calculated intimacies 66, 80, 127, 163, 172, 174, 176
candles 59, 71, 102–3, 109, 126
cherry blossoms 31, 54, 56–7, 58, 59, 69, 80, 128, 150, 156
*Chicago* (Takarazuka version) 66
Chikamatsu Monzaemon 4, 50–1, 78–9, 88
  love suicide plays 4, 50–1, 202 n.2
  *The Woman Killer and the Hell of Oil* 78–9
Chin, Daryl 29, 192, 194–5
Chinese characters 25
Chinese opera 70, 71
*commedia dell'arte* 77, 146, 147, 164
Coveney, Michael 74, 75, 205 n.28
cutting plays 88

Daimon Goro 70, 71
Davis, Miles 108
Deguchi Norio 86, 88, 202 n.6

Egan, Peter 110
*enka* 51, 115

Fellini, Federico 43, 98
first three minutes 49–50, 127 (*see also* pre-show induction)
flowers 31, 75, 128–9, 153, 156, 170
Fujiwara Tatsuya 4, 13, 15, 21, 105–9, 110, 112–14, 118–22, 133, 181
Fukazawa Atsushi 71
*fukikae* (dummy actor) 81, 132
Fukuda Tsuneari 86, 204 n.7, 207 n.15
  *Hamlet* (dir. 1955) 86, 204 n.7
Fukushima nuclear disaster 156

Gardner, Lyn 202 n.5
Gekidan Seihai 2, 6, 7
Gendaijin Gekijo 6, 7, 41, 42, 46, 86
Ginkaku-ji 82
Ginza Saison Theatre 96–100, 199
Giotto *Seven Vices* 184
Girls' Day (3 March) 92
Gower, John 131–2, 133
Greenblatt, Stephen 192
Grotowski, Jerzy 21

Hagiwara Ken'ichi 88–9
Hamana Emi 191, 192
*hanamichi* 40, 51, 80, 157
Handel *Sarabande* 48, 204 n.12
*hashigakari* 62, 126
Hatakeyama Hisashi 65
Hawthorne, Sir Nigel 74–7

223

## INDEX

*hayagawari* 81, 132
Hijikata Tatsumi 46
*hina-matsuri* (Doll Festival) 88, 92–3, 95, 99
*hinadan* 92, 93, 94, 95, 96, 98, 99, 101, 103, 121, 206 n.6
Hira Mikijiro 8, 46, 48, 63–4, 65, 78, 90–2, 106, 110, 118, 120–1, 127, 167
Hira Takehiro 110
Hokusai 81, 206 n.30
Holt, Thelma 27, 76, 111, 129, 134, 203 n.13, 208 n.5
Horio Yukio 72, 74, 126, 127
Horowitz, Arthur 204 n.5, 205 n.22, 209 n.2
Huang, Alexa 191, 209 n.2

Ichikawa Ennosuke III 153
Ichikawa Kamejiro 66, 153–6, 158–61, 165, 208 n.10
Ichikawa Sadanji II 158, 159
Ichimura Masachika 100–5, 106, 110, 114, 123, 127, 129, 131, 132
Ikeda Riyoko 149
Im Yeeyon 179–80, 191–2
Imai Toyoshige 79, 81, 206 n.32
Imperial Theatre 85, 89, 90–4, 95, 199
Inoue Hidenori 202 n.6, 209 n.2
Inoue Hisashi 14, 15, 16, 22, 88, 108, 180, 209 n.2
 *Dogen's Adventures* 175
 *Musashi* 14, 209 n.22

*Tenpo Juninen no Shakespeare* 14–18, 67, 88, 112–14, 139, 202 n.6, 206 n.30
Inoue Shonsho 184
Inoue Yoshie 204 n.4
Inoue Yoshio 106
interculturalism 10, 25–31, 59–61, 77, 82, 120, 121, 160, 180, 191–5, 196, 208 n.14
intertextuality 31–4, 114, 193–196
*Interweaving Performance Cultures* 30

Japanese language 25–26, 47, 60, 95, 97, 113, 126, 196, 203 n.10
Japanese sense of self 11–12, 25–6, 49, 54, 146, 203 n.10
*japonisme* 28, 60, 205 n.19
Jo Haruhiko 13, 15, 110
John, Elton 43, 94, 142, 210 n.2
Johnny & Associates 141, 208 n.7
*jyoshikimaku* (curtain) 80, 178–9

*kabuki* 2, 6, 10, 13–14, 17, 22, 30, 35, 36, 37–42, 43, 45, 47, 48, 50, 51, 54, 61, 64, 65, 66, 70, 71, 73, 78, 79–83, 85, 91, 94, 98, 102, 106, 112, 121, 122, 132, 135, 136, 140, 141, 142, 143, 145, 153, 154, 155, 156, 157, 158, 159, 160, 161, 174, 178–9, 183, 189, 203 n.3

Kabuki-za 36, 78, 79, 80, 82, 112, 126, 145, 153, 154, 200
*kagamiita* 167
Kajii Motojiro 56, 156
Kakei Toshio 155
*Kamen Rider* 163
Kanai Yoichiro 80, 82, 206 n.29
Kara Juro 22, 44, 46, 61, 86, 95
   *Black Tulip* 61
   *Shitaya Mannencho Monogatari* 61, 95, 119, 188
   *Water Magician, The* 3, 44, 50, 77, 107, 129
Karasawa Toshiaki 15, 114, 127, 139, 140, 173
Kasamatsu Yasuhiro 96, 147
Kashima single pine tree 177
Katsumura Masanobu 114, 139, 176
Kawabata Kaori 89
Kawai Shoichiro 87, 106, 107, 116, 125, 167, 170, 190, 207 n.15, 207 n.17
Keene, Donald 12
Kennedy, Dennis 30, 75, 101, 205 n.16
Kent, Jonathan 106
*ki* (clappers) 40, 48, 122, 178
Kiba Katsumi 15, 73, 113–14, 166, 170, 171
Kishi Tetsuo 33, 60, 61, 64, 89, 190, 192, 205 n.19, 205 n.21
kissing 151, 152, 155
Koide Keisuke 152
Kokami Shoji 67, 129, 205 n.24
Komadori Sisters 115–16, 117, 169

Komine, Lily 91, 101, 104, 108, 110, 111, 112, 138, 157, 168, 181
Korea, South 37, 179–80
Kott, Jan 43
*kougetsudai* (moonviewing platforms) 82
Kubozuka Yosuke 176
*kumadori* (make-up) 39, 73, 91, 136
Kurahashi Ken 2, 6
*kuroko* stagehands 40, 70, 131
Kurosawa Akira 17, 52, 53, 75
   *Dreams* 206 n.6
   *Throne of Blood* 17, 52, 75
*kyogen* 22, 62, 66, 77, 163

*Last Samurai, The* 96
Lepage, Robert 28
Lillehammer Winter Olympics 3
Lincoln Center 12, 66, 206 n.5
lotus blossoms 31, 128, 132, 134, 179
Luhrmann, Baz 44

*Madness of King George, The* 74
Madonna 37
Maeda Fumiko 108
Maloney, Michael 110–11
Manaka Hitomi 134
*manzai* comedy 164
Matsu Takako 96
Matsumoto Koshiro IX 43, 45, 50, 65, 73, 96, 166
Matsuoka Kazuko 87, 96–7, 126, 127, 159, 167, 170, 175, 181, 187, 188, 190, 207 n.15, 208 n.12
Matsuzaka Tori 171

Meiji Restoration 37, 85, 119
memory 2, 15, 187–8
*mie* (pose) 40, 48, 136, 154
Mikami Hiroshi 49
mirrors 63, 80, 81, 82, 98, 100, 114, 128, 131, 137, 139, 140, 145, 146, 147, 163, 175, 206 n.31
Mishima Yukio 3, 5, 12–13, 22, 41, 46, 53, 110
   *Modern Noh Plays* 3, 12–13, 46, 50, 110, 130, 141, 181
   *Sotoba Komachi* 12, 46, 47, 53, 69, 165
   *Yoroboshi* 12–13, 46, 108
Miura Ryosuke 163
Miyamoto Amon 67
Miyamoto Noriko 147
*mizugori* 121, 207 n.17
Mnouchkine, Ariane 9, 27, 208 n.14
*mono no aware* 56
Morley, Sheridan 75–6
music 40, 42, 43, 48, 49, 51, 57, 73, 87, 94, 108, 115–17, 121, 126, 128, 130, 142, 144, 153, 159, 163, 169, 178, 188, 195
musical theatre 8, 14, 36, 45, 65, 90, 100, 127, 148, 149

Nakagoshi Tsukasa 68, 95, 107, 137, 138, 140, 147, 151, 156, 162, 175, 180, 182, 184
Nakane Tadao 7, 15, 42, 43, 44, 52, 64, 68, 72, 88, 89, 187, 204 n.10
*naminuno* 40, 65, 132

Narimiya Hiroki 102, 105, 109, 141, 143, 144, 151, 206 n.10
Natsuki Mari 15, 100, 104, 110
Nenbutsu Temple 59
New Left 54, 57
Ninagawa Company 67–8, 136, 205 n.25
*Ninagawa Shakespeare Legend* 118, 161, 201
*Ninagawa x Cocoon* 5–12, 14–18
*ningyo-buri* 131
*nio* statues 58–9, 128, 138, 181
Ninagawa Yukio
  acting career 2
    *Funeral Parade of Roses* 2
    *Ubu Roi* 2
    *W's Tragedy* 2
  artistic director of Bunkamura Theatre Cocoon 5, 202 n.1
  artistic director of Saitama Arts Theatre 202 n.1
  education 2
  films
    *Snakes and Earrings* 209 n.16
    *Summer of Demons* 204 n.6
    *Warau Iemon* 204 n.6
  productions
    *Antony and Cleopatra* 178–80, 200
    *As You Like It* 3, 140–4, 147, 200
    *Blood Wedding* 61, 67
    *Byakuya no Valkyrie* 10, 19

*Caligula* 9, 117, 209 n.16
*Cherry Orchard, The* 9, 107, 133
*Coast of Utopia, The* 22, 167, 175
*Comedy of Errors, The* 18–19, 145–8, 151, 159, 163, 179, 200
*Coriolanus* 67, 137–40, 178, 180, 181, 200, 203 n.13, 206 n.31
*Cymbeline* 172, 174–8, 180, 201, 203 n.13
*Doctor Faustus* 188
*Dogen's Adventures* 175
*Electra* 10, 21, 133, 206 n.2
*Greeks, The* 9, 14, 21, 77–9, 80, 107, 128, 130, 156, 167
*Farewell My Concubine* 22
*Genroku Harbour Song* 5, 61, 129
*Hamlet* (1978) 27, 49, 87, 89, 90–4, 95, 97, 104, 122, 138, 199, 206 n.7
*Hamlet* (1988) 94–6, 97, 106, 122, 199
*Hamlet* (1995) 95, 96–100, 107, 120, 122, 199
*Hamlet* (2001) 95, 100–5, 106, 107, 108, 109, 110, 114, 122, 129, 141, 200
*Hamlet* (2003) 4, 95, 105–9, 114, 133, 147, 200, 206 n.10
*Hamlet* (2004) 3, 95, 109–12, 122, 200, 207 n.11, 207 n.12, 207 n.13
*Hamlet* (2012) 114–18, 122, 169, 201
*Hamlet* (2015) 91, 95, 108, 118–23, 201, 206 n.8, 207 n.16
*Hearty But Flippant* 5, 6, 11, 41, 54, 129, 180, 204 n.4, 204 n.5
*Henry IV* 170–1, 201
*Henry VI* 139, 166, 167–70, 200
*In That Rainy Summer, Thirty Juliets Came Back* 8, 22, 61, 187
*Julius Caesar* 112, 139, 180–3, 201
*Kafka on the Shore* 206 n.5, 209 n.22
*Kaison – Priest of Hitachi* 5
*King Lear* (1975) 3, 45, 48, 94, 199
*King Lear* (1991) 199
*King Lear* (1999) 3, 27, 71–7, 100, 101, 109, 110, 127, 130, 200, 208 n.5
*King Lear* (2008) 166, 167, 171, 200
*Kitchen, The* 8–10
*Let's Lay Flowers There Tomorrow* 7
*Love's Labour's Lost* 129, 148–51, 164, 165, 166, 200
*Macbeth* (2001) 114, 127–9, 139, 200

*Masakado Loses His Head* 7–8, 10, 22
*Measure for Measure* 183–5, 201
*Medea* (1978) 3, 5, 10, 13, 20, 27, 47–50, 54, 70, 73, 77, 87, 90, 91, 121, 141, 148, 155, 165, 202 n.3, 206 n.32
*Medea* (2005) 10–12
*Merchant of Venice, The* 158–61, 163, 166, 201
*Midsummer Night's Dream, A* 11, 67–71, 72, 76, 77, 82, 94, 101, 112, 127, 130, 164, 199, 207 n.2
*Modern Noh Plays* 3, 12–13, 46, 110
*Much Ado About Nothing* 151–3, 181, 182, 200
*Musashi* 14, 108, 109, 209 n.22
*My Soul is Shining Water* 22
*Namboku Love Story* 5, 61
*Never Let Me Go* 163
*Nigorie* 119
*Ninagawa Hi no Tori* 130
NINAGAWA *Macbeth* 5, 13, 26, 52–61, 63, 69, 70, 82, 94, 100, 123, 128, 129, 141, 156, 162, 164, 176, 181, 183, 188, 199, 202 n.4, 205 n.17, 206 n.5
NINAGAWA *Twelfth Night* 14, 17, 79–83, 112, 145, 153, 165, 200, 202 n.5

*Oedipus Rex* (1976) 3, 45, 77, 91
*Oedipus Rex* (2002) 3, 10, 11, 14, 107, 130, 206 n.31
*Oedipus Rex* (2013) 117, 202 n.7
*Orestes* 10, 20–2
*Othello* (1994) 73, 166, 199, 209 n.17, 209 n.19
*Othello* (2007) 166–7, 171, 200
*Peer Gynt* 3, 27, 60, 72
*Pericles* 100, 110, 112, 129–133, 141, 166, 167, 172, 173, 174, 176, 200, 203 n.13, 208 n.4, 209 n.1
*Raven, We Will Load Bullets* 202 n.9
*Richard II* 117, 162, 188–9, 195, 201
*Richard III* 75, 100, 127, 133, 163, 169, 170, 200
*Romeo and Juliet* (1974) 3, 8, 42–4, 48, 63, 89, 94, 97, 112, 204 n.9, 210 n.2
*Romeo and Juliet* (1998) 126, 127
*Romeo and Juliet* (2004) 3–4, 43–4, 108, 112
*Romeo and Juliet* (2014) 118, 161–2
*Seagull, The* 9
*Shintokumaru* 106, 107, 108

*Shitaya Mannencho Monogatari* 61, 95, 119, 188
*Sotoba Komachi* 12, 46, 47, 53, 69, 165
*Streetcar Named Desire, A* 107
*Suicide for Love* 4, 5, 50–1, 54, 70, 87, 115, 129, 175, 202 n.3, 205 n.28
*Taming of the Shrew, The* 153–6, 158, 173, 184, 200
*Tango at the End of Winter* 8, 10, 22–3, 27, 61, 71, 188
*Tempest, The* 19, 61–6, 68, 70, 71, 72, 77, 81, 94, 97, 98, 112, 127, 164, 166, 172, 188, 199, 205 n.21, 209 n.1, 209 n.2
*Ten Thousand Years of Memories of Japan* 41
*Tenpo Juninen no Shakespeare* 10, 14–18, 67, 88, 112–14, 139, 200, 206 n.30
*Three Sisters* 9, 67, 68, 77
*Threepenny Opera, The* 90, 129
*Tis Pity She's a Whore* 20
*Titus Andronicus* 10, 18, 19, 112, 133–7, 139, 166, 176, 178, 181, 182, 200, 204 n.12
*Total Eclipse* 22
*Troilus and Cressida* 156–158, 161, 201
*Trojan Women* 67, 202 n.7
*Twelfth Night* (1998) 126, 127, 199
*Twelve Angry Men* 22
*Two Gentlemen of Verona, The* 162–5, 166, 201
*Waiting* 68, 205 n.26
*Water Magician, The* 3, 44, 50, 77, 107, 129
*Winter's Tale, The* 129, 172–4, 184, 200
*Yoroboshi* 12–13, 46, 108
*Yotsuya Kaidan* 6, 42, 129, 133, 163
Nishioka Tokuma 114
Nissay Theatre 3, 7, 43, 47, 61, 68, 90, 162, 199, 200
Noda Hideki 5, 19–20, 67
  *Byakuya no Valkyrie* 10, 19–20
Noguchi Isamu 77
noh 12, 13, 36, 37, 41, 46, 62–4, 72–3, 76, 77, 100, 121, 126, 132, 140, 164, 167, 190, 209 n.2
Nomura Mansai 22, 66, 106, 208 n.8
Nunn, Sir Trevor 130
  *The Winter's Tale* (dir. 1970) 172

O-Bon (Festival of the Dead) 59, 206 n.4
Odashima Yushi 8–9, 20, 65, 79, 86, 87, 94, 95, 127, 207 n.15, 207 n.2
Ofuji 71

Oguri Shun 18–19, 106, 109, 123, 141, 142, 146, 147, 208 n.7
Ohtori Ran 121, 149
Okada Tadashi 178
Okawa Hiroki 136
Okuni 37–8
Okouchi Naoko 69
*onnagata* 10, 38, 47, 49, 78, 80, 141, 155, 204 n.14
Onoe Kikugoro VII 80
Onoe Kikunosuke V 14, 22, 66, 78–9, 80–1, 83, 153
Orientalism 29, 191, 192
*Oshin* 172
Otake Shinobu 10–11, 20, 127, 168, 175
*otokoyaku* 121, 140, 141, 178, 209 n.21
Oxford University Dramatic Society 129

Peach Blossom Festival 92
pre-show induction 19, 23, 55, 63, 97–8, 116, 130–1, 137, 142–3, 151, 154, 157, 159, 168–9, 170, 171, 173, 175, 178–9, 182, 188
postmodernism 192–7

red ribbons 20, 48, 131, 134–6, 148, 204 n.11, 206 n.32
Rei Asami 14, 19, 78, 135, 149
Rickman, Alan 8, 72
riot police 7, 23, 58
*Rose of Versailles, The* 149–50, 209 n.21
Roubine, Jean-Jacques 188

Royal Shakespeare Company 3, 18, 72, 76, 78, 100, 110, 112, 133, 134, 136
Ryoan-ji 69

Sado Island 62–64
Sagawa Tetsuro 168, 175, 176
Sai no Kuni Shakespeare series 1, 3, 18, 33, 71, 77, 96, 97, 100, 101, 107, 108, 112, 118, 125–86, 193, 203 n.13, 208 n.15
Said, Edward, *Orientalism* 27
Saitama Arts Theatre 1, 100–5, 116, 118–23, 125–86, 189, 205 n.26
Saitama Gold Theatre 116, 161, 188, 202 n.9
Saitama Next Theatre 114–18, 123, 188, 202 n.7
Sakura-sha 7–8, 42, 44, 46
Salz, Jonah 46, 66, 205 n.17
Sanada Hiroyuki 76–7, 96–100, 106
Sankai Juku 153
Senda Akihiko 4, 58, 204 n.13
Sengoku Period 52, 95
September 11th attacks 104
Shakespeare, William
  cutting texts 88
  plays
    *All's Well That Ends Well* 203 n.14
    *Antony and Cleopatra* 178–80, 200
    *As You Like It* 3, 26, 140–4, 147, 164, 174, 200
    *Comedy of Errors, The* 10, 18–19, 96,

145–8, 151, 159, 163, 179, 200, 206 n.32
*Coriolanus* 26, 67, 137–40, 178, 180, 181, 200, 203 n.13, 206 n.31, 209 n.2
*Cymbeline* 172, 174–8, 180, 201, 203 n.13
*Hamlet* 3, 4, 6, 9, 11, 26, 27, 33, 49, 50, 54, 63, 70, 72, 76, 81, 85–123, 129, 133, 138, 141, 147, 161, 162, 163, 169, 174, 183, 189, 199, 200, 201, 204 n.7, 204 n.13, 206 n.1, 207 n.16, 209 n.1
*Henry IV* 170–1, 201
*Henry V* 171, 203 n.14
*Henry VI* 139, 166, 167–70, 200
*Henry VIII* 203 n.14
*Julius Caesar* 112, 139, 180, 181, 182, 183, 201
*King Lear* 3, 17, 27, 45, 48, 71–7, 91, 94, 100, 101, 109, 110, 127, 130, 166, 167, 171, 199, 200, 208 n.5
*King John* 203 n.14
*Love's Labour's Lost* 129, 148–51, 164, 165, 166, 200
*Macbeth* 5, 7, 13, 17, 22, 26, 52–61, 63, 69, 70, 72, 75, 82, 94, 100, 114, 123, 127–9, 130, 139, 140, 141, 156, 162, 164, 176, 181, 183, 188, 199, 200, 202 n.4, 205 n.18, 205 n.21, 206 n.5, 209 n.1, 209 n.2
*Measure for Measure* 183–5, 201
*Merchant of Venice, The* 158–61, 163, 166, 201
*Merry Wives of Windsor, The* 75, 129
*Midsummer Night's Dream, A* 11, 43, 67–71, 72, 76, 77, 82, 94, 101, 112, 127, 130, 133, 144, 164, 168, 199, 207 n.2
*Much Ado About Nothing* 151–3, 181, 182, 200
*Othello* 22, 73, 166, 167, 171, 199, 200
*Pericles* 100, 110, 112, 129–33, 141, 166, 167, 172, 173, 174, 176, 200, 203 n.13, 209 n.1
*Richard II* 117, 162, 188–9, 195, 201
*Richard III* 75, 100, 127, 133, 163, 169, 170, 200
*Romeo and Juliet* 3, 4, 8, 22, 42–4, 48, 54, 63, 65, 89, 94, 96, 97, 108, 112, 118, 126, 127, 161–2, 199, 200, 201, 210 n.2
*Taming of the Shrew, The* 153–6, 158, 173, 184, 200

*Tempest, The* 19, 61–6, 68, 70, 71, 72, 77, 81, 94, 97, 98, 112, 127, 164, 166, 172, 188, 199, 205 n.21, 209 n.1, 209 n.2
*Timon of Athens* 97, 186, 203 n.14
*Titus Andronicus* 10, 18, 19, 112, 133–7, 139, 166, 176, 178, 181, 182, 200, 204 n.12
*Troilus and Cressida* 156–8, 161, 201
*Twelfth Night* 14, 17, 79–83, 112, 126, 127, 145, 153, 165, 199, 200, 209 n.1
*Two Gentlemen of Verona, The* 162–5, 166, 201
*Winter's Tale, The* 129, 172–4, 184, 200
Shiki Theatre Company 36, 100, 112
Shimizu Kunio 5, 6, 7, 8, 10, 22–3, 41, 42, 61, 67, 71, 86, 137, 187, 188, 202 n.9, 204 n.4, 209 n.2
  *Blood Wedding* 61, 67
  *Gakuya* 22
  *Hearty But Flippant* 5, 6, 11, 41, 54, 129, 180
  *In That Rainy Summer, Thirty Juliets Came Back* 8, 22, 61, 187
  *Let's Lay Flowers There Tomorrow* 7
  *Masakado Loses His Head* 7–8, 10, 22
  *My Soul is Shining Water* 22
  *Raven, We Will Load Bullets* 202 n.9
  *Tango at the End of Winter* 8, 10, 22–3, 27, 61, 71, 72, 188
  *Ten Thousand Years of Memories of Japan* 41
*shingeki* 2, 15, 16, 17, 19, 30, 35, 36, 41, 43, 46, 53–4, 62, 64, 86, 94, 126, 181–2
Shinohara Ryoko 15, 114
*shinpa* 36
Shinto 132, 207 n.17
Shiraishi Kayoko 15, 67, 70, 78–9, 114, 127, 131, 132, 140, 205 n.24
*shojo* manga 142, 149
Singleton, Brian 28, 203 n.12, 205 n.20, 208 n.14
slow-motion 23, 93, 103, 109, 122, 176, 177, 183, 185
Smethurst, Mae 47, 49
Spencer, Charles 74, 111, 207 n.12
Spiral Hall 94–6, 199
Stanislavski, Konstantin 2, 66
star casting 15, 31–2, 65, 110
steps 41, 91, 94, 95, 99, 103, 137–8, 140, 180
Stoppard, Tom
  *Coast of Utopia, The* 22, 167, 175
sunflowers 156–7
super *kabuki* 153, 206 n.29
Suzuki Anne 106, 112
Suzuki Tadashi 17, 26, 29, 30, 67, 77, 86, 88
Suzuki Yutaka 136

Tabe Mikako 185
*tachimawari* fight scenes 39, 40, 183
Takahashi Yasunari 86, 89, 90, 125
Takahashi Yo 13, 146, 147, 167
Takarazuka 8, 14, 36, 66, 121, 136, 140–1, 142, 148–51, 178, 209 n.21
*Tale of Genji, The* 142, 174, 175, 178
*Tale of the Heike, The* 7
Tanaka Nobuko 15, 207 n.3
Tanaka Yuko 65, 132, 172, 173
tango music 188–9
Taylor, Diana 30
Taylor, Paul 207 n.3
Taymor, Julie 67
Terajima Shinobu 78, 127
Terayama Shuji 22, 86
 *Shintokumaru* 106, 107, 108
*Thermae Romae* 181, 183
Togashi Makoto 126
Toho 7, 42, 88, 204 n.10
Tokugawa Shogunate 25, 52, 119
Tokyo Globe 96, 104, 199
Tomelty, Frances 110
Tsubouchi Shoyo 79, 85–6, 87, 90, 95, 106, 119, 158, 207 n.15
Tsujimura Jusaburo 48

Tsukikawa Yuki 102, 103, 108, 110, 141, 143, 148, 151–2, 154, 162, 163, 176
*tsukurimono* 73

Ubersfeld, Anne 24, 195
Uchida Kenji 118, 122–3
Uchida Shige 148, 151–2, 157
United Red Army 57–8, 164
Uzaki Ryudo 16, 73

Venturi, Robert 194

*wagoto kabuki* 38–9, 80
Watanabe Ken 94–6, 106
Wilson, Robert 28
Wirgman, Charles 113, 207 n.15

Yamagata Harue 10
Yamaguchi Hiroko 54–5
*yaoi* manga 109, 142, 148, 151, 156, 165
Yokota Eiji 118, 163, 168, 174, 181
Yomiuri Prize for Drama 117
Yoshida Kohtaloh 15, 17, 21, 133, 152, 166, 167, 168, 171, 175, 178, 181, 182, 186
*Yoshitsune Senbon Zakura* 142, 174
Yung-Biau Lin 70, 76

Zeami Motokiyo 62, 64
Zeffirelli, Franco 44, 111, 204 n.10

www.ingramcontent.com/pod-product-compliance
Lightning Source LLC
Chambersburg PA
CBHW072147290426
44111CB00012B/1999